D0860171

Toward a
Patriarchal
Republic

Toward a
Patriarchal
Republic

The Secession of Georgia

MICHAEL P. JOHNSON

LOUISIANA STATE UNIVERSITY PRESS

Baton Rouge and London

Publication of this book was assisted by the
American Council of Learned Societies under a grant
from the Andrew W. Mellon Foundation.

LIBRARY OF CONGRESS CATALOGING IN PUBLICATION DATA

Johnson, Michael, 1941–
  Toward a patriarchal Republic.

  Bibliography: p.
  Includes index.
  1. Georgia—Politics and government—1861–1865.
2. Secession. I. Title.
F290.J65   973.7′13   77–3029
ISBN 0–8071–0270–9

For
Anne Elizabeth Johnson

Contents

Contents

Tables

Maps

Preface

Secession gave the South a distinctive political definition. Until the winter of 1860–1861, arguments about what defined the South emphasized its distinctive climate, crops, labor system, biracial population, way of life, or typical personality traits. Although such arguments quickly became muddied by contradictions, it was clear that the South did not have a political definition. The South, like the North and West, was a part of the United States. Like those other regions, it was composed of states loosely bound together by certain common interests, as indeed was the United States itself. Historically, the United States had to a considerable degree been identified with the South. Southerners did at least their share, if not more, in the American Revolution, in the Constitutional Convention in Philadelphia, and in governing the new nation. Washington, Jefferson, and Madison were national heroes. But by the summer of 1861, seventy-four years after that summer in Philadelphia, the political polarity of the South had reversed. Eleven states had seceded from the Union to join the new Confederacy, an unmistakably separate political entity—with armies in the field, diplomats in foreign capitals, and new government officials in office, if not in charge, at home. Somehow, from the southern ingredients within the Union, a political precipitate had formed. But how? By what chemistry? Why?

At one level the answer is quite simple. The election of Abraham Lincoln to the presidency in November of 1860 precipitated the secession of the seven states of the lower South. Six weeks after Lincoln's election, on December 20, 1860, South Carolina led the exodus, to be followed in January, 1861, by Mississippi, Florida, Alabama, Georgia, and Louisiana, and on February 1 by Texas. The other four states that joined the Confederacy—Virginia, Arkansas, Tennessee, and North Carolina—remained in the Union until April and May of 1861 when they were provoked to secede by Lincoln's call for volunteers to suppress the insurrection that began with the firing on Fort Sumter, which had occurred on April 12 and 13. Indeed, it is tempting to oversimplify and argue that, given the election of Lincoln, all else followed more or less automatically. The degree to which this is oversimplification is determined by one's interpretation of the secession of the lower South and of the history of the antebellum South in general.

The burden of professional scholarship for the last generation has been somewhat ambivalent.[1] It has conclusively proved that to argue that secession followed Lincoln's election with an iron logic is an egregious oversimplification. Scholars have emphasized the contingencies, the moments when history turned away from a different past. Still, one is left with a taste of inevitability.

Since the 1930s, scholars have been impressed by the strong ties between the Union and the antebellum South as well as by the relative ease with which reunion followed Reconstruction. The problem posed by secession was to explain what went wrong. Why did the South act as if it were fundamentally different from the North when, in fact, it was not? After all, the argument ran, the differences between southerners and northerners were neither much greater nor much less than the differences between southerners themselves. In the Old South, even slaveholders were divided by region, religion, political party, and by differences in the number of slaves owned, in the quantity and quality of the land cultivated, and in the crops grown, among other ways. How could similarities between North and South lead to secession, the ultimate symbol of distinctiveness?

The answer proposed was that the South misperceived the intentions of Lincoln and the Republican party and of the North in general. Some

1. It is impossible in this brief discussion to do justice to the complex issues and rich historiography of secession. For a more extended treatment, see David M. Potter, *The Impending Crisis* (New York: Harper and Row, 1976), 448–513; William J. Donelly, "Conspiracy or Popular Movement: The Historiography of Southern Support for Secession," *North Carolina Historical Review*, XLII (1965), 70–84; Ralph A. Wooster, "The Secession of the Lower South: An Examination of Changing Interpretations," *Civil War History*, VII (1961), 117–27.

scholars linked the misperceptions to southern paranoia, rooted in the touchy defensiveness of a minority in a majoritarian government, in widespread guilt about owning slaves, or in a moist-eyed romanticism. Others pointed to the partisan southern press and to the shortage of objective news about Lincoln and the North. Still others have argued that Lincoln himself was remiss in not making his intentions more perfectly clear. Whatever their causes, the misperceptions were exploited by fire-eating secessionists whose skillful, race-baiting demagoguery excited the masses of southerners into propelling the South from the Union while cooler heads wisely but vainly counseled restraint. The divisions among southerners which had been a cohesive force for the Union became instead an internal weakness. The agents of disunion—demagogic politicians and the bulk of the southern electorate—exploited this weakness and wedged the sections apart for reasons which, above the level of selfish personal gain, were hopelessly confused and wrongheaded.

In the end, this interpretation elevated the Union to a primary moral value and, at least implicitly, lamented that reason was the first casualty of the Civil War. If reason had prevailed at each step in the process, the South would have remained in the Union. Thus the linkage between Lincoln's election and secession was less logical than circumstantial, composed of equal parts of misinformation, blundering, and the unpredictable forces of irrationality and historical contingency. Yet when this interpretation is coupled with its attendant assumptions about the nature of American society and politics, more than a trace of inevitability emerges. Implicit in the interpretation is the assumption that America's mass political culture made politics and government subject to abuse by misguided leaders and a misinformed electorate. Normally, government institutions and political parties cushioned the impact of an electoral majority which lurched from one position to another. Wise leaders could translate these electoral shifts into sensible policy. But by 1860 the political party system had disintegrated, the government and even the Constitution were discredited, and the political leaders were not distinguished by their wisdom. In this situation, politics was open to the uncushioned influence of the electorate, which had always been noted more for its numbers than its rationality. In a sense, then, secession was inevitable, since the mediating institutions of party and government and the guiding hands of wise leaders were stripped away, leaving history to the blind will of the people, North and South. This interpretation thus structured historical contingencies in a framework of assumptions about the nature and dangers of democracy. If, in this view, reason was the first casualty of the Civil War, then democracy was the first firing squad.

Since the 1960s the fundamental tenets of this interpretation have been provocatively challenged by Eugene D. Genovese. He began by asking what southerners' primary values were rather than what they should have been. Since southerners left the Union in the name of slavery, Genovese reasoned, it is only fair to take them at their word—slavery, not the Union, was first priority. For Genovese, the primacy of slavery had the most far-reaching consequences. "The confrontation of master and slave, white and black, on a plantation presided over by a resident planter for whom the plantation was a home and the entire population part of his extended family generated [a patriarchal and paternalistic] ethos" which suffused the entire society, touching not only masters and slaves but reaching out to slaveless whites as well.[2] The master-slave relationship and the ideology it generated not only made the antebellum South distinctive and unified, but it also meant that secession was a rational act that confirmed the hegemony of the planter class. At every point the former interpretation was contested.

The distinctiveness of the antebellum South resided in "the political hegemony and aristocratic ideology of the ruling class," the planters. The South was not only politically and ideologically unified; it was also fundamentally different from the North, since "the relationship of master to slave is fundamentally different from that of capitalist to wage worker and . . . this difference is decisive for an understanding of ideology and class psychology, as well as of economics."[3] Trapped between this basic difference between North and South and the internal contradictions of the slave economy, "the slaveholders slid into violent

2. Eugene D. Genovese, *The World the Slaveholders Made: Two Essays in Interpretation* (New York: Random House, 1969; Vintage ed., 1971), 96.
    3. *Ibid.*, 17.

collision with Northern interests and sentiments.'' For when slaveholders tried to prop up their economy either by seeking cheap labor through reopening the African slave trade or by advocating territorial expansion for new slave states, they ran headlong into conflict with the North. Secession, then, was logical, sensible, and far-sighted. Slaveholders' "only hope lay in a bold stroke to complete their political independence and to use it to provide an expansionist solution for their economic and social problems."[4] Secession not only resulted from the distinctive ideology and psychology of the planter class, it also confirmed their hegemony, for in "the decision to secede and to stake everything on an uncompromising fight for regional independence . . . the slaveholders recognized in other than an abstract way their existence as a ruling class and as the self-appointed guardians of a way of life."[5]

For Genovese, the relationship between Lincoln's election and secession is clear and direct. Lincoln's election necessitated secession because it doomed the territorial expansion of slavery, which was essential if the South was to remain the South as it was. The secessionists marched past Lincoln's election in files nearly as straight as their direction was predictable. Certainly there were contingent phenomena, but on the whole one is struck by the logical march of events. The social force behind the logic was neither the electorate nor self-serving politicians but the ruling class planters who, "in the fullest sense . . . were fighting for their lives."[6] Secession, then, was driven by the nature of the southern ruling class which had been shaped, ultimately, by the unique characteristics of the master-slave relationship and all that it implied. Reason was less the casualty than the cause of secession, and democracy, at least within the South, was more or less beside the point.

Previous interpretations of secession, then, have differed about the reasons for secession, about the active agents of disunion, and about the degree to which southerners were united both by a commitment to

---

4. Eugene D. Genovese, *The Political Economy of Slavery: Studies in the Economy and Society of the Slave South* (New York: Random House, 1965; Vintage ed., 1967), 35.

5. Genovese, *World the Slaveholders Made,* 101.

6. Genovese, *Political Economy of Slavery,* 270.

slavery as the essence of southern life and by the willingness to honor that commitment by leaving the Union. As I studied the secession of Georgia, I discovered that these previous interpretations did not fully account for what happened. To understand events in Georgia I have had to piece together a new interpretation. Although the details and, more importantly, the supporting evidence are in the pages that follow, it is perhaps worth noting briefly the differences between my interpretation and previous views.

On the question of motivation, I am persuaded by what Georgia secessionists said, and by what their opponents did, that secession was undertaken rationally and for good reasons. In this I agree with Genovese's view. But while Genovese focuses on the operative importance of territorial expansion—and in general on the tension between the South and events outside the South—I have been convinced both by what secessionists and their opponents said and by what secessionists did after they left the Union that the operative tension in the secession crisis was *within* the South. Far from being united, Georgia and the rest of the South was deeply divided on the question of secession. Thus, while I appreciate the older interpretation's emphasis on the divisions within the South, I do not believe that the operation of those divisions in the secession crisis has been properly understood. In Georgia it was not the electorate but something very close to Genovese's ruling class that led the state out of the Union. Secession was the ultimate test of the hegemony of the slaveholders. Yet secession was necessary precisely because the hegemony of slaveholders was not secure. According to secessionists, at least as I read them, secession was necessary because of the internal divisions within the South, divisions which focused on the degree to which the slaveholding minority could have its way in a government based ultimately on manhood suffrage. In particular, secessionists feared that many southerners would be receptive to Republican offers of patronage and would become the nucleus of a southern Republican party, making possible an internal counterpart of the Republican victory in the North.

In Georgia, secessionists translated that fear into a double revolution: a revolution for home rule—to eliminate the external threat; and a conservative revolution for those who ruled at home—to prevent the political realization of the internal threat. Men with conservative social and political ideas were instrumental not only in creating the small electoral margin the secessionists enjoyed in Georgia, but also in the definition and direction of the second revolution. The actions of the secession convention, including the new state constitution which they drafted, constituted the second revolution. It represented an attempt to preserve the social status quo by reconciling the tension between the slaveholding minority and the enfranchised slaveless majority.

This tension culminated in the secession crisis, but its roots extended back to the seventeenth century when slavery became well established both in practice and in law. Secession's ancestry in seventeenth-century slavery was linked in the eighteenth century to the American Revolution. Secession resulted, more than anything else, from the conflict between these two inheritances. While this conflict existed throughout the antebellum period, it was masked by the contradictory social, political, sectional, and national loyalties of southerners. But by 1860 the institutional and ideological consequences of the American Revolution had assumed a historical configuration—Lincoln's election—that posed an external threat to the established order of southern society. Lincoln's election forced southerners to choose among their loyalties, and their choices revealed a South which was united neither by racial fears nor by an ideological consensus, but which was divided along lines which coincided roughly with an interest in slavery and the established order. In Georgia, both the secessionists and their opponents spoke and acted as if they shared fully in the heritage of 1776. Secession was driven by political conflict not only between the South and the North but also between the black belt and the upcountry, slaveholders and nonslaveholders, and those who feared democracy and those who valued it. Without considering this internal conflict, it is impossible to understand why Georgia secessionists tried to create a patriarchal republic. For, by taking things into their own hands, Georgians tried to live with their history as both southerners and Americans. In the process, they put themselves ultimately into the hands of Abraham Lincoln.

Although this interpretation is obvious in the structure of the text, I have tried to write a history of the secession of Georgia rather than an analysis of the historiography of secession. I do discuss the pertinent historiographical issues in Chapter Five. But, with that exception, I have focused the text on events in Georgia, with the conviction that readers are persuaded by close attention to the historical evidence. Chapter One is a brief survey of Georgia as if viewed from some imaginary historical camera obscura on January 2, 1861, the day when most Georgians squarely faced the question of secession. Chapter Two canvasses the major events in Georgia during the presidential election of 1860—the unofficial beginning of the campaign for secession—and later during the official campaign which stretched from Lincoln's election until January 2, when Georgia voters chose delegates to the state convention which would decide whether to secede. Chapter Three analyzes the argument for secession, considering the viewpoints of both proponents and critics. Chapter Four discusses the social and political ecology of the January 2 election. This discussion is based on a thorough quantitative analysis of the election returns, which is explained in detail in the Appendix. Readers who are allergic to numbers will, I hope, be able to proceed safely through the text, which puts all the conclusions of the quantitative analysis into ordinary language. Those who have developed a resistance to the debilitating effects of quantification, or who have come to thrive on it, are encouraged to consult the Appendix, perhaps even before reading Chapter Four. Chapters Six, Seven, and Eight concentrate on the actions of the state convention delegates as they accomplished secession, the first revolution, and then turned toward the second revolution and the creation of a patriarchal republic. Chapter Nine explains how the second revolution was completed in July, 1861, by the ratification of the new state constitution and, perhaps more importantly, by the beginning of war. In a sense, then, the book opens and closes like a clamshell, revealing most somewhere in the middle.

There are many good reasons for studying Georgia. Although there have been recent studies of the secession of South Carolina, Alabama, and Mississippi, and although there are older works on the secession of all the other states, the secession of Georgia has never received extended treatment.[7] Yet it is easy to see why it should have. Except for

---

7. For recent studies, see Steven A. Channing, *Crisis of Fear: Secession in South Carolina* (New York: Simon and Schuster, 1970), and William L. Barney, *The Secessionist Impulse:*

Texas, Georgia was larger than the other states in the lower South and, except for South Carolina, it was older. In 1860 Georgia had more people (1,057,286), more voters (106,868 in the 1860 presidential election), more slaves (462,198), more slaveholders (41,084) and more nonslaveholders (more than 65,000) than any other lower South state.[8] Clearly the secession of Georgia was crucial to the success of the secessionists, just as the failure to bring Georgia along had stymied their success in 1850. Furthermore, Georgia is worth studying precisely because it was somewhat atypical. Research on the secession of the other lower South states has convinced me that what I have discovered in Georgia had counterparts elsewhere. But since the process of double revolution was most fully developed in Georgia, Georgia is the strongest test for the interpretation—if the interpretation is found wanting in accounting for the secession of Georgia, it will be even less adequate in explaining secession in the other states. Or, as I hope, if the interpretation is convincing for Georgia, it may help us ask some new questions about the rest of the South.

Nevertheless, when I began this study as a seminar paper in the spring of 1966, I chose to study Georgia not for all these good reasons but for a better one. David M. Potter observed to his seminar that Ulrich Bonnell Phillips had noted in *Georgia and State Rights* that Whigs and Democrats in Georgia had executed a political "somersault" in the secession crisis: Democratic counties which had voted for the Southern Rights candidate John C. Breckinridge in 1860 tended to oppose secession, while Whig counties which had voted for the Unionist candidates John Bell or Stephen A. Douglas in 1860 tended to

Alabama and Mississippi in 1860 (Princeton: Princeton University Press, 1974). For references to previous studies of Georgia, see note 14, Chapter Two herein.

8. The census takers counted people, slaves, and slaveholders, but not nonslaveholders as such. The number of nonslaveholders is therefore an estimate. It is based on two assumptions: (1) that there were at least as many adult white males in the population as there were voters in the presidential election of 1860, since one had to be adult white male to vote (because there were surely more adult white males than voters, the estimate is a minimum); (2) that on the whole, most slaveholders were adult white males. Undoubtedly the second assumption is less tenable than the first, since some women and children certainly owned slaves. But the validity of the second assumption is bolstered by the statement in the 1860 census that, "It would probably be a safe rule to consider the number of slaveholders to represent the number of families directly interested in the slave population." *Agriculture of the United States in 1860* (Washington: Government Printing Office, 1864), clxxii.

favor immediate secession.[9] Potter suggested the secession of Georgia might bear further investigation. As usual, he was right.

Many persons have helped me discover how right Potter was. Archivists and librarians at Duke University, Emory University, the Georgia Historical Society, the Georgia State Department of Archives and History, the University of Georgia, and the Southern Historical Collection at the University of North Carolina were invariably generous not only in making their holdings available but also in sharing their personal knowledge of their collections. I am especially grateful to Susan B. Tate of the University of Georgia for helping me get access to the Howell Cobb Papers and to Linda M. Matthews of Emory University for aid in deciphering Alexander H. Stephens' handwriting. Carl N. Degler guided this project from its inception as a dissertation and inspired any clarity of expression and conceptualization which may exist in the text. For his comments and the encouragement and support that came with them, I am deeply grateful. For helping me distinguish between what I wanted to say, what in fact I said, and what I should have said, I am indebted to Philip Dawson and Don E. Fehrenbacher, who served on my dissertation committee, to my friends Jim Roark and Mark Schwehn, and to my colleagues at the University of California, Irvine, Jonathan Dewald, Jack Diggins, Karl Hufbauer, Jon Jacobson, Keith Nelson, Spencer Olin, Mark Poster, Gerald White, and Jonathan Wiener. A Summer Faculty Fellowship from the University of California and grants from the Humanities Research Fund and the Graduate Council provided necessary and much appreciated financial support. Natalie Korp typed the manuscript more times than either of us wants to remember, maintaining her typing speed and, equally indispensable, her sense of humor. My largest debt is acknowledged by the dedication.

9. Ulrich Bonnell Phillips, *Georgia and State Rights: A study of the Political History of Georgia from the Revolution to the Civil War, with Particular Regard to Federal Relations* (Washington: Government Printing Office, 1902; reprinted by Antioch Press, 1968), 206–207.

PART ONE

The Campaign for Secession

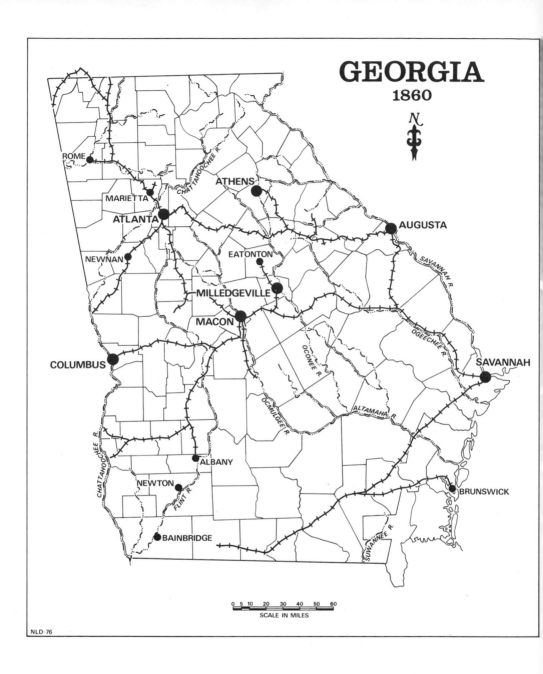

GEORGIA
1860

N

ROME
MARIETTA
ATLANTA
ATHENS
AUGUSTA
NEWNAN
EATONTON
MILLEDGEVILLE
MACON
COLUMBUS
SAVANNAH
ALBANY
NEWTON
BRUNSWICK
BAINBRIDGE

CHATTAHOOCHEE R.
SAVANNAH R.
OCONEE R.
OGEECHEE R.
OCMULGEE R.
ALTAMAHA R.
CHATTAHOOCHEE R.
FLINT R.
SUWANNEE R.

0 5 10   20   30   40   50   60
SCALE IN MILES

NLD-76

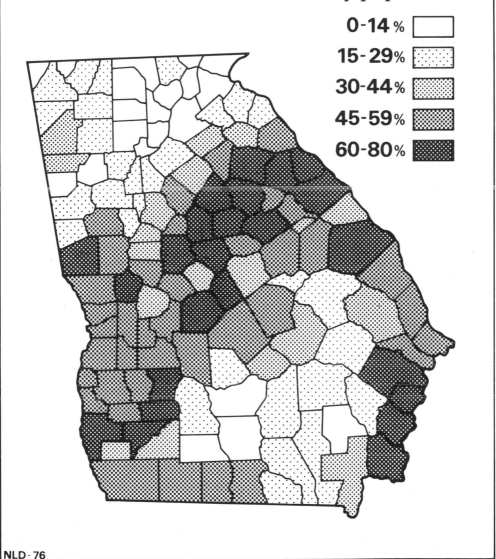

SLAVE POPULATION IN 1860

Proportion of slaves
in county population

0-14 %
15-29%
30-44%
45-59%
60-80%

NLD-76

1

Prologue:
Georgia, January 2,
1861

"This election day—raining—raining—raining—pouring—pouring," Alexander H. Stephens wrote his brother Linton on Wednesday, January 2, 1861. By the next day Stephens had concluded that, "Yesterday was the worst day for an election I ever saw in Georgia."[1]

The cold, hard rain was not confined to Stephens' Crawfordville home in east central Georgia. On the coast at Savannah, a newspaper reported "wet and stormy" weather; up the Savannah River about 100 miles, on the South Carolina border, Augusta was "very unpleasant, . . . part of the time rainy, chilly and damp; and the streets . . . very muddy"; west of Augusta about 150 miles, near the southern end of the Blue Ridge Mountains in north central Georgia, in Atlanta "the rain came down in floods" in the afternoon; southeast of Atlanta about 70 miles, in the center of the state and the heart of the cotton belt, at Macon, "heavy rains [kept the] . . . streets in an almost impassable condition"; in Albany, about 90 miles from Macon in southwest Georgia, it was "very rainy."[2]

In spite of the weather, most Georgia voters made their way to the polls. An election to choose delegates for the convention that would decide whether Georgia should secede from the United States was apparently incentive enough for men to risk getting wet. When Alexander Stephens, who had not planned to go out in the rain to vote, was called by his neighbors to share his views with them at the courthouse,

1. Alexander H. Stephens to Linton Stephens, January 2, 3, 1861, in Alexander H. Stephens Papers, Manhattanville College Collection on microfilm, Emory University.
2. Savannah *Republican,* January 3, 1861; Augusta *Daily Constitutionalist,* January 3, 1861; Macon *Daily Telegraph,* January 3, 1861; Albany *Patriot,* January 17, 1861. See also, Upson *Pilot,* January 5, 1861, and Alexander Means, *Diary* for 1861, ed. Ross H. McLean, *Emory University Publications* (Atlanta: Emory University, 1941), Ser. VI, No. 11, p. 12.

he arrived to find about a hundred men "standing about [,] some by the store [,] some on the stair steps—some in the jury boxes—some standing about in the Court Room—all dripping with wet." As these men and the other voters in Georgia walked or rode in the rain to the voting place, they no doubt thought of the weather.[3] Rain at the right time could mean a rich harvest; at the wrong time it could ruin the crop. How would the rain affect an attempt to raise a new government? Would it decrease the voter turnout, and, if so, how would that affect the result?

From Sparta in central Georgia, Linton Stephens reported to his brother that "the vote was thin, the day being a most unfavorable one for the turnout of voters." But the unfavorable day had had a favorable effect, he wrote. "The secessionists are terribly disappointed here," he noted, adding that he believed that "they may be as much so at the result in the State." Alexander Stephens came to the opposite conclusion. He wrote Linton that the rain had undoubtedly "told greatly against the Conservative cause." Linton, demonstrating the difficulty of arriving at a firm conclusion on the question, reversed his previous interpretation and agreed that indeed "the rain was greatly against us." "It really appears," Alexander speculated gloomily, "as if Providence were on the other side."[4]

Many secessionists would have agreed with Stephens' judgment about the favors of Providence. One rhapsodized that the January rains were a "secession freshet that would sweep away the past corruptions of the Government, and shower blessings on a Southern Confederacy." Even more reassuring to secessionists was the belief that, in addition to having God on their side, they also had most of the voters. The day after the election, a secessionist editor boldly predicted that "we are safe in estimating the success of the immediate secession ticket at fully *three-fourths* of the whole vote of Georgia—or say 80,000 for secession, to less than 30,000 for submission."[5] Governor

3. Alexander H. Stephens to Linton Stephens, January 3, 1861, in Stephens Papers, Manhattanville College Collection. For evidence of men's preoccupation with crops, weather, and politics, see the numerous letters reporting conditions from throughout the state in the Savannah *Republican* for July, 1860.

4. Linton Stephens to Alexander H. Stephens, January 3, 5, 1861, Alexander H. Stephens to Linton Stephens, January 3, 1861, in Stephens Papers, Manhattanville College Collection.

5. Albany *Patriot,* January 24, 1861; Atlanta *Daily Intelligencer,* January 3, 1861.

Joseph E. Brown contributed to secessionists' optimism when he wrote—three days after the election, before all the returns were in— that the results he had received "indicate beyond a doubt that the people of Georgia have determined, by an overwhelming majority, to secede from the Union." Given the weather and the predicted outcome of the election, United States senator Robert Toombs had chosen an apt metaphor when he telegraphed the "People of Georgia" late in December from Washington that, "Secession . . . should be thundered from the ballot box by the unanimous voice of Georgia"[6]

This confident optimism was not the predominant mood in Georgia shortly after the election, even among secessionists who believed their view had prevailed. From Montevideo, a plantation in the rice and sea-island cotton region along the Georgia coast, Mrs. Mary Jones wrote her son that although secession was necessary,"[a]n indescribable sadness weighs down my soul as I think of our once glorious but now dissolving Union!" While Mrs. Jones's resignation to the necessity of secession outweighed her reluctance to leave the Union, the balance was reversed for opponents of secession. Many cooperationists were reluctant "to leave a well established Government without any assurance of one half as good" to replace it, and they resigned themselves to what they feared was a position of futile opposition.[7] Some secessionists hoped to overcome this cooperationist reluctance with the promise that "from the ashes" of the Union "will spring up the most brilliant and powerful government that ever graced the face of the globe." Other secessionists avoided such promises since a secessionist victory was far from certain. A discouraged secessionist in northwest Georgia coupled his report that the local "secession ticket was defeated . . . by [a] two hundred majority" with the "hope [that] there are noble spirits enough [elsewhere] in Geo. to maintain the honor of

6. Joseph E. Brown to John Gill Shorter, January 5, 1861, in William R. Smith (ed.), *The History and Debates of the Convention of the People of Alabama Begun and Held in the City of Montgomery, on the Seventh Day of January, 1861* (Atlanta: Wood, Hanleiter, Rice and Co., 1861), 339; Robert Toombs to the People of Georgia (telegram), Washington, D. C., December 23, 1860, in Ulrich Bonnell Phillips (ed.), *The Correspondence of Robert Toombs, Alexander H. Stephens, and Howell Cobb* (Washington: Government Printing Office, 1913), 525.

7. Mrs. Mary Jones to Charles C. Jones, Jr., January 3, 1861, in Charles Colcock Jones, Jr. Collection, University of Georgia; John N. W. McRae to Dr. S. H. Latimer, January 25, 1861, in S. H. Latimer Papers, Duke University.

Georgia."[8] This cautious hope that secessionists reserved for their private correspondence was an expression of how difficult it was to be certain about the results of the election.

Newspapers noted the uncertainty, saying it was "impossible to foretell the result," especially since there had been "a close run between the parties." From the uncertainty other Georgians divined that the tide of popular opinion ran away from secession rather than toward it. A Georgia legislator wrote cooperationist Herschel V. Johnson that three-fourths of the people were "on conservative grounds" and, he predicted, "when unbridled [they] will speak in thunder tones." Johnson himself wrote Alexander Stephens "that the conservative feeling is in the ascendant." But Johnson, like nearly everyone else, was uncertain. Uncertainty was so pervasive that even those who did not think that "the people are miserably divided and distracted" would have nonetheless agreed that "the excitement heightens daily."[9]

Excitement, reports of "bewildered and distracted" people, and uncertainty about the future pushed many conservative men to despair. "This is a cheerless Christmas for me," one wrote, reflecting "the dark and doubt" that many felt. Other conservatives accepted the "appalling calamity" of secession as "inevitable" and concluded that rather than despair they should seek "to temper the calamity as much as may be done, and shape events which can not be prevented, towards the best possible results." The lawyer and educator Richard Malcolm Johnston tried to console his friend Alexander Stephens with the observation that the "majority of the extremists is not so great that they will not need the counsel and cooperation of the wisest of the moderates." But Stephens' despair was deep. "All is now dark and gloomy," he confided to a friend on New Year's Eve. "I see no ray of hope. What is to become of us I know not."[10]

8. C. H. Sutton to John S. Dobbins, January 14, 1861, in John S. Dobbins Papers, Emory University; Edward R. Harden to Mother, January 3, 1861, in Edward Harden Papers, Duke University.

9. Savannah *Republican,* January 4, 1861; Rome *Weekly Courier,* January 11, 1861; George A. Hall to Herschel V. Johnson, January 7, 1861, Johnson to Alexander H. Stephens, January 9, 1861, in Herschel V. Johnson Papers, Duke University; J. D. Waddell to Alexander H. Stephens, December 17, 1860, in Stephens Papers, University of Georgia.

10. A. H. Wyche to Alexander H. Stephens, December 25, 1860, Richard M. Johnston to Alexander H. Stephens, January 10, 1860, in Stephens Papers, Library of Congress; Alexander

The factors which contributed to the pessismism and despair of men like Stephens were many and complex. But one was simple—the rain. Stephens' biographers report that he remarked to a friend that the storm had cost the cooperationists ten thousand votes.[11] If one thought that rain was dissolving ties which might have held Georgia in the Union, uncertainty might easily become despair.

Aside from whatever difference the rainstorm actually made in the election, it was the one experience common to all Georgians early in the new year. Condensed in their comments on the rain and the election is an image of Georgians registering their opinions about secession, an image of a divided people, some exultant, some ambivalent, some uncertain and expectant, and others frightened and despairing. If Georgians were unanimous on anything, it was probably nothing more than that they were Georgians.

H. Stephens to Linton Stephens, January 3, 1861, Linton Stephens to Alexander H. Stephens, January 7, 1861, in Manhattanville College Collection; Alexander H. Stephens to J. Henly Smith, December 31, 1860, in Phillips (ed.), *Correspondence,* 527.

11. Richard Malcolm Johnston and William Hand Browne, *Life of Alexander H. Stephens* (Rev. ed.; Philadelphia: J. B. Lippincott, 1883), 378.

2

The
Campaign for
Secession

The election of delegates to the state convention was the culmination of a forty-two-day campaign for secession, a campaign officially begun November 21, 1860, when Governor Brown signed the law authorizing the election. Unofficially the campaign for secession had been a frequent topic of political conversation as Georgians considered the four candidates for president of the United States. For nearly a generation before 1860 secession had been a staple of southern political rhetoric, being used periodically as a threat, a deterrent whose effectiveness presumably depended upon its undesirability to both North and South. By 1860 the very frequency with which secession had been discussed led some persons to regard talk of secession as a ritualistic posturing, rather than as an actual alternative for action. They referred to the threat of secession as crying wolf, as "nothing more than the watch cry of politicians," and as "some spectral vision that haunted the minds of evil-suspecting men."[1] At the same time, many other persons were becoming convinced that secession should be transformed from a threat into a policy. Familiarity with the idea of secession hastened this transformation and strengthened the secessionists. How could an act which had been discussed and analyzed by so many prominent Southerners for so long be anything other than well considered and relatively harmless? While secessionists were galvanized by such questions, their opponents were disarmed.

Would the threat become a policy? That was the question facing

1. Augusta *Chronicle and Sentinel,* September 25, 1860; Greene County resolution, in Allen D. Candler (ed.), *The Confederate Records of the State of Georgia* (Atlanta: Charles P. Byrd, 1909), I, 71; A Southerner to editor, Macon *Telegraph,* November 5, 1860.

Georgia voters during late November and December, 1860, as the short, hotly contested campaign developed. By then, opponents of secession were convinced that they confronted a threatening policy rather than merely an empty threat. Yet, according to secessionists, the greatest threat lay in failing to secede. Whether secession was to be a threat or a policy was only partially resolved by the election of January 2, 1861. The voters were choosing delegates who would ultimately decide whether Georgia would leave the Union. The election, then, was both an end and a beginning. In another sense it was only a midpoint, for the ideas with which Georgians had framed the issues of secession for a generation continued to structure thought and action through the spring of 1861, when they were finally overwhelmed by war.

The Presidential Election of 1860

Thoughts of secession did not greatly exercise most Georgians early in 1860. "There is really not the least excitement in the public mind upon public affairs," Alexander Stephens wrote a friend at the beginning of the year.[2] Even seven months later in July, after the Democratic party had split into the national-Douglas and southern-Breckinridge parties, and after the Republicans had nominated Abraham Lincoln, and the Constitutional Unionists had selected John Bell, a letter writer from southeast Georgia reported that the "great mass of people" were "not much excited on political questions." "They take things quite philosophically," he wrote, "and are engaged mainly in going about their own business." While there may not have been much excitement, there was a growing awareness by July that secession was an issue in the presidential election. The correspondent, who signed his letter "Quandry," outlined his own views: "But in truth I find it hard to decide, myself, between Bell and Breck; I have *almost* got to the point to consent to a dissolution of the Union. If I get there between this and the 1st Monday in November next, I shall vote for Breck, for I find about seven in ten of his supporters (leaders) are for it;—but if not—if I want the Union, I shall vote for the only truly national candidates,

---

2. Stephens to J. Henry Smith, January 5, 1860, in Phillips (ed.), *Correspondence,* 454.

Bell and Everett"[3] The question of who was the "truly national" candidate tended to become the center of the debate in the presidential contest in Georgia. Barely submerged beneath this discussion was the implicit issue of secession.

Bell supporters lumped the Lincoln and Breckinridge parties together as "enemies of the country" and argued that only Bell could "restore peace to our distracted Union." The reason the "country is in trouble," wrote an "Old Whig," was that, "old and effete political parties have preyed on its vitals and brought it to the verge of dissolution." While the Republican and Southern Democratic politicians displayed a dangerous lust for office accompanied by a regrettable partisan spirit, the Constitutional Union party had nothing more nor less than the good of the country at heart, its supporters claimed. "This cry of protection [of slavery in the territories] is a masked battery behind which the disunionists have rallied to concoct their dark plots," wrote a Bell man, echoing the common view among Constitutional Unionists that the dispute about the expansion of slavery involved "nothing but an abstract question." If one realized that the heated controversy over a mere abstraction threatened the "peace, prosperity, and plenty" that the country presently enjoyed, then a vote for Bell was inescapable, his advocates believed. With this appeal to "the Old Whigs of the Union," Bell partisans hoped to rally support for ignoring the slavery extension controversy, focusing on the here and now, and preserving the Union.[4]

The Bell press concentrated most of its rhetorical salvos on the Breckinridge party. There was no need to woo Georgia voters away from Lincoln, and the Douglas Democrats had virtually no chance to win a plurality in Georgia. In fact, the Bell press was openly friendly to

3. Quandry to editor, July 26, 1860, Savannah *Republican,* July 28, 1860. See also Augusta *Daily Chronicle and Sentinel,* September and October, 1860.

4. Savannah *Republican,* July 2, 1860; Old Whig to editor, July 20, 1860, *ibid.;* J. S. Dobbins to W. H. Dobbins, October 13, 1860, in John S. Dobbins Papers, Emory University; W. W. Paine to Alexander H. Stephens, October 7, 1860, in Stephens Papers, Library of Congress Collection on microfilm at University of Georgia. For a complete list of the Bell, Douglas, and Breckinridge newspapers in Georgia, see Donald E. Reynolds, *Editors Make War: Southern Newspapers in the Secession Crisis* (Nashville: Vanderbilt University Press, 1970), 223–24. Reynolds' book and Ollinger Crenshaw, *The Slave States in the Presidential Election of 1860* (Baltimore: Johns Hopkins Press, 1945), are indispensable sources of southern newspaper opinion on the secession crisis.

Douglasites, ostensibly because Douglas too was a "national" candidate and, more realistically, because a sizable Douglas vote would lessen the chances that the Breckinridge Democrats would carry Georgia. The primary Bell charge against the Breckinridge Democrats was that they were disunionists. By trying to tar Breckinridge with the brush of secession, the Bell press was apparently estimating that there were enough Georgians who were "national and Union loving in their sentiments," to whom secession was undesirable, that Bell might win Georgia's electoral votes. In part, that is, the charge of disunion was less an expression of genuine concern about the Union than simply a Bell campaign tactic designed to provide victory in the traditional fashion of political rivalry. But behind this Bell tactic lay an element of positive, though conditional, unionism. A pro-Bell Savannah editor expressed this unionism in his observation that "the slavery issue has been wrongfully thrust upon us in this election. All that the South has demanded, or had a right to demand, has been granted. Every department of the government, legislative, executive and judicial, has responded to our call, and their action secures every constitutional right. The whole controversy is settled; the only question, is, whether or not, we will support the constitution and the laws of the land."[5]

Similar statements of conditional unionism were made by the Breckinridge press, with the difference that Breckinridge papers emphasized the conditions and the Bell papers, the Union. A pro-Breckinridge reporter in Atlanta wrote that a Breckinridge spokesman, "repelled the stale and threadbare charge of disunion indignantly with prodigious effect, and proved that the Union could only be preserved by maintaining the Constitution and observing its compromises and enforcing the decision of the Supreme Court." It was the *only* that marked the difference. In general, the Breckinridge press dismissed Bell charges of disunion as "claptrap" and referred to Breckinridge and Lane as "the only National candidates in the field." "The way to preserve the Union," Georgians were told, was to vote for Breckinridge and Lane, "the only ticket that stands the least chance to defeat

5. See for example Savannah *Republican,* July 7, 25, August, 1860.

Abe Lincoln."[6] Always lurking behind the Breckinridge press's professions of unionism was the threat of secession, a threat which Breckinridge supporters had to keep visible to maintain its threatening quality without making it so visible that a vote for Breckinridge was a vote for secession.

It was this volatile mixture of union and disunion that the Breckinridge press had to control, and, to do it, they called on party tradition, claiming that this mixture was what the Democratic party had supported for thirty years. "We are for the Union as Gen. Jackson understood it," an Atlanta editor wrote. "A Union of equal rights to every citizen of this Confederacy; a Union which secured to the slave-holder the same privileges as a non-slaveholder; a Union which afforded protection to slave property throughout the length and breadth of our vast domain; a Union which guarantees the right of property of *every kind* in the common Territories of the Union." Breckinridge spokesmen apparently calculated that this interpretation of the Democratic party and the Union would distinguish their party from the Douglasites and still capitalize on voters' party loyalty. At the same time, party loyalty was emphasized to repel voters from Bell. After charging that Bell men were Know-Nothings, an Atlanta editor concluded that, "in the same organization, you find Tariff men, United States Bank men, and every sort of men, who for the last quarter of a century have been fighting the Democracy."[7]

With this formula the Breckinridge press seemed confident of victory in Georgia. Their confidence rested not only on their rhetoric, but also on their organization. Within each of Georgia's eight congressional districts one person was apparently responsible for locating areas of Breckinridge strength and weakness and for keeping a close watch on political developments, particularly whether "any of our leading men [are] likely to take after Douglas." Such efforts gave credibility to the report that reached Secretary of the Treasury Howell

6. Atlanta *Daily Intelligencer,* September 10, 26, November 2, 1860. See also Milledgeville *Federal Union,* April 10, June 26, 1860; Macon *Telegraph,* November 6, 1860.

7. Atlanta *Daily Intelligencer,* September 10, 14, October 22, 31, 1860. See also November 1, 1860. A similar argument has been advanced in Richard H. Brown, "The Missouri Crisis: Slavery, and the Politics of Jacksonianism," *South Atlantic Quarterly,* LXV (Winter, 1966), 55–72.

Cobb in Washington, D. C. in early August that it was going to be "easy" to carry Georgia for Breckinridge. By October an Atlanta editor even predicted that a national Breckinridge victory was "certain." [8]

Confidence in a Breckinridge victory was reluctantly shared by many Breckinridge opponents. Alexander Stephens predicted in early July that Breckinridge "will carry much the larger portion" of the state. Even though Stephens personally favored Douglas, he wrote a friend that, "of course there is no prospect of his getting the vote of the state." Expectation of a Breckinridge victory in Georgia sapped the energy that might otherwise have gone into more effective Bell or Douglas organizations. Neither group matched the Breckinridge effort, in part because of reports like the one from northeast Georgia that "the Democracy [is] almost unanimous for Breckinridge." Even the popular former governor of Georgia, Herschel V. Johnson, Douglas' running mate, could not overcome the grass-roots opposition to Douglas. [9]

Uncertainty about the outcome of the presidential election was focused less on Georgia than on the nation. Breckinridge opponents in Georgia claimed that the leaders of the Breckinridge party hoped that by splitting the constituency of the national Democratic party they would insure Lincoln's election, which would in turn "result in the dissolution of the Union." [10] But whether Lincoln would be elected president by a majority of the electoral college was up to northern voters. The way Georgians distributed their votes among Bell, Douglas, and Breckinridge was an important expression of voter sentiment, but it had little to do with whether Lincoln would get the votes he needed. The uncertainty about the presidential election in Georgia,

---

8. J. T. Irvin to Colonel D. C. Barrow, July 14, 1860, also Folder 19, in Colonel David C. Barrow Papers, University of Georgia. Barrow was in charge of the Eighth Congressional District. His correspondence during the late summer and fall of 1860 is full of political intelligence. J. W. Spullock to Howell Cobb, August 7, 1860, Cobb-Erwin-Lamar Letters, University of Georgia; Atlantic *Daily Intelligencer,* October 3, 1860.

9. Stephens to J. Henly Smith, July 4, August 8, 30, September 10, 1860, in Phillips (ed.), *Correspondence,* 484, 491, 493, 494; A Southern Democrat to editor, July 14, 1860, in Milledgeville *Federal Union,* July 31, 1860; [?] to Alexander H. Stephens, October 18, 1860, in Stephens Papers, Library of Congress.

10. E. to editor, September 19, 1860, Savannah *Republican,* September 22, 1860. See also *ibid.,* July 7, 1860, and Rome *Weekly Courier,* November 2, 1860.

then, was the uncertainty of a people who were on the sidelines of a contest in which they had a deep personal interest. There were few, if any, who doubted that if Lincoln were defeated, then the secession crisis would pass, at least for the time being. As the presidential campaign matured, Georgians' attention tended to be drawn away from the vote in Georgia toward that in the nation.

To many Georgians, the election of Lincoln seemed "inevitable." Others continued to "hope [that] Lincoln will be defeated." As Georgia's November election day neared and reports of Republican successes filtered in from some northern states, the probability of Lincoln's election loomed ever larger. This prompted proposals, especially among Bell supporters, for a "fusion" of all Georgia parties behind one electoral slate pledged to cast Georgia's electoral vote for whatever candidate had the best chance of defeating Lincoln. Although "the fusion" was vigorously pursued, particularly by Bell leader Benjamin H. Hill, it came to nothing. Breckinridge spokesmen ridiculed the idea as an attempt to defeat their candidate. Not even Bell and Douglas leaders could agree on the terms of "the fusion." [11]

This maneuvering misled many Georgians into thinking that they might somehow prevent Lincoln's election. Others, who were aware of the futility of such notions, could do little but wait for the verdict from the North. As Georgians waited, their mood was dark and tense. Ardent secessionist Thomas R. R. Cobb wrote his brother Howell that either the Union or the South would be "irretrievably gone if Lincoln is elected." "I confess I feel *very sad*," he added, "the forebodings of my mind are of the most depressing character." [12]

By November 8 nearly all Georgians knew that Lincoln had been elected. That knowledge created a consensus in Georgia, and across

11. R. M. Johnston to Alexander H. Stephens, October 15, 1860, J. Henly Smith to Stephens, October 30, 1860, in Stephens Papers, Library of Congress; A. R. Lawton to Howell Cobb, November 5, 1860, in Howell Cobb Papers, University of Georgia. For examples of Bell supporters see Savannah *Republican,* October 1, 22, 1860; Augusta *Chronicle and Sentinel,* October 6, 20, 24, 1860; Rome *Weekly Courier,* October 26, 1860. Breckinridge press coverage of "fusion" activities can be sampled in Atlanta *Daily Intelligencer,* September 10, 13, 1860; Macon *Telegraph,* October 6, 24, 27, November 1, 3, 1860. For a discussion of Hill's role see Haywood J. Pearce, Jr., *Benjamin H. Hill: Secession and Reconstruction* (Chicago: University of Chicago Press, 1928), 38–40. Atlanta *Daily Intelligencer,* October 22, 23, 24, 30, 1860.

12. T. R. R. Cobb to Howell Cobb, November 5, 1860, Howell Cobb Papers.

the South, about the question at hand: *"What shall be done?"* [13] With that question, the campaign for secession began in earnest.

The Campaign for Delegates to the State Convention

As they tried to decide what should be done, Georgians suffered from no shortage of advice. Accompanying news of Lincoln's election were reports of Governor Brown's message to the legislature urging immediate secession, an appropriation of a million dollars for defense, and the calling of a state convention to consider measures necessary for the protection of Georgia's rights. Although the legislature quickly responded with the defense appropriation and the authorization for a convention, it did not pass a proposed immediate secession resolution, in spite of the presence in Milledgeville of many prosecession Breckinridge leaders from Georgia and of Edmund Ruffin of Virginia, Robert Barnwell Rhett of South Carolina, and W. L. Harris of Mississippi, who were seated by the Legislature as delegates from their states.[14] In addition to these counsels, the legislature, and the rest of the state via extensive newspaper coverage, were the beneficiaries of a series of speeches by prominent Georgians.

13. Rome *Weekly Courier,* November 10, 1860. In Georgia, Breckinridge received a plurality (52,172), and Bell (43,069) and Douglas (11,627) shared the majority. See Walter Dean Burnham, *Presidential Ballots* (Baltimore: Johns Hopkins Press, 1955), 332.

14. Governor Joseph E. Brown, *Special Message to the Legislature of Georgia, on our Federal Relations, Retaliatory State Legislation, the Right of Secession, &c, November 7, 1860* (Milledgeville, Ga.: Boughton, Nisbet, & Barnes, 1860), reprinted in Candler (ed.), *Confederate Records,* I, 19–57. There are a number of accounts of the issues, personalities, and events of the campaign for secession. See for example: I. W. Avery, *The History of Georgia From 1850 to 1881* (New York: Brown and Derby, 1881), 130–48; Phillips, *Georgia and State Rights,* 193–202; Philip J. Green, "Secession in Georgia, 1860–1861," *North Dakota University Quarterly Journal,* XVII (1927), 248–65; E. Merton Coulter, *A Short History of Georgia* (Chapel Hill: University of North Carolina Press, 1933), 296–99; George V. Irons, "The Secession Movement in Georgia, 1850–1861" (Ph.D. dissertation, Duke University, 1936); T. Conn Bryan, "The Secession of Georgia," *Georgia Historical Quarterly,* XXXI (1947), 89–111; Horace Montgomery, *Cracker Parties* (Baton Rouge: Louisiana State University Press, 1950), 243–47; T. Conn Bryan, *Confederate Georgia* (Athens: University of Georgia Press, 1953), 1–8; William E. Bates, "The Last Stand for Union in Georgia," *Georgia Review,* VI (1953), 455–67; Ralph A. Wooster, *The Secession Conventions of the South* (Princeton: Princeton University Press, 1962), 80–84; N. B. Beck, "The Secession Debate in Georgia; November 1860-January 1861," in J. Jeffrey Auer (ed.), *Antislavery and Disunion, 1858–1861: Studies in the Rhetoric of Compromise and Conflict* (New York: Harper and Row, 1963), 331–59; Herschel V. Johnson, "From the Autobiography of Herschel V. Johnson," *American Historical Review,* XXX (1925), 323.

The speeches, all of which were delivered in the hall of the House of Representatives in Milledgeville, were begun on November 6 by Henry L. Benning, an eminent jurist who had recently completed a six-year term as an associate justice of the Georgia Supreme Court. Benning's advocacy of immediate secession was seconded the following day by Governor Brown in his special message to the legislature, which was followed five days later, on the twelfth and thirteenth, by the prosecession addresses of Thomas R. R. Cobb and Robert Toombs. Opposition to immediate secession was expressed on the following three days, November 14, 15, and 16, by Alexander Stephens, Benjamin Hill, and Herschel V. Johnson.[15] In these speeches spread over ten days, Georgians had presented to them as concentrated, complete, and intelligent a discussion of secession as was available anywhere else in the South. In a sense, the speeches were a series of state of the union addresses which more or less officially began the campaign for delegates to the state convention. Printed as pamphlets, the speeches were distributed throughout the state, and, judging from the many appreciative letters received by the speakers, they reached a wide audience.[16]

Meanwhile, many Georgians were gathering in public meetings in their counties, adopting resolutions recommending appropriate action

15. Henry L. Benning, *Speech on Federal Relations, November 6, 1860,* reported by A. E. Marshall, University of Georgia. Brown, *Special Message, Nov. 7, 1860;* Thomas R. R. Cobb, *Substance of Remarks Made in the Hall of the House of Representatives, Monday Evening, November 12, 1860* (Atlanta: John H. Seals, 1860); Robert Toombs, *Speech on the Crisis Delivered Before the Georgia Legislature, December 7, 1860* [an incorrect date; the speech was actually delivered November 13, 1860] (Washington: Lemuel Towers, 1860), University of Georgia. For Stephens' speech, see *Prophecy and Fulfillment: Speech of A. H. Stephens, of Georgia, in Opposition to Secession in 1860* (New York: Holman, 1863), University of Georgia or Candler (ed.), *Confederate Records,* I, 157–82. Hill's speech is in Benjamin H. Hill, Jr., *Senator Benjamin H. Hill of Georgia* (Atlanta: n.p., 1890), 365–24. Johnson's speech is reported in his "Autobiography," 323–24.

16. See the discussion of the Georgia speeches in William W. Freehling, "The Editorial Revolution, Virginia, and the Coming of the Civil War: A Review Essay," *Civil War History,* XVI (1970), 64–72. Mary Ann Cobb wrote her husband Howell that their house was "filled with secession Documents" including the speeches of Toombs, T. R. R. Cobb, and Benning. Mary Ann Cobb to Howell Cobb, December 10, 1860, in Howell Cobb Papers. The Telamon Cuyler Collection, University of Georgia, contains several letters to Governor Brown thanking him for his speech. For appreciation of Hill's speech, see William S. Dobbins to John S. Dobbins, December 23, 1860, in Dobbins Papers, Emory University. For the dozens of letters to Alexander Stephens, see the Stephens Papers, Library of Congress Collection and Manhattanville Collection on microfilm at Emory University.

and, after the legislature had provided for the election, nominating candidates. Around the state, especially in the towns, groups of Minute Men were organized. By November 10 the Atlanta Minute Men had over four hundred members pledged to use "all lawful and honorable means to bring about a peaceable secession of the State of Georgia . . . [and] to unite our people as a band of brothers—in resistance to Northern aggression—and in defense of ourselves, our property and our firesides."[17] Some charged that the Minute Men were overzealous in uniting Georgians as a band of brothers. Reports of intimidation of opponents of immediate secession were common. In Albany, a bricklayer who had voted for Bell was suspected of helping Lincoln and was "ordered" to leave town; an "enterprising Book merchant" piled a bundle of *Harper's* magazines in the middle of Broad Street, "sprinkled" them with "camphere" and "burned [them] to ashes amid the plaudits of the crowd." Reports of "abolition emissaries" and of possible slave insurrections rippled through Georgia as they had since late in the summer. From Savannah a woman wrote her mother that "several men [had been] tarred and feathered, then sent away" for "tampering with the negors [sic]." "One was even persuading them to rise and kill the whites on Skidaway Island and," she added, "he told them as soon as Lincoln was President they would all be free [;] I think such men should be hung" While some were in a hanging mood, most Georgians were "taken up . . . thinking and talking about the present state of affairs." Mary Ann Cobb wrote her husband that her brother John "thinks of nothing but secession—and is working all day for it." Instead of proclaiming their sentiments with campaign buttons (or bumper stickers), ladies wore homespun and men sported blue secession cockades as ordinary Georgians experienced what Herschel V.

17. For reports from these nominating conventions, see nearly any Georgia newspaper for November and December 1860. For a selection of the resolutions passed at county meetings, see Candler (ed.), *Confederate Records*, I, 58–156. For firsthand accounts of the meetings see Rev. C. C. Jones to Mrs. Mary S. Mallard, December 13, 1860, in Robert Manson Meyers (ed.), *The Children of Pride* (New Haven: Yale University Press, 1972), 633–35; and the letters to Alexander Stephens from J. R. Sneed, November 8, James D. Russ, November 13, Porter Ingram, December 18, 1860, in Stephens Papers, Library of Congress, and from Linton Stephens, December 9, 1860, in Stephens Papers, Manhattanville College Collection. Atlanta *Daily Intelligencer*, October 30, 31, November 2, 10, 1860. A long list of names of members was published November 16, 1860.

Johnson referred to as the "bewildering" excitement of the campaign for secession.[18]

By the first or second week in December nearly all of the counties had nominated two sets of candidates for their delegates to the convention, although eleven counties were presented with only one set.[19] On the whole, the candidates were nominated by groups of like-minded men either to favor or to oppose immediate secession in the convention. Thus, the purpose of the short campaign was less to acquaint voters with the candidates than to obtain voters' support for one policy or another. With editorials, reports of speeches, and news the press was instrumental in defining the various policies and articulating the issues of the campaign. In general, the former Breckinridge papers were vigorous, even vehement in their support of immediate secession, while the former Bell and Douglas papers tended to oppose immediate secession and to favor some plan of staying in the Union at least until a united South could be created.

Many prominent Breckinridge leaders, who had just carried the state for their candidate, were back in the field campaigning for secession. "[T]o hold our own," a secessionist wrote from Columbus, "we want enthusiasm that can only be created by speaking." The speaking they got. "The secessionists all over the state are active and noisy," cooperationist Herschel V. Johnson accurately observed. T. R. R. Cobb, for example, kept a speaking schedule during December that would seem jammed even to a politician in an age of air travel. And

18. J. A. Stewart, a self-proclaimed "Union man" from Atlanta wrote the editor of the Nashville *Democrat* (March 2, 1861) that organizations like the Minute Men "have had in view the coercion of Union men into the support of their revolution, and that such was and is their chief object." Atlanta *Daily Intelligencer,* March 9, 1861; Albany *Patriot,* December 6, 1860. Rome *Weekly Courier,* August 28, September 7, 1860; South to editor of Gainesville *Air-Line Eagle,* October 27, 1860, in Atlanta *Daily Intelligencer,* November 6 1860; Macon *Telegraph,* September 4, October 16, 1860; H. J. Wayne to Mama H., December 3, 1860, in Edward Harden Papers, Duke University; Mary Ann Cobb to Howell Cobb, December 10, 1860, Lamar Cobb to Howell Cobb, November 14, 1860, in Howell Cobb Papers. See Johnson, "Autobiography," 323. On the use of homespun and cockades, see for example Milledgeville *Federal Union,* January 1, 1861; Atlanta *Daily Intelligencer* for December, 1860.

19. The legislature set representation in the convention at three delegates for those thirty-seven counties with two representatives in the house, and two delegates for the other counties which had one representative. *An Act to Authorize and Require the Governor of the State of Georgia to Call a Convention of the People of this State,* Sec. III, in Candler (ed.), *Confederate Records,* I, 207.

Cobb gave four-hour speeches with "great effect," a sympathizer reported, noting that, remarkably, "nobody was tired!" Impelling the secessionists was the belief that a "desperate battle has to be fought in Georgia," and that the outcome was by no means certain.[20]

Secessionists were encouraged by reports from Macon that "the secession feeling is waxing warmer daily," from Savannah that "the greatest portion are for secession," from Newnan that "secession is growing like wild-fire up in this [west-central] part of the state," and that in general, "[e]verything is cheering for secession—Georgia is certain to go out." News that South Carolina would secede and, after December 20 that she had, added to secessionists' perception that "the prairie is on fire" and that "most people have become convinced that we mean to go out of the Union." Evidence that this perception was accurate was provided by numerous reports of conservative unionists, former Bell and Douglas men, who had recently embraced immediate secession, or, as cooperationists viewed it, who had "yielded to the clamorous howl."[21] Yet the impassioned efforts of secessionists demonstrated that they did not interpret these encouraging trends as indications that a secessionist victory was assured. If they had been certain of victory, they would not have worked so hard.

Doubts drove the secessionist campaign efforts. After the failure of the secession resolution in the state legislature, it seemed to a secessionist observer as if "[a]ll is confusion . . . among our friends while the submissionists are concentrating their strength and will give us a strong fight for the Convention." While some feared the cooperationists were more unified, others worried that the "cry of cooperation is injuring us—while it means submission it deceives a

20. Herschel V. Johnson to Alexander H. Stephens, November 30, 1860, in Johnson Papers, Duke University; A. Hood to Howell Cobb, December 19, 1860, T. R. R. Cobb to Howell Cobb, December 18, 1860, John B. Lamar to Howell Cobb, December 11, 1860, all in Howell Cobb Papers; Jno. M. Richardson to Robert N. Gourdin, December 5, 1860, in Robert Newman Gourdin Papers, Emory University.

21. John B. Lamar to Howell Cobb, November 19, 1860, T. R. R. Cobb to Howell Cobb, December 8, 1860, John B. Lamar to Howell Cobb, December 11, 1860, all in Howell Cobb Papers; H. J. Wayne to Mama H., December 3, 1860, Harden Papers; W. R. Fleming to Robert N. Gourdin, November 27, 1860, in Gourdin Papers; Ben to Bel, November 27, 1860, in Joseph Belknap Smith Papers, Duke University; Herschel V. Johnson to Alexander H. Stephens, November 30, 1860, in Johnson Papers, Duke University.

great many." Some secessionists were troubled less by the specifics of
the cooperationist position than by the general nature of the polity. "So
demoralized have our people been by their previous party strifes," one
secessionist brooded, "and so ignorant are the masses, and so basely
corrupt are some of the leaders (Hill, Johnson, and Stephens) that it
will be almost an unexpected blessing to carry a majority in the Convention." Still others worried that time was on the side of the
cooperationists, that in late November Georgia was "all right, but that
it will be difficult to keep her so." To counteract the potentially
moderating effect of time, Governor Brown wrote a private letter to
Howell Cobb urging him to impress upon the South Carolina convention that if South Carolina "goes out promptly her actions will cause a
thrill to pass through the great popular heart of Georgia, and we shall
certainly succeed in the elections and follow her. But if she passes an
ordinance to take effect at some future day we are beat and all lost." [22]

These secessionist concerns about the momentum of their movement, the demoralization of the polity, and the appeal of the
cooperationists were focused on two areas of the state. One was north
Georgia, a relatively poor region of small farmers and few slaveholders
which was enclosed within the Fifth and Sixth congressional districts,
where the "great trouble lies," T. R. R. Cobb wrote his brother Howell. Shortly after the elder Cobb had resigned from Buchanan's cabinet
to come home to Georgia to strengthen the secessionist campaign, his
brother urged him, "By all means come *directly to Athens. . . .* We
have trouble above here [in north Georgia], and *no one* but *yourself* can
quell it." Late in December, Howell Cobb toured the upcountry on a
strenuous schedule, speaking to large audiences who listened with "the
greatest attention." "I found the union or *submission* sentiment *overwhelming,*" he wrote his wife, adding, "but I am satisfied that a great
change was made." A supporter wrote Cobb that he had indeed "done
a great deal of good by speaking in our country"; secessionists were

22. A. H. Prince to Mrs. Howell Cobb, November 22, 1860, A. Hood to Howell Cobb,
December 19, 1860, Governor Joseph E. Brown to Howell Cobb, December 15, 1860, all in
Howell Cobb Papers; James Mercer Green to Robert N. Gourdin, December 15, 1860, Louis G.
Young to Gourdin, November 27, 1860, in Gourdin Papers. See also, May Spencer Ringold,
"Robert Newman Gourdin and the '1860 Association,'" *Georgia Historical Quarterly,* LV
(1971), 501–509.

"gaining ground" although they were still in the minority. The problem, the man reported, was that "some of our Old Democrats was determined that you should not open thare Eyes; They would not come to Here you."[23] The stubbornness of these old Democrats was a hint that Cobb's speaking tour had not quelled the trouble in the upcountry, as his brother had hoped.

The second area of potential trouble for the secessionists existed throughout the countryside of Georgia. A Rome editor warned that "revolutions of public sentiment are sometimes exceedingly rapid in the Towns and along the railroad lines where the people are in the habit of reading the daily papers, of thinking quick, and where, not infrequently, one leading spirit gives tone and direction to the whole place." In contrast, the editor noted, the "great mass of people who live in the country... come to conclusions more slowly and dispassionately. They *think,* every man for himself, and do not act to any considerable extent upon the prejudices of each other." Whether or not the editor was right about the considered judgment of country folk, there were numerous reports that secession sentiment was stronger in the towns than in the countryside. T. R. R. Cobb had anticipated this in his November speech when he urged the legislators to pass a secession ordinance themselves rather than to "wait... till the grog-shops and cross-roads shall send up a discordant voice from a divided people." But the legislature waited and gave the grogshops and crossroads an opportunity to speak in the January 2 election. To bring these country voices into harmony with disunion, secessionists worked all the harder, trying to drown out the strains of the "syren [*sic*] song of Union." The secessionists "were more than zealous," Herschel V. Johnson remembered in 1867, "they were frenzied."[24]

Johnson's memory was colored by the sense that the years since

23. T. R. R. Cobb to Howell Cobb, December 8, 15, 1860. See also John B. Cobb to Howell Cobb, December 14, 1860, T. R. R. Cobb to John B. Lamar, December 15, 1860, and T. R. R. Cobb to Howell Cobb, December 18, 1860, Howell Cobb to Mary Ann Cobb, December 26, 29, 1860, A. M. Evans to Howell Cobb, December 26, 1860, all in Howell Cobb Papers. See also, John Eddins Simpson, *Howell Cobb: The Politics of Ambition* (Chicago: Adams Press, 1973), 131–45.

24. Rome *Weekly Courier,* December 1, 1860. Cobb, *Substance of Remarks,* 17; Atlanta *Daily Intelligencer,* November 23, 1860; Johnson, "Autobiography," 324.

1860 had vindicated his opposition to secession, and his characteriza-
tion of secessionist activity was correspondingly exaggerated. Yet, in
comparison to the efforts of the cooperationists, it was accurate
enough. Cooperationist leaders were closer to resignation and paralysis
than to frenzy and zeal. Neither Johnson nor Stephens actively campaigned against secession. Johnson, feeling "prostrate and powerless
on account of my adhering honestly to the fate of the Nat. Democracy
in the late election," took solace from having "done right" and decided to be "content with the consequences . . . [to] diligently abide the
tide of events, without much effort to give it direction." Alexander
Stephens spoke for many cooperationists when he wrote a friend that
he was "inclined to let those who sowed the wind reap the whirlwind,
or control it, if they can."[25]

Letters came to Stephens from throughout the state, pleading with
him to speak in their area, and attesting to the disorganization and
demoralization among opponents of disunion. "[T]here is no one to
raise his voice to give the masses confidence in the position their hearts
dictate to them to assume," wrote one cooperationist. Speaking out
was "perilous" since "Those who favor moderation are branded as
cowards or traitors."[26] The result, as another cooperationist put it, was
that "*we have no leader in this county* all timmid men not a man of our
party in the county can get up—or that will do it—and give his views
you see at once the difficulty we are laboring under."[27] But Stephens,
pleading illness, remained at home, observing the harvest of the
whirlwind, and cooperationists remained unorganized.

Although the cooperationists resigned themselves to drift through
the campaign, they still had hope that the secessionists would be defeated. Abraham Lincoln himself was a source of hope to some, including one who was "*not at all* alarmed as to secession or dissolution
being a [con]sequence [of Lincoln's election]." Lincoln, he wrote,

25. Herschel V. Johnson to Alexander H. Stephens, November 30, 1860, in Johnson Papers;
Alexander H. Stephens to J. Henly Smith, November 23, 1860, in Phillips (ed.), *Correspondence,* 503.
26. James Atkins to Alexander H. Stephens, December 10, 1860, in Stephens Papers, Duke
University.
27. James N. Montgomery to Linton Stephens, December 5, 1860, in Stephens Papers,
Library of Congress.

would "shape his course to conciliate the South. And by a *free use* of *'Pap'* will be obliged to succeed in harmonizing the secessionist generally." Others rested their hopes on "popular feelings," seeing "indications [that] are unmistakeable that *Cooperation* will prevail, by an unprecedented majority." Linton Stephens wrote his brother that "Georgia of herself is *largely* opposed to immediate secession," an opinion that Herschel V. Johnson shared.[28] But cooperationists' hopes, like their organization, were diffuse and unfocused.

Challenging these vague hopes was a fairly well-defined development that threatened to undermine what little confidence the cooperationists could muster. Coupled with reports that "we are gaining ground and outside of the City [of Columbus] we can get along well enough" was the troubling news that "we have a hard time in the City." Or, as the citizens of Coweta and Heard counties put it, "Hear in hour County the hasty men are verry sever on the prudent men of the County and are useing evry means to forse the most quiet man to take theire position and hour Country people are all opposed to hasty action." The most disheartening news was that prudent men in towns, "gentlemen of talent and ability," men "regarded as the bell weather [*sic*] of the Union party," whose Union "sentiments at one period were regarded by some as obnoxious and even dangerous," had undergone a "conversion" and were advocating secession. The reports of these conversions were so numerous that Herschel V. Johnson, after reviewing them, wrote Alexander Stephens, "Indeed, I do not know who are left." With cooperationist ranks being deserted by many prominent former unionists, and with fear that the voters "will be misled by the noisy advocates of immediate secession," cooperationist hopes dimmed. "If you have any hope," Johnson wrote Stephens late in December, "reflect its rays on me."[29]

---

28. George W. Lamar to Gazaway Bugg Lamar, November 12, 1860, in Gazaway Bugg Lamar Papers, University of Georgia; George W. Lamar to Alexander H. Stephens, December 27, 1860, John Billings to Alexander H. Stephens, November 30, 1860, James P. Hambleton to Stephens, November 29, 1860, all in Stephens Papers, Library of Congress; Linton Stephens to Alexander H. Stephens, November 26, 1860, in Stephens Papers, Manhattanville College Collection; Herschel V. Johnson to Alexander Stephens, December 22, 1860, in Johnson Papers.

29. Porter Ingram to Alexander H. Stephens, December 18, 1860, Wm. T. Patterson to Stephens, December 6, 1860, Citizens of Coweta and Heard counties to Stephens, December 13,

Yet, the greatest difficulty confronting the cooperationists was probably neither hopelessness nor disorganization but lack of agreement
about what should be done. Their general strategy was simple enough.
The southern states would cooperate in presenting a southern ultimatum to the North, a move cooperationists believed would, in turn,
marshal conservative northern support for the southern position, reassure the South, and save the Union. But when cooperationists translated this strategy into a concrete plan, their position became confused
and ambiguous. There were too many answers to the questions raised
by the cooperationists. Should the South wait until all the slave states
could agree on an ultimatum, or was it enough for all or some of the
states of the lower South to agree? How would agreement be reached?
By congressional representatives? By a special convention? When and
where should such a convention meet, and how would the delegates be
chosen? And, if a southern consensus were achieved, how would
northern support be manifested? By a similar northern convention?
Could the South depend upon mere professions of northern support, or
were certain actions required? If action was necessary, what specific
northern actions would reassure the South? How long should the South
wait for these reassuring words and deeds? A few months? A year?
Two years? In short, cooperationist answers to these questions added
up to various plans for unifying the South, any number of lengths of
time to remain in the Union, and all manner of tests of northern
opinion. About the only thing beyond dispute in the cooperationists'
position was opposition to unilateral, separate state secession.

Unable to agree on an appropriate tactic, cooperationists were
doomed to respond to events rather than to shape them. It was virtually
impossible for cooperationists to take the political offensive. Instead,
their position was progressively narrowed and undermined by events in

---

1860, J. R. Sneed to Stephens, November 8, 1860, James D. Russ to Sephens, November 13,
1860, Benj. R. Reese to Stephens, November 26, 1860, Citizens of Macon to Stephens, December 6, 1860, James J. Scarborough to Stephens, November 28, 1860, A. H. Wyche to
Stephens, December 25, 1860, all in Stephens Papers, Library of Congress. The quotations are
from an article describing the conversion of James Johnson, Columbus *Weekly Times,* November
30, 1860, *ibid.* See also, A. R. Lawton to Howell Cobb, November 5, 1860, in Howell Cobb
Papers. Johnson to Stephens, November 30, 1860, Johnson to Stephens, December 22, 1860, in
Johnson Papers.

November and December: the resignation of Howell Cobb from Buchanan's cabinet to campaign for secession in Georgia, the secession of South Carolina, the campaigns throughout the states of the lower South for delegates to state conventions, and then finally on election day, January 2, by order of Governor Brown, the seizure of Fort Pulaski in the Savannah harbor. It is little wonder that cooperationists came more and more to believe that "all seems to be lost" and that they "must yield to what seems to be inevitable."[30] Perhaps the greater wonder is that there were any cooperationists at all.

Indeed, that perplexed secessionists, some of whom had "no use politically with a man who deviates one degree from the true line of secession."[31] The campaign for secession gave Georgians an opportunity to decide whether secession was the true line. While their choices were clear-cut—immediate secession, yes or no—the reasons for their choices were complex. To understand why Georgians favored or opposed immediate secession requires knowing not only what secessionists and cooperationists said but also why they said it as they did.

30. Governor Joseph E. Brown to Colonel A. R. Lawton, January 2, 1860, in Telamon Cuyler Papers; Herschel V. Johnson to Alexander H. Stephens, December 22, 1860, in Johnson Papers.

31. W. N. Hutchins to Dear Fritz, December 19, 1860, in Nathan L. Hutchins Papers, Duke University.

3

The
Secessionist
Argument

The secessionist argument was a litany disguised as historical analysis, an incantation which promised to create a South that never would be out of a South that never was. Appropriately, the form of the argument resembled a rhythmic liturgical chant. Tedious constitutional arguments and repetitious lists of grievances were the verses of the chant which gave the argument what secessionists hoped was an irresistible, hypnotic quality. Without this quality, the intellectual obstacles which the argument confronted might have been actual roadblocks to secession. It contributed more to the goal of the secessionists to chant *Te Dixium* than to consider exactly what the chant implied. To identify the implications and to explore their meaning we must focus on the interplay between theme and variation in the secessionist argument.

Secession as Revolution

"If [secession] is, as I esteem it, revolution, then I am for it," Judge Eugenius A. Nisbet announced to an audience in Macon, as he proclaimed his conversion to the cause. In public, other secessionists were more cautious about calling secession revolution, perhaps because, as one secessionist privately wrote another, late in January, 1861, "it is desirable that our revolution should be attended with as slight a jar as possible to the habits of our people." To many Georgians it was jarring enough that secessionists called upon them to exercise their "inalienable right of revolution." Many cooperationists opposed secession precisely because, in their judgment, it was "revolution, with all [its] imaginable horrors." Few Georgians doubted that the call for the convention in Georgia was indeed the first step, as one editor noted,

28

"toward the great revolution upon which we are now entering—for a *revolution* it surely *is.*" Although they differed profoundly over its desirability, Georgians shared the perception that the "spirit of revolution is rampant."[1]

Secessionists' choice of revolutionary rhetoric is somewhat surprising. Rather than revolt in the name of the protection of slavery and the rights of slaveholders, secessionists turned to the Founding Fathers for their revolutionary message. They sought to protect the liberties of all Georgians, they claimed. By invoking the "precious heritage" of 1776, secessionists emphasized that their "Second Revolution" was in the tradition of "Adams, Franklin, Sherman, Livingston and Jefferson, the authors of the immortal Declaration." Calling upon the immortal Declaration not only located secession within a sanctified and successful tradition, but it also rested the case for secession on the oppression of an entire people. Thus secession, like independence from Britain, was a remedy that was both appropriate and safe. Secessionists argued that the only thing revolutionary about secession was independence. Georgians who were "patriotic conservatives" should do "as Washington, Hancock, and other conservative Americans did, when coercive measures were adopted by the King and Parliament to collect a three-pence tax on tea imported into Boston—join the resisting party and aid in achieving perfect independence."[2] Like the Boston Tea Party, secession was a bold, militant, and—because of the tea party—thoroughly traditional step, according to secessionists. "Perfect inde-

1. Nisbet explained that he did not believe that secession was a constitutional right. E. A. Nisbet, Speech to citizens of Macon, Macon *Telegraph,* December 12, 1860; Julius Hillyer to Howell Cobb, January 30, 1861, in Ulrich Bonnell Phillips (ed.), *The Correspondence of Robert Toombs, Alexander H. Stephens, and Howell Cobb* (Washington: Government Printing Office, 1913) 535; W. N. Hutchins to Dear Fritz, December 19, 1860, in Nathan L. Hutchins Papers, Duke University; N. M. Crawford to Alexander H. Stephens, November 23, 1860, in Stephens Papers, Library of Congress Collection on microfilm, University of Georgia; Rome *Weekly Courier,* November 24, 1860; Herschel V. Johnson to Alexander H. Stephens, November 30, 1860, in Johnson Papers, Duke University. On the theme of revolution see Emory M. Thomas, *The Confederacy as a Revolutionary Experience* (Englewood Cliffs, N.J.: Prentice-Hall, 1971), 23–42.

2. Robert Toombs, *Speech on the Crisis, Delivered Before the Georgia Legislature, December 7, 1860* (Washington: Lemuel Towers, 1860), 14; Milledgeville *Southern Federal Union,* May 21, July 2, 1861; A Conservative to editor, Augusta *Daily Constitutionalist,* January 18, 1861. Patrick Henry's liberty or death speech was reprinted by the Atlanta *Daily Intelligencer,* November 23, 1860.

pendence" from the North would preserve the heritage of all Georgians just as American independence had guaranteed the rights of all Americans.

The social consequences of secession would be just as salutary as those which followed independence from Britain. But the social threat of the British was small compared to that posed by the Lincoln administration for, as Henry L. Benning explained to the state legislators, "the meaning of Mr. Lincoln's election to the Presidency is the abolition of slavery as soon as the Republican party shall have acquired the strength to abolish it." To the degree that the word "revolution" connoted social upheavals comparable to the French Revolution, secessionists sought to identify such frightful consequences with staying in the Union. Cooperation, not secession, was revolutionary. The "law of self-preservation" mandated secession, Benning said to the cheering legislators. While the dictates of that law were revolutionary, they were nothing more than the dictates of 1776 made even more compelling by imagining how the dictates of 1789 might be rendered in a racially divided, slaveless South. "Let us follow the example of our ancestors," said Benning, "and prove ourselves worthy sons of worthy sires."[3]

Just as British "tyranny" had been described in 1776 as an external threat, the secessionists portrayed "Black Republicanism" as a foreign menace which should be treated as if it were an infectious disease. If Georgia were isolated from the source of the infection—the North— then the disease could be purged and cured. Secession was recommended both as a prophylactic measure and as a genuine remedy for the infection. But implicit in secessionists' views was the recognition that Georgia was not presently healthy. Why, after all, was the Republican virus contagious in southern climes? Why weren't Georgians ideologically immune?

In a sense, cooperationists denied that Black Republicanism was a dangerously contagious disease. At least, they urged, Georgia should wait for an appropriate incubation period to see if precipitate action

---

3. Henry L. Benning, *Speech on Federal Relations, November 6, 1860,* reported by A. E. Marshal, University of Georgia, 2, 16.

was in fact necessary. T. R. R. Cobb complained that he heard "on every side the bold assertion that 'Lincoln will make a good President' and all the timid men are saying 'Let us wait for an *overt* act.'" Meanwhile, the most immediate danger, according to conservative cooperationists, was not external but internal, the result of the "dying out" of the "spirit of the Revolution" of 1776. The "spirit of mutual forbearance, mutual concession and mutual fraternity" had "decayed" in both Georgia and the nation, and in its place had "arisen a spirit of radicalism, of innovation, of restlessness, and of intolerance," which ultimately threatened "to destroy our experiment of self-government, and to write *failure* on all our works." Both the public and its leaders were responsible for the general advance in "corruption" that these cooperationists sensed. On the one hand, "the people [are] mad, and drunken, and crazy," while "lawlessness runs riot, liberty is but another name for licentiousness, and patriotism is swallowed up in partyism." On the other hand, these conservative cooperationists believed, public leaders excited rather than cooled the passions of the people. Repeating an analysis of the prerequisites of a republic that the revolutionaries of 1776 had developed, Alexander Stephens wrote that "Republicks [*sic*] can only be maintained by virtue, intelligence and patriotism. We have but little public virtue, heroic virtue or patriotism now amongst our public men," he continued. "They are generally selfish, looking not to country but to individual aggrandisement." These dangers that conservative cooperationists perceived were, in their view, the result of the very nature of man and governments. At best, secession was no remedy for these dangers. At worst, these cooperationists feared, secession could turn a lamentable state of affairs into a catastrophe. As one secessionist accurately characterized this cooperationist criticism: "The submissionists say . . . [that] if the Union is disolved, the bloody scenes of the French revolution will be re-enacted on American soil. They say if this government is abandoned, we can never construct another so good."[4]

---

4. T. R. R. Cobb to Howell Cobb, November 5, 1860, in Howell Cobb Papers, University of Georgia; Augusta *Chronicle and Sentinel,* October 7, 1860; Alexander H. Stephens to J. Henly Smith, January 22, August 25, September 15, 16, 1860, in Phillips (ed.), *Correspondence,* 458, 493, 496, 497–500; Clarke to editor, Athens *Southern Banner,* December 27, 1860.

Secessionist responses echoed sentiments that had matured with the
nation the secessionists were preparing to leave. Secessionists were
willing to acknowledge publicly some internal weaknesses. "Luxury
and extravagance, were fast becoming with us National evils and National Sins," which, one editor grimly noted, "a civil war may cure."
While secession would require many "sacrifices," the "discipline will
do us good," secessionists predicted. And rather than increase the
present dangers, as cooperationists feared, secession would "sweep
away the past corruptions of the Government." Deliverance from these
internal evils required no more than remaining true to the ideals of
self-government set forth in the Declaration of Independence, secessionists argued. Cooperationist doubts, one secessionist wrote,
amounted to saying, "I believe, men of Georgia, that you are ripe for
anarchy and crime, I have you in a government where you can be
controlled, and I intend to hold you there, [because] I have no confidence in your capacity to govern yourselves or to form a government
for yourselves."[5]

Indeed, many conservative cooperationists did doubt that the ills of
self-government could be remedied merely be withdrawing from one
government and setting up another one exactly like the one they had
left. "I doubt the capacity of the people for self-government, and, as
you once said to me," J. Henly Smith wrote Alexander Stephens, "I
fear that if this government is destroyed we will never be able to make
one as good, in its stead." "Our government is too democratic for
stability—though it might be more corrupt and aggressive if stronger
and less popular," Smith added. "We are in a dilemma, and I fear we
will never see which horn it is best to take," he wrote, echoing the
doubts of many conservatives.[6]

Most secessionists did not share those doubts, partly because they
relied upon the optimism about men and history that was central to the

5. Milledgeville *Federal Union,* January 15, 1860; Albany *Patriot,* January 24, 1861; Clarke
to editor, Athens *Southern Banner,* December 27, 1860. For similar sentiments expressed during
the American Revolution, see Edmund S. Morgan, "The Puritan Ethic and the Coming of the
American Revolution," *William and Mary Quarterly,* XXIV (1967), 3–18.

6. J. Henly Smith to Alexander H. Stephens, November 16, 1860, in Stephens Papers,
Library of Congress.

revolutionary ideology of 1776. But they carefully restricted that optimism to the South. Henry R. Jackson responded to Alexander Stephens' cooperationist views by agreeing that "while there was no question as to the fitness of the [United States] government for a highly civilized people, there was a question, and a serious question, as to whether the people would be fit for the government." While Stephens doubted the fitness of all Americans, Jackson focused on "the hideous sea of political corruption at the North" where "public plunderers [were] growing more venal, more profligate, more shameless and rampant." The doubts that restrained Stephens propelled Jackson. Secession would restore government to a highly civilized people, southerners. This public optimism about southerners masked secessionists' private fears that their optimism was unwarranted. Some secessionists feared that Georgians were "so demoralized," "so ignorant," and their leaders "so basely corrupt" that secession would be difficult to achieve. "I confess my confidence in Southern men and Southern principles is daily losing strength," T. R. R. Cobb wrote his brother early in November.[7] But secessionists confined such confessions to their private correspondence. They apparently believed that public skepticism and caution would restrain their revolution while hope would drive it on.

When secessionists tied their hopes to the ideas of the Founding Fathers rather than to the proslavery argument, they implicitly acknowledged the limited hegemony of slaveholders. The ideology of 1776 did what proslavery ideology apparently could not do. It translated the issue of the rights and privileges of slave owners into the rights and privileges of southern society. If there had been a broad consensus on the proslavery view that slavery was the fundamental basis of southern society, secessionists would have had to demonstrate only that the Lincoln administration threatened slavery. By using in-

7. For the most complete recent analysis of the ideology of 1776, see "Part One: The Ideology of Revolution," in Gordon Wood, *The Creation of the American Republic, 1776–1787* (Chapel Hill: University of North Carolina Press, 1969), 1–124; Henry R. Jackson, *Letters to the Hon. Alex. H. Stephens* (Savannah, John M. Cooper, 1860), 19, 22; James Mercer Green to Robert N. Gourdin, December 15, 1860 in Gourdin Papers, Emory University; T. R. R. Cobb to Howell Cobb, November 5, 1860, in Howell Cobb Papers.

stead the rhetoric of a national independence movement and emphasizing that the rights of all Georgians were threatened by a Republican president, secessionists implicitly suggested that any consensus about the social necessity of slavery was not strong enough to rest their case on. Although they frequently referred to tenets of the proslavery argument, apparently hoping to create a consensus, they shaped their appeal for immediate secession around an ideology which they apparently felt was more likely to command common assent.

The ideology of 1776 served secessionists, then, as a weapon against the old government, a tool for building a new one, and a defense against cooperationist critics. It even helped explain why secession was an appropriate response to the election of Abraham Lincoln. It was a venerable and convenient framework both for emphasizing that the threats to the South were of external origin and for avoiding a full confrontation with what the secessionist argument implied: that the Republican disease was dangerous mainly because certain inherent features of southern society made southerners susceptible to it.

Secession and Conspiratorial Tyranny

To avoid that implication, the secessionists focused on the nature of the external threat. Using arguments that their revolutionary forefathers had made about Britain, the secessionists asserted that Lincoln's election was the most recent event in a sustained conspiracy to tyrannize the South. Since the conspiracy was hidden, of course, the secessionists had to convince Georgia voters that what was apparent—Lincoln's election—only hinted at the hidden reality of tyranny. Had Lincoln's election occurred "forty, twenty, nay perhaps even ten years ago, it might have been silently acquiesced in," secessionist Henry R. Jackson wrote. But now, Lincoln had "the electoral votes of states occupying a position of open rebellion against the fundamental law, and thus disenfranchised of all constitutional right to cast them" and the Republican party was "organized upon grounds altogether sectional, and for an object treasonable and revolutionary." Lincoln's election was therefore "void," Jackson concluded, "because of what lies behind it and before it—because of its origin and its objects—the significance of the former and the vast overshadowing moment of the latter."[8] Secession was mandatory.

Cooperationists were unconvinced. "Lincoln is just as good, safe and sound a man as Mr. Buchanan," Alexander Stephens wrote before the election. "I know the man well," he added, "He is not a bad man." In fact, Stephens predicted, "He will make as good a President as Fillmore [the last Whig president] did and better too in my opinion." A cotton planter who owned three hundred slaves agreed. He pointed out that Lincoln had been legally elected and that southern interests would be protected in Washington by Congress and the Supreme Court. Many Georgians were "among that number who believe that the bare election of a Black Republican to the presidency is not a sufficient cause for a rupture."[9] It was difficult for cooperationists to believe that the South had lost more than a presidential election.

The task of the secessionists was to demonstrate that, on the contrary, the election of Lincoln was but the last in a long string of losses, and that the losing trend outlined the conspiracy. To prove this point, secessionists included as a standard part of their argument a long review of the nation's history, beginning with the compromises of the Constitutional Convention of 1787 and running through a detailed summary of the events of the prolonged struggle over the protection and extension of slavery: the nullification controversy, the Wilmot Proviso, the Compromise of 1850, the Kansas-Nebraska Act, John

8. Jackson, *Letters to Stephens,* 23. See also T. R. R. Cobb, *Substance of Remarks made in the House of Representatives, Monday Evening, November 12, 1860* (Atlanta: John H. Seals, 1860), 3–5. For a more systematic treatment of the theme of conspiracy, see David Brion Davis, *The Slave Power Conspiracy and the Paranoid Style* (Baton Rouge: Louisiana State University Press, 1969). On the use of the notion of conspiracy in the American Revolution, see Bernard Bailyn, *The Ideological Origins of the American Revolution* (Cambridge: Harvard University Press, 1967), 144–59, and Wood, *The Creation of the American Republic,* 36–43. On the South's view of Lincoln, see Michael Davis, *The Image of Lincoln in the South* (Knoxville: University of Tennessee Press, 1971).

9. Stephens to J. Henly Smith, July 10, 1860, in Phillips (ed.), *Correspondence,* 487; A Southern Cotton Planter to editor, *National Intelligencer,* in Augusta *Chronicle and Sentinel,* November 17, 1860; M. D. Cody to Alexander H. Stephens, November 18, 1860, R. M. Johnston to Stephens, October 15, D. G. Cotting to Stephens, November 22, H. S. Williams to Stephens, December 1, Geo. S. Robinson to Stephens, December 3, Wm. T. Patterson to Stephens, December 6, 1860, all in Stephens Papers, Library of Congress.

Brown's raid on Harpers Ferry, and, finally, Lincoln's election.[10] The purpose of this recital of history was to show that the South was losing, that it had won only the skirmishes which were preludes to the more important strategic losses to come. With this reading of the nation's past, the secessionists tried to deflate the cooperationists' confidence in the Union by pointing out that northern reliability in the past had been but a disguise for ultimate betrayal.

While a review of history might disclose the conspiracy, the secessionists could not depend on the fine distinctions of the slavery extension controversy to communicate the conspirators' goal of tyranny. To express the tyranny Lincoln's election would bring, the secessionists depended on language that cut through to the personal experience or observation of nearly every Georgian. "On the 4th of March, 1861 [Lincoln's inauguration]," one secessionist editor remarked, "we are either *slaves in the Union or freemen out of it.*" "Submission is slavery, and slavery is worse than death," another secessionist warned. Separation alone could keep black Georgians enslaved and white Georgians protected from enslavement, secessionists promised. "These people [northerners] hate us, annoy us, and would have us assassinated by our slaves if they dared," T. R. R. Cobb wrote his wife.[11] Rumors of plots to do just that circulated through the state, aiding the secessionist argument with their implicit message of black revenge for white tyranny.

As men familiar with the principles of the proslavery argument, the secessionists revealed the fragility of their defense of slavery with their portrayal of the dual consequences of Lincoln's tyranny: slavery for whites and murderous freedom for blacks. On the one hand, slavery was beneficial for blacks. "Our slaves are the most happy and contented, best fed and best clothed and best paid laboring population in the world, and I would add," T. R. R. Cobb told the state legislators, "also [they are] the *most faithful* and least feared." Yet secessionists

10. See Toombs, *Speech on the Crisis,* 3–11.

11. Athens *Southern Banner,* November 8, 29, December 6, 1860; Albany *Patriot,* December 20, 1860; T. R. R. Cobb to Marion Cobb, October 11, 1860, in T. R. R. Cobb, "The Correspondence of Thomas Reade Rootes Cobb, 1860–1861," *Publications of the Southern History Association,* XI (1907), 157.

used the symbol of slavery, which was supposedly mild and benefi-
cent, to communicate the tryanny that they hoped would drive white
southerners from the Union. The symbol of white slavery was potent
only if secessionists could maintain the fundamental racial distinction,
that slavery was heaven for blacks and hell for whites. Yet, when
secessionists spoke of freed slaves seeking to assassinate their benefac-
tors, they revealed their recognition that slavery was a form of tyranny
for both whites and blacks. Cobb asked the legislators to "Notice the
anxious look when the traveling pedlar lingers too long in conversation
at the door with the servant who turns the bolt—the watchful gaze
when the slave tarries long with the wandering artist who professes
merely to furnish him with a picture—the suspicions aroused by a
Northern man conversing in private with the most faithful of your
negroes, and tell me if peace and tranquility are the heritage which this
Union has brought to your firesides,"[12] Introspection of this sort could
lead to secession only if it were easy to believe that even the most
faithful slave was receptive to the dangerous ideas of these outsiders
from the North. Secessionists' fears of northerners could only be expressed when coupled with fears of slaves. This implicit fear of slaves
and the use of slavery as a symbol of the coming Republican tyranny
betrayed secessionists' claims that slavery was benign, even for
blacks, or perhaps, especially for blacks. For even if one were to grant
the common assertion that it was in the character of black persons to
murder and maraud, a form of servitude that would repress that charac-
terological trait would be closer to tyranny than to beneficence.

In this, as in so much else of the secessionist argument, the more the
secessionists said about the North, the more they revealed about the
South. The more they spoke of the anticipated northern tyranny, the
more they revealed of their perceptions of southern tyranny. The fragil-

---

12. Cobb, *Substance of Remarks*, 6–7. See also Thomas R. R. Cobb, *An Inquiry into the Law
of Negro Slavery in the United States of America* (Philadelphia: T. & J. W. Johnson, 1858;
reprinted 1968), 17 *passim*. Race alone, Cobb explained, made black slavery harmonious with
natural law and white slavery a violation. For a thorough modern study which basically agrees
with Cobb about the material conditions of slavery, see Robert William Fogel and Stanley L.
Engerman, *Time on the Cross: The Economics of American Negro Slavery* (2 vols.; Boston:
Little, Brown, 1974). But see also Herbert G. Gutman, *Slavery and the Numbers Game: A
Critique of Time on the Cross* (Urbana: University of Illinois Press, 1975).

ity of their argument suggested that beneath it they perceived a fragile social structure. It was easy and tempting for them to say either too little or too much. If slaves were indeed "the most happy and contented . . . laboring population in the world," then separation from the North was unnecessary. No matter what allegations might be made about the susceptibility of slaves to demagoguery, material and spiritual contentment would provide ample security against the whispers of itinerant Yankees. Yet if these conversations aroused the suspicions of slaveholders, as Cobb claimed they did, masters must have feared that their slaves were dissatisfied enough to listen and possibly even to respond to Republican ideas. To provide an argument for secession, it was thus necessary to imply that slaves were not so happy and contented that they would shrug off Republican heresies. But if secessionists portrayed slaves as too susceptible to the lure of freedom, then it might seem that Republican criticisms of slavery, besides being dangerous, were also probably correct. To avoid such a disastrous conclusion, the secessionist argument had to maintain a fine balance. Secessionists tried to strike that balance by making their argument as routine as a catechism, and then repeating it over and over again. They apparently hoped that repetition would make their fragile argument appear substantial.

As if they recognized the shakiness of their argument, some secessionists refused to rely ultimately on the success of their rhetoric. Early in 1860 Robert Toombs wrote Alexander Stephens that, "For one I would raise an insurrection, if I could not carry a revolution, to save my countrymen, and endeavor to save them in spite of themselves." [13] Toombs was not alone. Another secessionist leader was quoted as telling an audience " 'that if the convention did not declare the State out of the Union then there would be civil war in Georgia.' " During the presidential campaign there were rumors that if Lincoln were elected, there was "a scheme on foot . . . to plunge the South into

13. Robert Toombs to Alexander H. Stephens, February 14, 1860, in Phillips (ed.), *Correspondence,* 462. Commenting on a paraphrase of this sentiment, the cooperationist Upson *Pilot* (December 8, 1860) remarked, "Toombs says that if Georgia does not give him the sword he will take it—Let him take it, and, by way of doing his country a great service, let him run about six inches of it into his left breast."

a revolution . . . and maintain the army of the South by confiscating the property of Douglas men, and all such as may oppose the measure." Just before Lincoln's election, a Breckinridge man had warned a public meeting that "if Lincoln is elected we will go for revolution, and if you (the Bell party) oppose us, we will wring you into it, and if you refuse us, we will brand you as traitors, and chop off your heads." [14]

These threats of rolling heads, insurrection, and civil war in Georgia were but variations on a theme, variations used with Georgia voters in much the same way that the threat of secession had been used in national politics. The theme was unity. The variations revealed that the secessionists were aware that the rhetorical theme was mostly rhetoric.

Secession and Southern Unity

From the resolutions of county meetings, from speakers' rostrums, and from editors' desks came appeals "for unanimity among the people of Georgia" and for an end of "partyism." [15] Savannah gave the appearance of unity, as did several other areas, by having only one set of candidates. "The unanimity of sentiment in Chatham County is so great that we have but one ticket in the field," a Savannah editor wrote, perhaps mistaking the consequence for the cause. A man who had announced his candidacy in a Georgia coastal county decided to withdraw "as the running of two tickets in McIntosh County might give the impression that there was a diversity of opinion among us." In some counties, harmony was sought by choosing a slate of candidates for the convention that included a man from each of the Bell, Breckinridge, and Douglas parties. [16]

No matter how strenuously harmony was sought, it was not achieved.

14. Francis S. Bartow, Speech to citizens of Rome, Georgia, December 29, 1860, quoted in Rome *Weekly Courier*, January 1, 1861; J. Henly Smith to Alexander H. Stephens, October 18, 1860, in Stephens Papers, Library of Congress; Wilde C. Cleveland, quoted in Amicus to editor, Upson *Pilot*, October 20, 1860.

15. The quoted words are from Linton Stephens to Eli H. Baxter, November 29, 1860, quoted in Alexander H. Stephens, *A Constitutional View of the Late War Between the States* (2 vols.; Atlanta: National Publishing Co., 1868), II, 317, and from Augusta *Chronicle and Sentinel*, November 13, 1860.

16. Charles Spaulding to editor, December 29, 1860, Savannah *Republican*, January 1, 1861; Linton Stephens to Eli H. Baxter, November 29, 1860, in Stephens, *A Constitutional View of the Late War Between the States*, II, 320; Albany *Patriot*, December 13, 1860.

Even in Savannah, where "unanimity" was claimed, the secessionist mayor Charles Colcock Jones, Jr., admitted to his father that "there is no doubt that there are those in our midst who do not sympathize with us upon the question of state action and secession." Another Savannah secessionist noted, "We are all of one opinion here, unless perhaps the northern class of merchants, of whom there may be some, who still cherish the idea of Union, it being inseparable when viewed in the light of dollars and cents." Outside Savannah, in spite of urgings that there be no parties in the contest for the convention, that each county nominate only one ticket composed of the "ablest, wisest, most discreet, and most reliable men," almost all counties did have two sets of candidates, and each set received a considerable vote. Some saw harmony in the similar positions of the two sets of candidates, claiming that the cooperationists agreed on the right of secession and only disputed the timing. From this point of view one could find harmony even between supporters and opponents of a war as long as the opponents agreed that a society has the right to make war. But cooperationists, far from being in harmony with secessionists, did not even agree among themselves. Some cooperationists said secessionist assertions of the right to secede were "humbug"; others were incredulous—"I cannot fathom the designs of these disunionists—do you believe they are in earnest?"; still others, though they desired unity, saw in the secession movement "the 'raw head and bloody bones' of Democracy."[17] The existence of unity, harmony, unanimity, and an absence of party spirit had to be asserted vigorously lest the evidence convince the voters otherwise.

Cooperationists had a vested interest in the unity plea. Their program called for action by some kind of coalition of the southern states. This generalized cooperation scheme was consistent with the secessionists' assertions of unity and harmony in the slave South. But

17. Hon. Charles C. Jones, Jr., to the Reverend and Mrs. C. C. Jones, December 17, 1860, in Robert Manson Meyers (ed.), *Children of Pride* (New Haven: Yale University Press, 1972), 633–35;[?] to John M. Kell, December 11, 1860, in John McIntosh Kell Papers, Duke University; Augusta *Chronicle and Sentinel,* October 9, November 22, 1860; D. G. Cotting to Alexander H. Stephens, November 22, 1860, in Stephens Papers, Library of Congress; Albany *Patriot,* November 29, 1860.

when secessionists advocated immediate, unilateral secession, they implicitly denied the unity of the South. Indeed, cooperationists charged them with dividing the South with their agitation for precipitate, radical action. Cooperationists argued that southern unity provided the only certain protection for southern rights. "One may talk as flippantly or as seriously as one pleases of disunion," Alexander Stephens wrote a friend, "but one thing is evident to my mind, it will render confusion worse confounded unless our people can agree upon some line of policy together in its maintenance. And if they will do this," he added, "there will be no necessity for disunion."[18] Implicitly, cooperationists asked secessionists to abandon either their assertions of southern unity or, preferably, their commitment to separate state action.

Secessionists could not comply with either request. On the one hand, their commitment to secession was firm. On the other hand, they had to insist upon the organic unity of the slave South since, according to their rhetoric, they were determined to make a revolution along the lines set forth in the "immortal Declaration," that is, a revolution to protect the whole of a slave society from tyranny. If southern society was not portrayed as a harmoniously functioning organism, then the tyranny that the secessionists foresaw might seem to be directed only at slaveholders. In a society like Georgia where nonslaveholding voters outnumbered slaveholding voters three to two, the secessionists had no choice but to demonstrate that tyranny for slaveholders was tyranny for all—no choice, that is, short of openly repudiating the democratic political values on which there had been a public consensus for nearly two generations. Some secessionists were prepared to go that far, if necessary. But if a revolution to protect the interests of slaveholders could be achieved by maintaining public obeisance to democratic values, so much the better. In fact, if the secessionists could do that, they would not only demonstrate the organic unity of the slave South, but,

18. See Alexander Stephens to J. Henly Smith, September 16, 1860, in Phillips (ed.), *Correspondence,* 458, 499; Greene County resolution, in Allen D. Candler (ed.), *The Confederate Records of the State of Georgia* (Atlanta: Charles P. Byrd, 1909), I, 71–72; George A. Hall to Herschel V. Johnson, January 7, 1861, in Johnson Papers, Duke University; Old Whig to editor, Savannah *Republican,* July 20, 1860.

to a degree, they would create it. The first step in that direction was to assert the unity which they feared did not exist.

"Our whole social system," Governor Brown reminded the legislature in November 1861, "is one of perfect homogeneity of interest, where every class of society is interested in sustaining the interest of every other class." To a group of citizens he intoned, "We all, poor and rich, have a common interest, a common destiny."[19] Eugenius A. Nisbet, a prominent conservative jurist who had supported Douglas in 1860, was more rhapsodically pointed as he announced to a Macon audience his conversion to the program of immediate secession:

> Our merchants, artisans, day laborers and small farmers are sustained and grow in wealth through the general prosperity of the country; and that springs from slave labor. . . . This they know. It is not too much to say that we love the institution of slavery, as we love our laws and social life, our sunshine and our showers—our soil and its fruits. This feeling pervades all classes. It has grown up with our polity—we have inherited it as a people—it is made vital and vigorous by daily association—it is an heirloom of the State—it is part of our religion.[20]

Most cooperationists agreed with this secessionist vision of the organic unity of the South, that the "people of the South are a homogeneous race—they have but one interest and one feeling."[21] In the early spring of 1861 these visions of southern unity and harmony would become transient dreams of a southern utopia; but in the winter campaign for secession they created the central intellectual dilemma for the secessionist argument.

As cooperationists never tired of asking secessionists, if the South was unified, why should the mere fact of Lincoln's election necessitate secession? "Is there not some secret reason kept hidden from the poorer and humbler classes, for the advocacy of secession which it seems to me would bring ruin upon us, without in the slightest alleviating any ills we may unconsciously labor under but aggravating them

19. Governor Joseph E. Brown, Message to Senate and House of Representatives, November 1, 1861, in Candler (ed.), *Confederate Records,* II, 124. See also Brown to David Walker, April 19, 1861, Milledgeville *Southern Federal Union,* April 30, 1861; Brown to A. H. Colquitt and others, December 7, 1860, Macon *Telegraph,* December 24, 1860.
20. E. A. Nisbet, Speech to citizens of Macon, Macon *Telegraph,* December 12, 1860.
21. Augusta *Daily Constitutionalist,* March 16, 1861.

instead?,'' an old Whig asked his friend Alexander Stephens. Indeed, why should a united South secede? To answer this telling question, secessionists implicitly denied the very unity they had asserted. Cooperationists were not convinced by the secessionists' general statement that the Lincoln administration would be a "*hostile* government," which was "founded on a deadly antagonism to everything in our social science or economy—to everything in our interest and feelings—to almost everything in our belief and practice." Stephens' friend complained that the secessionists "do not tell us, except in vague promises of prosperity and security, what I, as a slaveholder, am to gain by going with them," and asked, "Can you explicitly point out the advantages of disunion.''[22] Information about the operational details of Lincoln's tyranny was what the cooperationists demanded. In response, the secessionists disclosed their perceptions of the fundamental disunity of southern society.

As a variation on the theme of unity designed to demonstrate the necessity of immediate secession, the secessionists pointed to the potential traitors in the midst of their "harmonious" organic social unit. "We have a heavy Northern element, and a Southern element Northernized to contend with in our borders," one secessionist noted. These elements in the South and a Republican president in Washington meant that "it is not hostile legislation that we have most to fear," a secessionist predicted, but rather "the insidious influence of the Executive Department, through its thousands of functionaries, sewing discord, insubordination and insecurity throughout the South." "[T]he new dynasty will be sleeplessly engaged in building up a party in our midst," another secessionist warned. "Thus a Lincoln party will be built up in the South," another secessionist foresaw, a party based on the "over 1200 office holders receiving their offices and emoluments from his hands"[23]

The significant result of Lincoln's election was, according to the

22. D. G. Cotting to Stephens, November 22, 1860, in Stephens Papers, Library of Congress; Macon *Telegraph,* October 3, 1860.
23. Rev. C. C. Jones to Hon. Charles C. Jones, Jr., November 15, 1860, in Meyers (ed.), *Children of Pride,* 628; Macon *Telegraph,* November 5, 20, 28, 1860; A Union Man for Twenty Years to editor, Atlanta *Daily Intelligencer,* November 15, 1860.

secessionists, the "certainty, that submission to Lincoln, with or without new constitutional guarantees, must lead, first, to the formation of a black republican party in our midst, and then to a civil and servile war." The Lincoln administration would use its "patronage for the purpose of organizing in the South a band of apologists," Howell Cobb wrote in a public letter early in December, "the material around which Black Republicanism hopes, during his four years, to gather an organization in Southern States to be the allies of this party in its insidious warfare upon our family firesides and altars." But in a society where "all classes of society are harmonized with each other, and linked together by the chain of interest," what classes would provide the recruits for a Southern Republican party?[24] In an article which a secessionist editor said "fairly and honestly depicted" the situation, a writer for the Charleston *Mercury* was explicit:

> The thousands in every county, who look up to power, and make gain out of the future, will come out in support of the Abolition Government. . . . They will organize; and from being a Union party, to support an Abolition Government, they will become, like the Government they support, Abolitionists. They will have an Abolition party in the South, of Southern men. The contest for slavery will no longer be one between the North and the South. It will be in the South, between the people of the South.[25]

Secession *had* to be immediate because as soon as Lincoln was in office he could use his patronage to build a Republican party in Georgia. This was the most compelling argument the secessionists had. All their other charges about such northern outrages as personal liberty laws or the lack of federal protection of slavery in the territories amounted to little more than alerting Georgians to Republican threats

---

24. Jno. M. Richardson to Robert N. Gourdin, December 14, 1860, in Gourdin Papers; Howell Cobb, *Letter to the People of Georgia on the Present Condition of the Country* (Washington, D.C.: McGill and Witherow, 1860), 14; Governor Joseph E. Brown to David Walker, April 19, 1861, in Milledgeville *Southern Federal Union,* April 30, 1861.

25. Charleston *Mercury,* October 11, 1860, reprinted in Atlanta *Daily Intelligencer,* October 15, 1860, and Athens *Southern Banner,* November 1, 1860. For nearly twenty years antislavery radicals had advocated such action as a constitutional blow against slavery. "We believe," James Russell Lowell wrote, "that the 'irrepressible conflict' . . . is to take place in the South itself." Lowell quoted in Eric Foner, *Free Soil, Free Labor, Free Men: The Ideology of the Republican Party Before the Civil War* (New York: Oxford University Press, 1970), 120, and, in general, 116–23.

and harassment. Even if such external actions spelled the ultimate death of slavery, which was extremely questionable, they did not necessitate immediate secession, for little was likely to change in a few months or even in Lincoln's four-year term of office. Likewise, secessionist charges that slavery was already dying in the border states and would soon be confined to the eight cotton states, allowing an antislavery amendment to be added to the United States Constitution, still allowed a number of years before the slave states would be face to face with their supposed fate.[26] Again there was time to wait. Immediate secession was not necessary. But to escape the extraconstitutional consequences of a constitutional process—the creation of a southern Republican party by the use of the newly elected president's patronage—immediate secession *was* necessary.

Thus, the strongest part of the secessionist argument directly contradicted secessionist assertions about Georgia's society. It suggested some weak links in the "chain of interest" that supposedly bound all Georgians together. Specifically, the "thousands in every county, who look up to power, and make gain out of the future" were the potential southern abolitionists. Although the argument for the necessity of immediate secession rested directly upon the recognition of these potential abolitionists, the secessionists could not very often afford to say so. One reason was that secessionists could not be sure that these persons would be more trustworthy out of the Union than they were in it. For this reason, among others, many cooperationists agreed with Alexander Stephens' judgment that "slavery [was] much more secure in the Union than out of it."[27] Secessionists, on the other hand, believed that it was worthwhile to remove these potential southern abolitionists from the temptation of the federal patronage at the disposal of a Republican administration.

If secessionists had emphasized that secession was necessary because of the latent disloyalty of some southerners toward slavery, then it would have been difficult for them to maintain that their revolution was for the good of the whole society. Instead, they would have been

---

26. See Benning, *Speech on Federal Relations,* 3.

27. Stephens to J. Henly Smith, July 10, 1860, in Phillips (ed.), *Correspondence,* 487. See also Augusta *Chronicle and Sentinel,* December 15, 1860.

forced to admit what they preferred to gloss over: that slaveholders had more to lose from a Republican administration and more to gain from secession than did nonslaveholding Georgians. Such an admission would have undermined the argument the secessionists made at the same time that it would have solidly established a good reason for immediate secession, a reason the secessionist argument usually left implicit. Of course, it was the better part of political wisdom for secessionists to leave it that way. Also, the political experience of the last three-quarters of a century gave secessionists reason to hope that the latent disloyalty they detected would remain latent until after secession, when there would be an opportunity to look for some formula to create the actual linkages of interest that in 1860 were mostly imagined. Evidence that the secessionists recognized that they were seceding to protect slavery from other southerners is therefore found less often in overt public discussion of the problem than in the frequently expressed denials that there was a problem at all. The purpose of the denials was to forge a chain of interest that secessionists feared either did not exist or, if it did, was not strong enough to withstand the stresses of disunion.

Secession and Racial Fears

To fire the forge that they hoped would weld white Georgians together, the secessionists raked the coals of racial fear. Secessionists tried to intensify the racial fears of white Georgians not because they feared that nonslaveholders and slaves might unite out of mutual regard and common interest; secessionists were fully aware that such a possibility was extremely remote. Instead, secessionists turned to the racial fear arguments because they hoped to prevent a linkage between nonslaveholders and slaves that might be based on a mutual antagonism toward slaveholders. Secessionists thought that such a white-black alliance was possible, as they hinted in the ambiguous warnings they issued about the consequences of Lincoln's election. They said that there were "no other alternatives than a political revolution [secession] on the one hand or a social revolution on the other," and that "now, with the sword over us [the Lincoln administration] and volcanic fires beneath, we sleep on." The terms "social revolution" and "volcanic fires" had a double meaning.[28] The possibility that white Georgians might be among the incipient revolutionaries in the "volcanic fires" was a meaning that had to remain implicit. On the other hand, secessionists enthusiastically portrayed the horrors that would result from a "social revolution" perpetrated by black Georgians. The very enthusiasm with which secessionists predicted racial horrors disclosed that they were well aware of the unspoken implications behind their appeals for racial unity.

Using ideas about race that were old long before ideas about secession existed, the secessionists tried to prove that what seemed a fact was only illusory, that it was wrong to believe that Lincoln's election threatened only the rights of slaveholders. With characteristic moderation, Eugenius A. Nisbet pointed out that the "ultimate aim" of the Republican party was "to free" the slaves "and leave them in our midst, upon a footing of social and political equality with the whites," a "danger" he found "more appalling than death."[29] More pointed was a secessionist whose letter was headlined, "The Effects of Abolitionism—Poor Men of Georgia Read It!" He warned that if Georgians remained "in a government ruled by Lincoln and his crew . . . [then] in TEN years or less our CHILDREN will be the *slaves* of negroes. For emancipation must follow and negro equality is the same result."[30] More direct and more classically rabid in tone was a secessionist plea from "A Union Man for Twenty Years." "I wish to say a word to the common people, the masses, the voters, to the non-slaveholder, if you please," he wrote, "and ask him what interest have you got in this question [of Lincoln's election]." "You own no negroes," he reminded these Georgians; therefore, he asked, "how are you to suffer?" "I will tell you," he continued: "Do you love your mother, your wife, your sister, your daughter? Can you look your

28. Macon *Telegraph*, November 8, 1860; Conciliation to editor, *ibid.*, October 6, 1860.

29. E. A. Nisbet, Speech to citizens of Macon, Macon *Telegraph*, December 12, 1860. For a range of similar opinion see the resolutions from White, Spaulding, Elbert, and Clay counties, in Candler (ed.), *Confederate Records*, I, 90, 103, 105, 128; Atlanta *Daily Intelligencer*, November 23, 1860; Albany *Patriot*, December 13, 1860; Governor Joseph E. Brown to A. H. Colquitt and others, December 7, 1860, in Macon *Telegraph*, December 24, 1860; Augusta *Daily Constitutionalist*, January 1, 1861; Milledgeville *Southern Federal Union*, March 12, 1861.

30. A Georgian to editor, Atlanta *Daily Intelligencer*, December 13, 1860.

fellow man in the face and say, 'I am a man?' Are you not better than a negro? Did God not make you better?" Yes, yes, yes, his readers were presumably expected to respond, followed by no, no, no. "Are you willing to be looked upon as no better than a negro by others?" No! "Is your daughter the equal of a negro waiting maid or a corn field hand?" No! "Are you willing that you or she shall be put in such a position of equality?" God forbid! It was obvious then, this secessionist argued, that "the non-slaveholder" had a compelling interest in Lincoln's election, for "IN FOUR YEARS BY ABOLITION ENACTMENT THE NEGRO WILL BE TURNED LOOSE, AS YOUR EQUAL AND MY EQUAL, and the tragedy of St. Domingo will be enacted upon the soil of our beloved Georgia— you, I, the common classes of society will be the sufferers, by being reduced to a state of perfect degradation, and more than probably inhumanly butchered. Our mothers, wives, and daughters, debauched and murdered, our children slain, and our humble cottages reduced to ashes."[31]

In short, black Georgians coveted white status, thirsted for white blood, and lusted after white women. No matter how unequally the benefits of slavery might seem to be distributed among white Georgians, slavery was obviously infinitely more desirable than the horrendous inequities of a slaveless future. After all, secessionists argued, slavery guaranteed the continuation of the only equality that really mattered—equality of white superiority. "Among us the poor white laborer is respected as an equal," Governor Brown told the legislators. "His family is treated with kindness, consideration and respect. He does not belong to the menial class. The negro is in no sense of the term his equal. He feels and knows this. He belongs to the only true aristocracy, the race of *white men.*" These poor, white, laboring aristocrats would "never permit the slaves of the South to be set free among them," Brown predicted, because they "know, that in the event of the abolition of slavery, they would be greater sufferers than the rich, who would be able to protect themselves."[32]

Other secessionist arguments had the same intended function as the

---

31. A Union Man for Twenty Years to editor, Atlanta *Daily Intelligencer,* November 15, 1860.

32. Governor Joseph E. Brown, *Special Message,* 21.

one based on the fear of racial equality: to demonstrate to men who were not slaveholders that they had a direct, personal, visceral, even genital interest in protecting the threatened interests of slaveholders. For example, the constant reference to the South as the slave states and to issues as those of states' rights subtly suggested that the states and all who lived in them were interested in slavery and its associated benefits. A less subtle and more intentional approach was to transform the question of slavery in all its symbolic richness into a nuts-and-bolts issue of economics. One form of this approach was the secessionist appeal to those with substantial wealth but minimal economic interest in slavery. "Slave property is the foundation of all property in the South," one secessionist wrote. "When security in this is shaken, all other property partakes of its instability. Banks, stocks, bonds, must be influenced." More generally, he argued, the loss of slavery would mean "the loss of liberty, prosperity, home, country—everything that makes life worth having." In a statement with a similar function, E. A. Nisbet said that the "man of Southern birth considers the privilege of buying or inheriting negroes, as upon the same footing with the privilege of buying or inheriting lands." Making the point crystal clear, he added, "I am wholly mistaken in this class of our people [nonslaveholders], if they would not as promptly, and decisively, repel interference with our institutions, as would the slave proprietors themselves."[33]

The most revealing observations about the economic benefits of slavery for "poor white people" were made by Governor Brown. Brown, like many of the "poor white people" he addressed, was from the mountainous, slave-poor region of north Georgia where the secessionists knew they would have trouble. To allay the trouble, Brown was an ideal man. "He stands high in the up-country and deserves it," Linton Stephens had written of Brown in 1857. Brown pointed out that "our poor white people . . . now get higher wages for their labor, than the poor of any other country on the globe. Most of them are landowners and they are respected." The reason for the high wages enjoyed

---

33. Charleston *Mercury,* October 11, 1860, reprinted in Atlanta *Daily Intelligencer,* October 15, 1860; E. A. Nisbet, Speech to citizens of Macon, Macon *Telegraph,* December 12, 1860.

by white labor in the South was that "every white laborer is interested in sustaining the institution of slavery," and consequently "he makes it in the interest of every slaveholder to strive to sustain and keep up the price of labor." With slavery legal, Brown argued, high wages were supported by slaveholders in return for support for slavery from white laborers, and the bargain was sealed by the blood of white brotherhood. But "abolish slavery, and you make the negroes their [poor whites'] equals, legally and socially (not naturally, for no human law can change God's law) and you very soon make them all tenants and reduce their wages for daily labor to the smallest pittance that will sustain life." The reason for such instant "degradation" was that, "In every case, if the negro will do the work the cheapest, he must be preferred"[34] Straining the argument to the embarrassing breaking point, Brown said, in effect, that the "poor white man" was not the brother of the slaveholder but only the brother-in-law. Without slavery, the blood of white brotherhood was very thin indeed. To Brown, the alleged political bargain struck by slaveholders and white laborers was more important than their common race. When slavery was gone, nonslaveholders would have nothing to recommend them to their employers except their race, which was not much of a recommendation.

Turning away from the economic issues and directly toward the functional point, Brown portrayed the terrors of submission for North Georgia: "So soon as the slaves were at liberty, thousands of them would leave the cotton and rice fields in the lower parts of our State, and make their way to the healthier climate in the mountain region. We should have them plundering and stealing, robbing and killing; in all the lovely vallies [*sic*] of the mountains."

He admitted that, "Some who do not know them [the people of north Georgia], have doubted their capacity to understand these questions, and their patriotism and valor to defend their rights when invaded." "It is true, the people there are generally poor; but they are brave, honest, patriotic and pure-hearted," he wrote. Their patriotism,

---

34. Linton Stephens to Alexander Stephens, quoted in Louise Biles Hill, *Joseph E. Brown and the Confederacy* (Chapel Hill: University of North Carolina Press, 1939), 8; Brown, Public Letter, Albany *Patriot,* December 13, 1860; Brown to David Walker, April 19, 1861, in Milledgeville *Southern Federal Union,* April 30, 1861. See also Brown, *Special Message,* 21.

Brown implied, consisted of their support for slavery which was undergirded by nightmares of an exodus of bloodthirsty former slaves from the cotton and rice fields to the mountains. The patriotism of those who most directly reaped the benefits of slavery was uncertain, Brown argued, because "Wealth is timid, and wealthy men may cry for peace, and submit to wrong, for fear they may lose their money." To the degree that class antagonism toward wealthy Georgians existed among the poor, Brown tried to turn it toward support for secession. Unlike wealthy Georgians, "the poor, honest laborers of Georgia can never consent to see slavery abolished, and submit to all the taxation, vassalage, low wages and downright degradation which must follow. They will never take the negro's place; God forbid."[35]

Secessionists were well aware of the purpose of Brown's arguments. His "appeal to the poor men of the mountains [was] well calculated to arouse them," one secessionist wrote Howell Cobb, "and to fortify their minds against those appeals of demagouges [*sic*] which arouse the basest passions of the human heart, and array the poor against the wealthy—the non-slaveholder against the slaveholder." An admirer wrote Brown that his views had "done more to secure the votes of the masses than every other production combined." They had "done the cause immense good," T. R. R. Cobb wrote Brown, reporting that the "political signs are cheering for secession."[36] Whether Brown's arguments deserved the confidence secessionists had in them would be tested in the January 2 election. But the arguments themselves disclosed secessionists' perceptions both of the cleavages in Southern society and of the rhetoric that would bridge them.

Aside from the social cleavages which the secessionist warnings of racial equality were designed to overcome, the appeal to racial unity could easily be pushed too far, for behind it lay a logical pitfall for the secessionists' plan of action. What was it that made white southerners so similar to each other but so different from white northerners that white southerners were united by a common interest which repelled

35. Brown, Public Letter, Albany *Patriot,* December 13, 1860.
36. T. Allan to Howell Cobb, December 10, 1860, in Howell Cobb Papers; John W. Evans to Brown, January [?], 1861, in Telamon Cuyler Papers, University of Georgia; Cobb to Brown, December 25, 1860, in Thomas Reade Rootes Cobb Papers, University of Georgia.

them from white northerners? The answer proposed by one editor who found the other secessionist arguments hard to swallow was "the absolute and apparently irreconcilable *incompatibility* of temper, character, interest and feeling between the Northern and Southern sections." But when one probed into the components of that incompatibility, the delicacy of the secessionist policy and its associated view of society was exposed. Suppose that it was true, as one editor remarked, that "We of the South and they of the North are two people: essentially different in all that makes a white man, except the color. Different interests divide us, different sentiments animate us, and a different destiny awaits us."[37] As the secessionist argument demonstrated, the secessionists knew well that there were plenty of men in the South with different interests, sentiments, and destinies from those of slaveholders. Did that mean that these southerners were "essentially different in all that makes a white man?" If so, then secession could not eliminate the differences; if not, then there was no reason to secede from northerners.

To maintain the delicate balance between such inconsistencies the secessionists resorted to a routinized argument. The routine structure allowed them to avoid explicit disclosures of the white and black fuels they saw smoldering in the "volcanic fires beneath." Yet to achieve their goal, the secessionists had to make some of those disclosures. Otherwise, their argument would have made little sense and probably would have collapsed, the victim of its own folly.

Secession and Cooperationist Fears

Fear was what the cooperationists had in common during the campaign for secession. Many of them feared the war they saw on the horizon after secession more than they feared a Republican administration. Some secessionists tried to allay this fear with the soothing balm of King Cotton and peaceful secession: "the *cotton bag* will be the cannon in the hands of the South," one secessionist wrote. But cooperationists accurately perceived that nearly all secessionists were

37. Augusta *Chronicle and Sentinel,* December 15, 1860; Milledgeville *Southern Federal Union,* April 9, 1861. See also T. R. R. Cobb to Marion Cobb, October 11, 1860, in Cobb, "Correspondence," 157.

willing to go to war, even "to make one grand charnel house in Geo. from the Savannah to the Chattahooche." If it came to a choice between "suffer[ing] death in a few years by the hands of our slaves" and "fall[ing] in battle with the enemies of *my country*," secessionists preferred heroism to ignomity. Cooperationists wondered whether such a choice was necessary. To them it seemed that secessionists asked them to trade a "career of prosperity, peace, happiness and domestic security" in the Union for nothing but uncertainty outside the Union.[38]

Although cooperationists were united by their fears of the uncertain consequences of secession, they were more decisively divided by their fears of how the uncertainties might be resolved. From opposite ends of the social spectrum, cooperationists expressed fears of two quite different internal results of secession—monarchy and anarchy. In a way, cooperationists feared each other. Those in the lower social strata—most of them dirt farmers—feared the monarchical sympathies of their conservative social betters. Conservatives, looking down from higher social positions in law, politics, commerce, or planting, feared the anarchic impulses of the lower orders. Both groups were afraid that the social forces that had been held in check by the political alignments of the antebellum South would be loosed, unwittingly or not, by the secessionists. "Revolutions are much easier started than controlled, and the men who begin them, even for the best purpose and objects, seldom end them," Alexander Stephens observed. "The wise and good who attempt to control them will themselves most likely become the victims," he added, expressing in the abstract the common feature of cooperationist fears.[39]

Giving voice to the fear of monarchy that became more predominant after Georgia had seceded, a cooperationist public meeting in Upson County in November 1860, resolved that, "we are uncompromisingly opposed to the overthrow of our present republican form of Government and the establishment in lieu thereof of a "Constitutional

---

38. Albany *Patriot*, December 27, 1860; M. [?] to Alexander H. Stephens, December 8, 1860, in Stephens Papers, Library of Congress; Herschel V. Johnson to Alexander H. Stephens, December 22, 1860, in Johnson Papers.

39. Stephens to [a friend in the North], November 25, 1860, in Phillips (ed.), *Correspondence*, 504–505.

Monarchy' in these Southern States, as recommended by some advocates of immediate disunion." Other cooperationists charged that "there are many in favor of stronger Government in the present excited state of public feeling," a charge that secessionists tried to discredit by claiming, rightly, that it showed little faith in secessionist leaders.[40]

There was no denying that there were Georgians who favored a retreat from republican government. "I am one of the few who ever dared to think that Republicanism was a failure from its inception," one man wrote. "I have never wished to see this Union disrupted," he continued, "but if it must be, then I raise my voice for a return to a Constitutional Monarchy." "I do fear that our experiment of self-government is likely, at the end of eighty years to prove a failure," an "Old Democrat" wrote. "I have often, lately, been surprised at the questions: 'Are the people truely [sic] capable of governing themselves?' 'Would not a constitutional monarchy best secure the peace and quiet of our homes?' and much more of the same tenor," he added. To conservative cooperationists who believed that the "government is too democratic for stability," these questions were directly to the point. The United States Constitution set absolute limits which were beyond the reach of electoral majorities, these cooperationist believed. But if no law was above the popular will, as Lincoln's election proved, according to secessionists, then these conservatives might find it necessary to act on their "wish [that] our government was stronger."[41]

Yet conservative cooperationists feared that secession would lead not to a stronger government, but to the opposite, "to licentiousness and to a weak and contemptible government." Upon secession, "all the bad and destructive elements of the South, will be unbridled and turned loose upon us with no power to check or control [them]," one cooperationist wrote, with the cautious indirection and double meaning that characterized the secessionist exploitation of racial fear. He warned that anyone "who supposes that these elements are not

40. Upson County resolution, in Candler (ed.), *Confederate Records,* I, 65; Rome *Weekly Courier,* December 21, 1860; Athens *Southern Banner,* December 27, 1860. See also, Rome *Weekly Courier,* November 8, 1860; Jackson, *Letters to Stephens,* 18.
41. Constitutional Monarchy to editor, Columbus *Times,* reprinted in Rome *Weekly Courier,* December 21, 1860; An Old Democrat to editor, Savannah *Republican,* October 24, 1860; J. Henly Smith to Alexander H. Stephens, November 16, 1860, in Stephens Papers, Library of Congress.

amongst us, or, if they are, to such a limited extent as to be powerless for mischief, will, in a coming day, be under the necessity of making a new calculation; perhaps when it is too late to arrest their wildness and madness."[42] This fear of unchecked "destructive elements" particularly plagued the cooperationists who believed in the organic society the secessionists portrayed. They feared that when "love of country sours into a rabid passion of undefined rage and hate without aim or object," then the "unfortunate subjects [would be driven] to the wildest and most reckless ends." It was such fears that brought Alexander Stephens to comment: "I can but look upon the alternative [of disunion] as little better than jumping out of the frying pan into the fire." The choice, according to others, was *"Red* against *Black* Republicanism."[43]

These fears affirmed rather than contradicted conservatives' belief in an organic society. Ideally, each member of southern society contributed to the greater social good by accepting both the responsibilities and benefits of his particular social position. The problem, according to conservatives, was not the ideal but the real. Leaders should seek "the wisest, safest and soundest policy looking to the security of the rights, interest, welfare and prosperity of all parts and sections of the country." Instead, leaders in both North and South put personal and party considerations above the public welfare. Government could not be safely entrusted to such men, conservatives believed. Many of them would have agreed with the cooperationist who wrote that he "would feel quite a sympathy with [a] very determined resistance movement, if I could have confidence in those who are leading them."[44] This distrust of secessionist leaders reflected not simply conservatives' judgment of the individual men. At bottom it rested on conservatives' social theory, on their belief that their organic society was harmonious,

---

42. '76 to editor, Augusta *Chronicle and Sentinel,* December 28, 1860; D. R. Mitchel to editor, Rome *Weekly Courier,* January 8, 1861.

43. Alexander H. Stephens to J. Henly Smith, January 22, September 16, 1860, in Phillips (ed.), *Correspondence,* 458, 498; Wm. F. Samford to editor, Rome *Weekly Courier,* January 11, 1861. See also, Nepos to editor, November 20, 1860, Augusta *Chronicle and Sentinel,* November 22, 1860; H. C. Massburgale to Alexander H. Stephens, December 2, 1860, in Stephens Papers, Library of Congress.

44. Alexander H. Stephens to J. Henly Smith, September 16, 1860, in Phillips (ed.), *Correspondence,* 499; Richard Malcolm Johnston to Alexander H. Stephens, December 28, 1860, in Stephens Papers, Library of Congress.

that basic conflict between political leaders was illegitimate. Leaders were supposed to seek the general welfare rather than some more narrow, selfish goal defined by the interests of a specific group. In general, conservatives found it difficult to comprehend the legitimacy of a political party interested in anything other than the public welfare.

Secessionists had no difficulty comprehending an interest-based political party. After all, secession was necessary precisely because such a party existed in the North and might soon exist in the South. "So soon as the Government shall have passed into Black Republican hands, a portion of our citizens, must, if possible, be bribed into treachery to their own section by the allurements of office," Governor Brown explained.[45] The reality of political conflict between different social groups was all too evident to secessionists. While an organic society based on slavery was the social ideal of secessionists, they were well aware that secession represented their only chance to work toward that ideal. Dangerous internal divisions separated the South as it was from the South as they wished it were. Secessionists understood that their political agitation was likely to intensify social tensions and, in that way, to lead away from their social goal. Yet from the secessionists' perspective, this means was not only entirely appropriate to their social goal but it was absolutely necessary to preserve the potential in their society for social harmony on their terms.

Conservative cooperationists thus shared with secessionists a sympathy for an harmonious organic society. But, unlike secessionists, conservative cooperationists feared the disharmony that was created by political conflict. Still, since slavery was fundamental to the society they treasured, they could easily imagine advantages to separation from the North. Their social theory persuaded them that the slave states should secede together, lest their social organism be missing vital parts. But their social theory also plagued them with recurrent reminders that unless political leaders judiciously sought the public welfare, events could slide unpredictably toward disaster.

Conservative social theory not only shaped these cooperationists' criticisms of the secessionist argument, but, even more important, it helped them formulate their response to the secession crisis itself. In-

45. Brown, *Special Message,* 17.

creasing numbers of conservative cooperationists came to believe that secession would be safe if *they* assumed leading roles. "The people are wild," one wrote," [and] . . . the only hope of influencing them is to unite in the movement . . . in order that it may receive the proper direction after the excitement of the hour shall have passed away." With conservative leaders, the proper direction might well be a new one. Conservative cooperationists agreed that, "It becomes us then to make provision for the future and to so advance our future government that we will not secede . . . into a state of anarchy and discord." To the questions, "What government shall we adopt? Shall it be our present form, which everybody now declares is such a magnificent failure?" conservative cooperationists had no ready answers. They were certain that "To tear down and build up again are very different things and before tearing down even a bad Government we should first see a good prospect for building up a better." To them, a better government was, in general, a "stronger" government, in which, for example, "full power [was] centralized, held by one individual." A stronger government was necessary if the South's slave society was to be more harmonious out of the Union than in it. The general conservative complaint that "the people [have] too much power" had a quite specific meaning that was so well understood it was usually left implicit. The meaning was stated candidly in a letter J. Henly Smith wrote to Alexander Stephens. "I have no slaves to lose, but I neither want to live nor leave my posterity to live in any country where African slavery does not exist," Smith confided. "I think I understand the advantages of slavery to a poor man," he continued. "I am certain that the poor men of the South do not; and when the time comes that nonslaveholders begin to calculate the value of slavery to them, it is ended. They will fail to solve the problem correctly. Our government is too democratic for stability," he concluded. As one secessionist put it, with unintended irony, "Fealty to slavery, is as all pervading a sentiment as allegiance to the country." [46]

46. J. R. Sneed to Alexander H. Stephens, November 8, H. C. Massburgale to Stephens, December 2, J. Henly Smith to Stephens, November 16, 1860, in Stephens Papers, Library of Congress; S. to editor, Savannah *Republican,* November 21, 1860; Stephens to [a friend in the North], November 25, 1860, in Phillips (ed.), *Correspondence,* 505; E. A. Nisbet, Speech to citizens of Macon, Macon *Telegraph,* December 12, 1860.

Stronger government with better leaders was necessary, then, to insure that poor men got the right answers to their social calculations. Only then would social conflict be avoided and social harmony guaranteed. As the prospects for a better government improved, many conservative cooperationists began to relax their opposition to what they initially feared as a "wild secession crusade." [47]

47. A Farmer to editor, Augusta *Chronicle and Sentinel,* December 23, 1860.

PART TWO

The Election of Delegates to the State Convention

COUNTIES CATEGORIZED BY
SLAVEHOLDING, POLITICS,
AND TOWNS

POLITICS

SLAVEHOLDING

Democratic   Whig

Low

High

T = Town County

NLD-76

VOTE FOR SECESSION

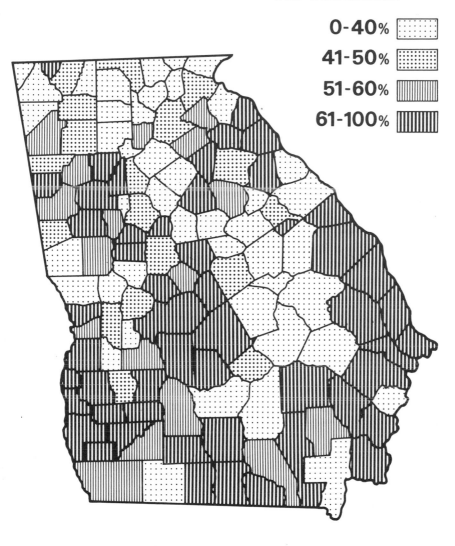

Percent of voters
for secession

0-40%

41-50%

51-60%

61-100%

4

The
Ecology of
Secession

The Election Results

If the voters in the January 2 election had been deciding whether
Georgia should secede, then it is likely that Georgia would have stayed
in the Union, at least for the time being. Using the most generous
estimate of the vote for immediate secession, the result of the election
was a 44,152 to 41,632 victory for the secessionists, a popular majority of just over 51 percent of those voting. A less generous and more
realistic estimate of the vote for immediate secession yields a 42,744 to
41,717 cooperationist victory, a majority of just over 50 percent.[1]
Whatever the true result of the election, we need only assume that it
was not far from either of these estimates to conclude that Georgians
were so equally divided by the question of secession that the voters'
judgment can be justly termed a paralyzing indecision. If the true result
had been made known shortly after the election, as was the routine
practice after other elections, it seems likely that even the ardent secessionists might have been forced to hesitate, and that hesitation
might have been just enough to stall, if not to prevent, the secession of
the lower South.

But the true result of the January 2 election was never made public.
An attempt in the state convention to require the governor to publish
the election returns was voted down by the secessionist delegates.[2] Not

---

1. For an explanation of the estimates, see Michael P. Johnson, "A New Look at the Popular
Vote for Delegates to the Georgia Secession Convention," *Georgia Historical Quarterly,* LVI
(1972), 259–75.
2. *Journal of the Public and Secret Proceedings of the Convention of the People of Georgia,
Held in Milledgeville and Savannah in 1861* (Milledgeville, Ga.: Boughton, Nisbet, and Barnes,
1861), 26–31.

until late in April, 1861, after the Confederacy was well underway, did Governor Brown release any information about the election, and then only in response to a request from a group of inquisitive citizens. Brown wrote the citizens that the secessionists received 50,243 votes, a comfortable 13,120 vote margin over the 37,123 cooperationist voters.[3] Yet more remarkable than Brown's gross exaggeration of the secessionist victory on January 2 was the doubt that continued to linger among Georgia voters for almost four crisis-racked months after the polls had closed. That doubt, demonstrated by the citizens' request, was a more accurate reflection of what Georgia voters had decided than was the *post hoc* report of Governor Brown or the magnificent secessionist majorities predicted by secessionist newspapers.

The doubt and indecision indicated by the estimated election returns did not prevent Georgia from seceding, in part because the voters were not holding a plebiscite, but were instead choosing delegates who would decide the question of secession in the state convention. Early in January, it was very difficult to "decide from the returns what is the complexion of the Convention."[4] But it was clear that the complexion of the convention was the vital issue. The number of voters arrayed on either side of the election was more or less beside the point. However, for an analysis of the social groups who favored and opposed immediate secession in Georgia, the election returns of January 2 are the essential source. With the results of a thorough quantitative analysis of the returns (explained in detail in the Appendix),[5] we can focus on the

3. Governor Brown to A. J. Whitten *et al,* April 25, 1861, Milledgeville *Southern Federal Union,* April 30, 1861. For an analysis of the accuracy of Brown's report, see Johnson, "A New Look at the Popular Vote."

4. Herschel V. Johnson to Alexander H. Stephens, January 9, 1861, in Johnson Papers, Duke University.

5. Readers interested in the exact quantitative details of the analysis are encouraged to read the Appendix herein, perhaps before continuing with the text. I have consigned the quantitative material to the Appendix partly for the convenience of those readers who are more interested in the results than in the analytical details. Yet I am well aware that other readers may be inconvenienced. The primary reason I have not included the tables in the text is that, if I had done so, the text would have had to be focused on explaining the tables rather than explaining the past. Not only would the text have become bogged down with a discussion of numbers, but also the tables themselves would have become the categories of analysis. To avoid that and to maintain a focus on what is important and interesting, I have simply brought into the text the results of the quantitative analysis. In a sense, I have generalized on the basis of the evidence presented in the Appendix. To check the accuracy of my generalizations, please read the Appendix.

degree of consistency between the rhetoric of the campaign for secession and the social reality disclosed by the actions of Georgia voters.

Social Groups and Secession

When Georgians slogged through muddy streets to the polls, stamped the muck from their feet and shook the rain from their hats before voting, they also, in their voting, shook off some old loyalties and exposed the ligaments of interest and fear that the politics of a generation had effectively clothed in ambiguity.[6] No matter how voters framed the issues in the January 2 election—union versus disunion, cooperation versus secession, republican versus oligarchical or monarchical government, federal versus states' rights, slavery versus freedom, a unified organic slave society versus a fragmented society of competing interests, racial tranquility versus racial chaos, or peace versus war—the nature of the issues forced voters to choose from among the welter of conflicting loyalties that claimed their allegiance, those values that did not command the highest loyalty. By voting against those values, Georgians disclosed their secondary, conditional loyalties and suggested which of their loyalties ultimately took precedence. As never before, Georgians had to decide what they most feared and most valued. After they made their decisions and cast their votes, Georgia voters left behind a dim, intricate image of men acting as if their society was actually as riven as the rhetoric of the secession campaign had implied.

VOTERS IN LOW SLAVEHOLDING COUNTIES

Those whose loyalties were most in doubt, if the rhetoric of the secession campaign was a reliable guide, were the nonslaveholders. Secessionists feared them as potential recruits for a southern abolition party. Conservative cooperationists feared them as potential members of an unruly mob exercising social and political powers rather than delegating those powers and deferring to their exercise. Both kinds of fears derived from the widespread doubts about the ultimate loyalties

6. For a careful and convincing analysis of the loyalties of antebellum southerners, see David M. Potter, *The South and the Sectional Conflict* (Baton Rouge: Louisiana State University Press, 1968), 30–33, 66–83.

of nonslaveholders. Many Georgians feared that most nonslaveholders did not identify with the southern slave society strongly enough to support leaving the Union and setting up a new government designed to defend and buttress that society. Many doubted whether the potential threats to the social and economic interests of slaveholders and to the racial interests of whites were clearly perceived and intensely felt by nonslaveholders.

In general, the doubts were well founded and the fears were realized, at least in part. Where voters were preponderantly nonslaveholders, secession was decisively opposed. In the poorest areas, in areas producing the least amount of staple crops and with the fewest slaves and slaveholders—areas located largely in the pine barrens of south central Georgia and the mountains of north Georgia—between two-thirds and three-fourths of the voters expressed a lack of interest in secession that closely matched the relative lack of the actual institutions of a slave society in their midst. Indeed, as the proportions of slaveholders increased in these low slaveholding counties, so did the vote for secession.

Voters in these low slaveholding areas, who numbered one out of every three or four voters in Georgia, were nothing short of remarkable in the way they resolved their conflicting loyalties. For over twenty years they had voted resoundingly for Democratic presidential candidates, a tradition they continued in 1860 by giving very large majorities to Breckinridge, the Southern Rights candidate. For almost a generation they had acted as if southern rights and the rights of slaveholders were inseparable primary values. But when over five thousand of these voters who had voted *for* Breckinridge voted *against* secession, they demonstrated that their support for Southern Rights Democrats did not translate into repulsion from a Union which threatened the rights of slaveholders.

But perhaps previous Democratic voters were less a function of loyalty to slaveholders and southern rights than of ignorance and inertia. During the presidential campaign a man wrote that he belonged to that "large class of our citizens[,] mostly small farmers[,] that have no ready access to political information; who seldom read a paper or book, and who quietly pursue their avocation of toil, without a correct knowledge of the real political issues before the people." Cutoff from political information, these voters may have voted with their reflexes rather than their minds. "In voting," the small farmer continued, "most of us are controled [*sic*] by old party prejudice; we vote for the Democratic party because we have always belonged to that party, or because our fathers did."[7] If tradition governed the Democratic vote in these areas, as indeed it did in 1860, then that tradition was broken in the secession election. By voting even more resoundingly against secession than they had for Breckinridge, these voters not only overcame the inertia of tradition. They also demonstrated that they had information enough to decide against secession, against leaving the Union to protect what secessionists claimed were the interests of southern society. These voters acted as if their primary values were different from the secessionists', as if they believed secession would serve their interests less than the interests of slaveholders. Cooperationist voters in these low slaveholding areas, then, were as disloyal to slaveholders as secessionists were to the Union.

The actions of these voters were frightening to those who worried about the organic unity and social stability of a slave society. J. Henly Smith's prediction that nonslaveholders "will fail to solve the problem correctly" had turned out to be all too accurate. The time had come for nonslaveholders "to calculate the value of slavery to them" and they had arrived at an alarmingly low value.[8] They were not convinced by Governor Brown's portrayal of the benefits of slavery for nonslaveholders. Most voters in low slaveholding areas acted as if they agreed with a Virginia unionist's response to Brown's claim that "among us the Poor white Laborer is Respected as an Equal." "[I]f you mean Equal in Association you say that which is not so." the Virginian wrote. "We all know that every man is Equal in Respect to Law," he continued; "you say that the families of the Poor white Laborer of the South is treated with kindness consideration and Respect[.] When Did the Aristocracy of the South become so Charitable so kind so considerate

7. Little Farmer to editor, Upson *Pilot,* September 1, 1860.
8. J. Henly Smith to Alexander H. Stephens, November 16, 1860, in Stephens Papers, Library of Congress Collection on microfilm, University of Georgia.

considering the Poor white Laborer any more than they are at the North [?]"[9] Such questions disclosed that Brown's rhetoric was recognized for exactly what it was. The social benefits of slavery for nonslaveholders were more apparent to those who owned slaves than to those who did not.

Voters in low slaveholding areas, then, ignored the advice of the Democratic leaders they had followed for years, nearly all of whom were fire-eaters. They remained skeptical that the protection of slavery was of primary importance to them. Perhaps most surprising of all, they shrugged off secessionists' warnings of the racial rapine and bloody servile insurrection that failure to secede would entail. To Governor Brown's charge that "it is the Design of the North as a general thing to Put the People of the south on an equality with a Negro," the Virginian responded in terms that voters in low slaveholding countries might well have agreed with. Northerners, the Virginian wrote, "can Not put the People of the South on an Equality with a Negro Worse than what the People of the South Practice every Day for there are men of the south that have Negro Women for their Wives Buy them for that Purpose I know that Personally to be a fact[.] What are the Propriety of accusing a People [northerners] of a Design that we all Ready Practice more than they Do [?]"[10] Such questions, coupled with the actions of voters in low slaveholding counties, suggested that many Georgians were well aware that the racial fear arguments were attempts to create a racial unity that would overarch the social and political divisions in Georgia. The voters' opposition to secession demonstrated that there were chasms of interest the racial fear arguments would not bridge. It was also evidence that the structure of loyalties in Georgia's social system was actually in the shambles that the secession campaign had hinted at. Yet it is doubtful that these voters had relinquished either their strong belief in white supremacy or their commitment to its social and political protection. For individuals, what has since been called the central theme of southern history probably remained psychologically

9. A Virginian to Mr. Brown, November 20, 1860, *ibid*.
10. *Ibid*.

central.[11] Many voters simply acted as if that commitment was not at issue in the secession election, or, if it was at issue, it was of secondary importance. Thus, the central theme of white supremacy proved of marginal value in closing the social divisions that the secession crisis had exposed.[12]

By relegating their traditional party and racial loyalties to a secondary position, voters in these low slaveholding areas asserted the primacy of their fear of the oligarchic tendencies of secessionists, at least if their words during the secession campaign were any indication. If their political ideology was that of a *"Herrenvolk* democracy,"* as it has been called, then these voters demonstrated that they feared threats to democracy more than threats to the *Herrenvolk*.[13] But if they feared a secessionist oligarchy outside the Union, they valued, by implication, the degree of political and social democracy they had enjoyed within the Union. For when they said that "our Government is a Democracy, and not an Oligarchy, and we hope it never will be," they were noting both the value they put on what "is" and their fears of what might be.[14] Since these voters opposed leaving the Union which had developed along with the democratic practices they valued, they, in a sense, turned upside-down John C. Calhoun's notion of the role of the South in the Union. Calhoun had argued the value of the South as a conservative counterweight to the potentially disruptive white laborers of the North. These voters, on the other hand, suggested by their opposition to secession that the Union was a democratic counterweight to the inherent oligarchic tendencies of southern slave society.[15] Cal-

11. Ulrich Bonnell Phillips, "The Central Theme of Southern History," *American Historical Review,* XXXIV (1928), 30–43.

12. For an interpretation of secession that emphasizes the primacy of racial fears, see Steven A. Channing, *Crisis of Fear, Secession in South Carolina* (New York: Simon and Schuster, 1970).

13. The concept of *Herrenvolk* democracy is advanced and developed in George M. Fredrickson, *The Black Image in the White Mind: The Debate on Afro-American Character and Destiny, 1817–1914* (New York: Harper and Row, 1971), 43–70, following the suggestions of the sociologist Pierre L. van den Berghe in his *Race and Racism: A Comparative Perspective* (New York: John Wiley, 1967), 77–95.

14. Rome *Weekly Courier,* January 1, 1861.

15. The Jacksonian editor Hopkins Holsey had made this argument in the 1850s. See Horace Montgomery, *Cracker Parties* (Baton Rouge: Louisiana State University Press, 1950), 3.

houn's idea was subject to repudiation by the North and, in a way, Lincoln's election symbolized that repudiation. But the notion that the Union balanced antidemocratic tendencies within the South could only be repudiated by the absence of marked antidemocratic actions on the part of the newly seceded governments. Thus the opposition to secession among these cooperationists was conditional, not absolute. To the degree that Georgia out of the Union accorded as much respect to their interests and opinions as Georgia had in the Union, these voters would have reason to doubt their distrust of secessionists and to reassemble the taut web of pre-secession loyalties. But that test would come later, in the months between secession and war.

For the time being, the behavior of voters in these low slaveholding counties confirmed the accuracy of secessionists' perceptions of untrustworthy nonslaveholders. To the degree that secessionists themselves were aware of this confirmation, they would presumably take steps either to insure the trustworthiness of these voters or to eliminate them as a threat by, in some way, reducing their influence. Time and the actions of the delegates in the state convention would tell whether these secessionist actions would be necessary and forthcoming.

Voters in High Slaveholding Counties

In marked contrast to the strong opposition to secession in the low slaveholding counties, support for secession came from high slaveholding counties. In counties where about a third or more of the voters were slaveholders, or in the wealthier and more productive counties, voters apparently saw either a more menacing threat in Lincoln's election or a more enticing promise in secession than did voters in low slaveholding areas. Voters in these high slaveholding areas did not have to imagine their interests in a slave society; they could calculate them. A threat to slavery was a direct threat to them and to the society they lived in. Since slaves also lived in these counties in large proportions, the voters might have been very sensitive to their racial interests. But their racial interests tended to parallel their social and economic interests. It is impossible, with the evidence at hand, to isolate the influence of racial fears. Whether or not they agreed with the assertion that "slave insurrections . . . are all a delusion," a majority of voters in high slaveholding districts voted as if their ultimate loyalties were with their tangible interests, as if they cared more for their attachment to slavery than for their bonds to the Union.[16]

The majorities in these districts tended to be bare rather than sizable. The reason for the relatively close vote was not that voters failed to perceive what was at stake. Instead, the vote was close because men perceived the threats to their common, tangible interests from different political viewpoints. On the one hand, voters in high slaveholding Whig counties split their vote about equally.[17] On the other hand, in high slaveholding Democratic counties an overwhelming majority, two voters in three, supported secession.[18] Yet these differences in the proportion of the popular vote for secession understates the actual support for secession in Whig counties. Even more important, they mask the shift of voters in Whig counties toward support for secession. Somewhere between 630 and 5,169 voters in high slaveholding Whig counties shifted from opposition to Breckinridge in 1860 to support for secession in 1861.[19] In high slaveholding Democratic counties, in contrast, a maximum of 1,244 voters made such a shift.

The secession election, then, polarized Georgia. Thousands of voters in low slaveholding Democratic counties were driven away from their votes for Breckinridge into opposition to secession, while other

16. Augusta *Chronicle and Sentinel,* December 15, 1860.

17. "Opposition" counties might be a more accurate name for these counties since they are defined as those counties that gave half or more of their votes to the opponents of the Democratic presidential candidates in the six elections between 1836 and 1856. But since most voters in these counties were Whigs while the Whig party was alive, and since ideas associated with southern Whiggery were important in these areas in the secession election, I have chosen to call them "Whig" counties, recognizing that the label is not entirely accurate. Of the fifty-six Whig counties, all but three were high slaveholding counties. Democratic counties, then, were those that gave a majority of votes to Democratic presidential candidates in these elections. Of the seventy-six Democratic counties, forty were low slaveholding counties, and thirty-six were high slaveholding counties.

18. To maintain that these differences were the result of racial fear one would need to entertain the dubious notion that in equally slave-dense areas Democrats feared slaves more than Whigs did.

19. Even this may understate the actual shift in sentiment toward secession in Whig counties. For example, in counties that opposed both Breckinridge and secession, as the voter turnout increased, so did the support for secession. This suggests that those who failed to vote in these counties were actually in favor of secession. In sharp contrast, in all other sets of counties (that is, pro-Breckinridge–prosecession, pro-Breckinridge–antisecession, and anti-Breckinridge–prosecession counties) the vote for secession *decreased* as turnout increased.

thousands of voters in high slaveholding Whig counties shifted from opposition to Breckinridge to support for secession. In high slaveholding Democratic counties, voters seem to have voted in 1861 more like they voted in 1860, although there was still probably a small shift toward secession.

Thus the secession campaign appeals for an absence of party sentiment, like the calls for racial unity, were expressions of a hope set against reality. Political loyalties remained very much alive, although they were expressed in new ways. Overall, the secession election in Georgia came closer to creating a three- rather than a one-party state.[20] With the collapse of the loyalty of many traditionally Democratic voters in low slaveholding areas, Georgia was left with two competing political ideologies in high slaveholding areas and a third in low slaveholding areas. In the new alignment of political forces, slaveholding replaced traditional political allegiances as the central consideration. After secession was achieved, as never before, there would be an opportunity for voters in Democratic and Whig high slaveholding counties to reconcile their ideological differences and unite behind a program that would explicitly strive to protect the rights, privileges, and interests of slaveholders. Voters in high slaveholding Democratic areas had little to lose in such a development, since their traditional allies in low slaveholding districts were already lost. They stood to gain not only the support of their traditional Whig opponents but also the benefits of political allies who clearly shared their tangible interests in slavery. Likewise, should such a development occur, voters in Whig counties would have little to venture and much to gain. By becoming the postsecession allies of voters in high slaveholding Democratic areas, they would be able to exert a measure of control over the political and social consequences of secession. Fear of these consequences had made cooperationists of many of these Whig voters, according to their secession campaign rhetoric. "Disruption seems to me to be inevitable," Linton Stephens wrote his brother, "and the next

20. There were important quantitative exceptions to this general pattern, to be discussed shortly. For a discussion of the one-party interpretation, see Seymour Martin Lipset, "The Emergence of the One-party South: The Election of 1860," in his *Political Man: The Social Basis of Politics* (New York: Doubleday, 1960), 372–84.

thing is to temper the calmity as much as may be done, and shape events which can not be prevented towards the best possible results."[21] If Whig voters could temper the calamity and shape events, if they could help set the social and ideological tone of the postsecession government, their fears might disappear.

VOTERS IN TOWN COUNTIES

During the secession campaign many Georgians observed that "the secession sentiment is much stronger in and around the cities, than it is among the common people in the country."[22] The accuracy of these observations was confirmed when town counties gave secessionist candidates the overwhelming majority of 69 percent of their votes.[23] In the four counties which had the largest proportion of town population, the secessionist majority was an even larger 77 percent. Perhaps still more astonishing, in the rural countryside of Georgia—where most of the crops were grown, where most small farmers, slaveholders, planters, and slaves lived and worked, and where a full eighty percent of the 1861 electorate voted—a 53 percent majority opposed secession.

Clearly, the secession election polarized Georgia along a town-country axis as well as along political and slaveholding axes. The three axes reinforced and counteracted each other, depending on the relative position on the axes of a given set of counties. For example, although a majority of voters in country counties opposed secession, in those country counties that were both high slaveholding and Democratic, a 58 percent majority favored secession. That is, being country counties tended to reduce the vote for secession, while being high slaveholding and Democratic counties counter-balanced and outweighed that tendency.

Thus, Democratic counties, whether high or low slaveholding, town or country, consistently gave larger votes for secession than the corre-

21. Linton Stephens to Alexander H. Stephens, January 7, 1861, in Stephens Papers, Library of Congress.

22. L. F. to editor, Upson *Pilot,* December 22, 1860.

23. Town counties were defined as those with more than 10 percent of their population living in a town. Country counties were those with town populations of 10 percent or less. There were 113 country counties and 19 town counties. For the names and populations of the towns and a discussion of the definition of town and country counties, see the Appendix.

sponding Whig counties. Among low slaveholding country counties, Democratic counties gave only 42 percent of their votes for secession, but that exceeded the 32 percent in Whig counties. Among high slaveholding country counties, Democratic counties gave a 58 percent majority for secession, Whig counties only 47 percent. In high slaveholding town counties, the majority for secession was 61 percent in Whig counties and 79 percent in Democratic counties.

Equally consistently, high slaveholding counties gave a larger proportion of their votes for secession than the corresponding low slaveholding counties. Among country Whig counties, high slaveholding counties favored secessionists with 47 percent of their votes, low slaveholding counties with 32 percent. In country Democratic counties, low slaveholding counties gave secessionists 42 percent of their votes, while a 58 percent majority was recorded in high slaveholding counties. Since there were no low slaveholding Whig town counties, there is no appropriate comparison for the 61 percent secessionist majority in high slaveholding Whig town countries. But in Democratic town counties, high slaveholding counties favored secession with a 79 percent majority while low slaveholding counties registered a majority of 68 percent.

Finally, town counties consistently gave a larger share of their votes for secession than country counties of similar slaveholding and politics. Among high slaveholding Whig counties, country counties gave 47 percent of their votes for secession while town counties favored secession with a 61 percent majority. In high slaveholding Democratic counties, town counties surpassed country counties in their support for secession, 79 percent to 58 percent. In low slaveholding Democratic counties, town counties voted a 68 percent secessionist majority while country counties gave secessionists only 42 percent of their votes.

In sum, the largest secessionist majority was in high slaveholding Democratic town counties, closely followed by other town counties, and by high slaveholding Democratic country counties. Low slaveholding Whig country counties gave secession the smallest proportion of votes, but there were only three such counties. Much more important was the opposition to secession in the thirty-six low slaveholding Democratic country counties which gave secession 42 percent of their votes, less than the 47 percent in high slaveholding Whig country counties.

While the distribution of the popular vote for secession is extremely revealing, it understates the actual sentiment for secession in Whig counties. At a minimum, 928 voters in town Whig counties shifted from opposition to Breckinridge to support for secession. At a maximum, 1,520 voters in these counties shifted toward secession, exceeded only by the 2,683 voters who did likewise in high slaveholding country Whig counties. Even these estimates may understate the shift in sentiment in Whig town counties since, in these counties, unlike all others, the support for secession increased as voter turnout increased, which suggests that most of those who stayed away from the polls were in favor of secession.

The maximum voter shift toward secession in Democratic town counties and high slaveholding Democratic country counties was only about half that in Whig counties. The reason for the difference was that among high slaveholding country counties, the maximum voter shift in Democratic counties (618) was less than one-fourth that in Whig counties (2,683). In town counties, on the other hand, the maximum voter shift in Democratic counties exceeded that in Whig counties, 2,975 to 1,530.

At a mimumum, then, only Whig town counties showed a voter shift toward secession while at a maximum there was a substantial shift of voters toward secession in both Whig and Democratic town counties and high slaveholding country counties. In town counties, a maximum of 3,605 voters who had opposed Breckinridge favored secession, followed closely by a similar shift of 3,301 voters in high slaveholding country counties. In sharp contrast, the movement of voters in low slaveholding country counties was away from secession. In these counties between 6,229 and 4,947 voters who had voted for Breckinridge voted against secession. Clearly, we only need to assume that the actual movement of voters was somewhere between these maximum and minimum estimates to conclude that the secessionist votes of anti-Breckinridge voters in town and high slaveholding country counties were crucial to the degree of electoral success that the secessionists achieved.

Almost as important as the movement of voters toward and away from secession was the failure of many potential voters to cast their ballots. Throughout the state, as voter turnout increased, the support for secession decreased. In those counties where the turnout was less than 60 percent of that in the recent presidential election, secession was supported with an emphatic 80 percent majority. Where the turnout was between 60 and 79 percent, secessionists received a 52 percent majority. In the counties where the turnout equaled or exceeded 80 percent, secession was favored by only 47 percent of the voters.

This inverse relationship between turnout and support for secession suggests that perhaps Alexander Stephens was right about the cold January rain keeping the opponents of secession away from the polls. At least it seems true that, except in Whig town counties, many opponents of secession failed to vote. Yet the rain does not appear to have been the reason for their failure. In country counties, where the rain would have caused voters the greatest inconvenience, the turnout was higher than in town counties. Low slaveholding Democratic country counties, the staunchest opponents of secession, had the highest turnout, 93 percent. In contrast, turnouts in town counties, where secession received the largest majorities, ranged between 69 and 80 percent. In Democratic town counties, turnout alone accounted for a remarkable 70 percent of the variation in the vote for secession. Turnout was almost equally important in high slaveholding Democratic country counties, while it had a smaller but still significant influence in Whig town counties.

Whether potential voters chose to vote seems to have been determined mostly by the intensity of their opposition to secession and by their social environment. The most intense opponents of secession were apparently in low slaveholding Democratic country counties. When such men in these counties took their breakfasts on January 2 and considered the wet, cold, gloomy day, they apparently felt strongly enough to overcome the restraining effects of both the weather and the likelihood that the outcome of the local election was a foregone conclusion. In Democratic town counties, on the other hand, opponents of secession were restrained either by the relative weakness of their opposition or by the town environment—the rain, it seems, can have been little more than a convenient excuse for not voting. In Whig town counties, many prosecession voters apparently did not vote, again, presumably because of the weakness of their commitment to the cause or some influence of the town environment.

While many potential voters in town counties and high slaveholding country counties failed to vote, many other voters in these same counties, especially in Whig counties, shifted from voting for the national and unionist presidential candidates Bell and Douglas to voting for secession. Reports from throughout the state—from Macon that a group of "Douglas men" had "announced in favor of immediate secession"; from Rome that "an old-line Whig, then an American, and finally a member of the John Bell party" had "sacrifice[d]" his party loyalty and supported secession; from Atlanta that "many . . . good union men . . . look to separation as the nearest hope for peace and the only hope for preservation of our rights"; from Columbus, that "the bell weather [*sic*] of the Union party," a "gentleman of talent and ability," had made "a forceful [secessionist] appeal to his conservative friends"; from Athens that even a man who was "always so conservative seems to feel that the only course left us is to secede at once"—corroborate the quantitative evidence of the conservative ideology and Whig politics of the voters who shifted toward secession.[24] It was indeed, as one editor noted, "a remarkable indication of the times and state of feeling in Georgia . . . [that] in the ranks of the resistance men of the State . . . [are] men of such high intelligence who have heretofore been distinguished for conservatism and devotion to the

---

24. C. J. Harris to editor, Atlanta *Daily Intelligencer,* December 3, 1860; Rome *Weekly Courier,* December 7, 1860; W. F. Herring to Alexander H. Stephens, November 9, 1860, Columbus *Weekly Times,* November 30, 1860, Richard Malcolm Johnston to Stephens, January 10, 1861, in Stephens Papers, Library of Congress. See also the letters to Stephens from J. R. Sneed, November 8, 1860, James D. Russ, November 13, 1860, Benjamin R. Reese, November 26, 1860, in Stephens Papers, Library of Congress; John B. Lamar to Howell Cobb, November 26, 1860, in Howell Cobb Papers, University of Georgia; Mother to Son, December 2, 1860, in John McIntosh Kell Papers, Duke University; Wilson Lumpkin to public, Milledgeville *Federal Union,* January 1, 1861; Citizens of Atlanta to Senator Douglas (telegram), December 24, 1860, quoted in Ulrich Bonnell Phillips, *The Life of Robert Toombs* (New York: Macmillan, 1913), 211; Albany *Patriot,* November 29, December 6, 1860.

Union."[25] "The good Lord deliver us from any man who would cry 'Union' now, while such men . . . are leading a Southern Rights column," another editor pleaded.[26] From these conservatives—men who lived in town counties and high slaveholding country counties, many of them former Whigs—came the decisive electoral impetus to the secession movement in Georgia. They not only strengthened the secessionist delegation to the upcoming state convention, but they also, by their character, lured other conservatives toward secession. Understandably, secessionists found the support of these conservatives "especially satisfactory on account of the *impetus* it has given, and will continue to give, to the glorious cause of the Secession Party of Georgia."[27] In fact, these conservative, substantial men in town counties and Whig counties were harbingers of the coalescence of conservatives behind the secession movement which would occur as the secession movement itself coalesced around conservative ideas and practices.

But why did these conservatives embrace secession? Why did many other Georgians fail to vote? To what degree were both groups influenced by their social environment? These simple questions require prolonged answers that must begin with a look at historians' interpretations of the Old South.

25. Macon *Telegraph,* December 13, 1860.
26. Albany *Patriot,* December 6, 1860.
27. Columbus *Weekly Times,* November 30, 1860, in Stephens Papers, Library of Congress.

5

Secession and
the Internal Crisis
of the South

Interpretations of the Old South

The election of delegates to the state convention was no ordinary election, as Georgians were well aware. There had been hundreds of elections during the antebellum years, but in none of them had Georgia voters as squarely confronted the question posed by the secession election. Did being a southerner—an identity few, if any, disclaimed—necessitate secession?[1] As Georgians voted, they unwittingly left a record of how they resolved that question. Since the question is an important element in the major historical interpretations of the Old South, a brief historiographical foray should help us understand why Georgians voted as they did. It should also bring into sharper focus those features of voter behavior that remain problematic.

One major school of historical thought, more prominent in the 1930s than today, saw a Jeffersonian South, an agrarian section peopled by individualistic, freedom-loving dirt farmers who participated fully in the development of American democratic traditions. Among the merits of this view is that it helps explain why some southerners might have opposed secession, for why should the election of a Republican president necessitate separation from a Union which had fostered traits these southerners treasured. But the agrarian interpretation has the fault, among others, of making it difficult to understand why southerners would support secession.[2]

1. For the most judicious analysis of southern identity and secession, see David M. Potter, *The Impending Crisis, 1848–1861* (New York: Harper and Row, 1976), 448–84.
2. See for example, the chapter entitled "The Second Revolution" in Charles A. Beard and Mary R. Beard, *The Rise of American Civilization* (one-vol. ed.; New York: Macmillan, 1930),

79

Since, as we have seen, voters in high slaveholding areas gave secession sizable majorities, then one must either see these voters acting to protect the agrarian nature of their society, in which case slavery is seen as a peripheral institution (But if the secessionists were agrarians, why were they opposed so strongly by the quintessential agrarians in low slaveholding areas?), or one must acknowledge that slaveholding secessionists contradicted and subverted the agrarian South and were, therefore, not "essentially" southern.[3] One can attempt to avoid this dilemma by arguing that fire-eating extremists aroused the passions of the nonslaveholding farmers and misled them into supporting secession blindly and irrationally. But in Georgia, as we have seen, this is simply false since the large majority of voters in low slaveholding areas *opposed* secession. To avoid the conclusion that the secessionists who helped found a separate southern nation were in some fundamental way non-southern, one can simply separate one's judgments about the antebellum South from those about the Confederacy. Thus the Confederacy is seen as an abrupt departure from the Old South rather than a continuation of it. But to argue that the Old South was one thing and the Confederacy quite another seems as objectionable as the conclusion that the argument was designed to avoid. The agrarian interpretation, then, provides a possible explanation of why Georgians—especially those in low slaveholding areas—opposed secession, but its power for explaining the support for secession is severely limited.

A second major interpretation of the antebellum period emphasizes the degree to which the South was similar to the North. Slavery aside, the South shared with the North a vigorous two-party system, the

II, 52–121; Franklin Lawrence Owsley, "The Irrepressible Conflict," in *Twelve Southerners: I'll Take My Stand* (New York: Harper and Row, 1931), 66–91; Owsley's *Plain Folk of the Old South* (Baton Rouge: Louisiana State University Press, 1950); Fletcher M. Green, *Constitutional Development in the South Atlantic States, 1776–1860: A Study in the Evolution of Democracy* (Chapel Hill: University of North Carolina Press, 1930); and Green's "Democracy in the Old South," *Journal of Southern History*, XII (1946), 3–23, since reprinted in J. Isaac Copeland (ed.), *Democracy in the Old South and Other Essays by Fletcher Melvin Green* (Nashville: Vanderbilt University Press, 1969), 65–86. For a critique of the agrarian interpretation, see David M. Potter, *The South and the Sectional Conflict* (Baton Rouge: Louisiana State University Press, 1968), 7–15.

3. See David Hackett Fischer's discussion of the *"fallacy of essences"* in his *Historians' Fallacies: Toward a Logic of Historical Thought* (New York: Harper and Row, 1970), 68–70.

dominance of the countryside by the towns, and the overarching values of liberalism, Christianity, and American nationalism which created intense guilt about slavery in the minds of southerners. The South seceded, in this view, because of the "near-hysteria" among some elements of the population, because of "the paralysis of will, the despair, the sense of helplessness," and the desire to escape persistent insecurity that pervaded "more conservative" southerners, and, above all, because southerners' intellectual commitment to the same liberal and Christian values which abolitionists used to attack slavery had made the South's moral position on slavery "literally intolerable." As a result, southerners "passed the point of rational self-control" and reacted to Lincoln's election with irrational, "almost pathological violence."[4]

This view seems to provide a possible explanation for the strong support for secession among townsmen: namely, their desire for stability, for an end to the chronic insecurity that attended the sectional crisis. Yet this is only a step toward an explanation. We still need to know why merchants who, in this view, dominated towns—men whose commercial experience and former Whig party ties transcended sectional boundaries—believed that security and stability lay in secession rather than in union. Indeed, unless some other values took priority in the secession crisis, it seems that these men would have preferred the Union.[5]

The argument that "near-hysteria" led many to favor secession is less useful in understanding events in Georgia. As we have seen, the most important electoral shifts toward secession were made by conservative Bell and Douglas voters, sober men whom we would expect to be among the most resistant to hysteria. To argue that something approaching hysteria was an important factor in support for secession

4. See for example the two important essays by Charles Griers Sellers, Jr., "Who Were the Southern Whigs?" *American Historical Review,* LIX (1954), 335–46, and "The Travail of Slavery," in *The Southerner as American* (Chapel Hill: University of North Carolina Press, 1960), 40–71.

5. For an analysis of the conservative, unionist sympathies of urban voters in 1860, see Ollinger Crenshaw, "Urban and Rural Voting in the Election of 1860," in Eric F. Goldman (ed.), *Historiography and Urbanization, Essays in American History in Honor of W. Stull Holt* (Port Washington, N.Y.: Kennikat Press, 1968), 43–66.

implies that secession was less than rational, or, as one historian has put it, that it was "the product of logical reasoning within a framework of irrational perception."[6] But the assumption that either the act of secession or an important segment of its proponents was irrational hinges on the conclusion that Lincoln's election posed no threat to slavery in the states. Yet secessionists' campaign rhetoric, as we have seen, portrayed their fears that the Republican party would find numerous recruits within the South. The result of the secession election demonstrated that if support for secession was any measure of loyalty to slaveholders, then the nightmares of the secessionists were alarmingly realistic. Secessionists feared the Republicans not because southern psyches were unstable but because southern society was. If we begin with the assumption that secessionists were irrational, we will never be able to appreciate the fears in secessionist rhetoric, the portent in the election results, or the nature of southern society.

The interpretation of the Old South that is probably most widely accepted in one form or another by historians today is that slaveholders dominated southern society and politics throughout the antebellum period.[7] This interpretation has the great virtue of making the act of secession explicable. If we were to assume that slaveholders were not the dominant group in Georgia, it would be very difficult—without invoking irrationality—to understand why a threat to slavery led eventually to secession from the Union. It seems obvious that high slaveholding districts in Georgia registered support for secession because it was easy for slaveholders to perceive the genuine threat of Lincoln's election and the necessity of immediate secession. It seems equally obvious that secession would not have been accomplished if slaveholders had not been sufficiently dominant to translate their individual decisions into state policy.

Yet the view that slaveholders dominated the South can easily be

6. Stephen A. Channing, *Crisis of Fear: Secession in South Carolina* (New York: Simon and Schuster, 1970), 286; Robert E. Shalhope, "Race, Class, Slavery, and the Antebellum Southern Mind," *Journal of Southern History*, XXXVII (1971), 571.

7. The scholarship of Eugene D. Genovese has become the basic point of reference on this question. See especially, *The Political Economy of Slavery: Studies in the Economy and Society of the Slave South* (New York: Random House, 1965), and *The World the Slaveholders Made: Two Essays in Interpretation* (New York: Random House, 1971).

pushed too far and prevent us from understanding why Georgians behaved as they did. According to secessionists, the dominance of slaveholders was tenuous enough that only by secession could it be maintained. Indeed, secession was necessary precisely because, without it, the dominance of slaveholders might be contested by a southern Republican party. The potent opposition to secession in low slaveholding areas matched secessionists' fears with evidence that slaveholders were not sufficiently dominant to elicit political support for secession from those whose loyalty to slavery was most in doubt. If we simply assume slaveholders were dominant, it will be difficult to understand why many Georgians in high slaveholding areas thought secession was necessary while most voters in low slaveholding areas ignored the advice of respected political and social leaders and opposed secession, unconvinced that even "the cardinal test of a Southerner"—whether the South "shall be and remain a white man's country"—was at stake.[8]

Historians who emphasize the dominance of slaveholders argue that the Lincoln administration's threat to the geographical expansion of slavery was the fundamental reason why men supported secession. Expansion enlarged opportunities for both slaveholders and nonslaveholders, and it kept the concentration of blacks at a socially tolerable level by diffusing their ever-increasing numbers into under-populated areas. Secessionists favored independence, in this view, because they believed that the "continual maturation of slavery within a fixed geographical area created class and racial stresses that could be relieved only through expansion," which had been made impossible by Lincoln's victory.[9]

This is an attractive explanation for the secessionist votes of many Breckinridge voters, especially in high slaveholding areas. But if support for Breckinridge is a measure of intense interest in the expansion of slavery, then the thousands of Breckinridge voters in low slavehold-

8. Ulrich Bonnell Phillips, "The Central Theme of Southern History," *American Historical Review*, XXXIV (1928), 31.

9. William L. Barney, *The Road to Secession: A New Perspective on the Old South* (New York: Praeger, 1972), 6. See also Barney, *The Secessionist Impulse: Alabama and Mississippi in 1860* (Princeton: Princeton University Press, 1974).

ing regions who opposed secession must have been concerned about
something even more important to them than their previous endorse-
ment of the expansion of slave territory. It is also curious that during
the secession campaign Georgia secessionists did not emphasize the
fundamental necessity of expansion. Perhaps they believed that it was
a bad tactic to tie the necessity of an immediate action—secession—to
a cause whose influence was at best eventual. Or perhaps Georgia
secessionists did not attribute as much importance to expansion as this
interpretation claims. At least, if expansion was centrally important to
Georgia secessionists, they said very little about it. If it had been as
fundamental as this interpretation claims, it seems that secessionists
would have emphasized the alluring possibilities of expansion once
Georgia was separated from the Union.

But perhaps even more important than the lack of rhetorical evidence about secessionists' belief in the necessity of expansion were the
actions of conservative voters in town and Whig counties. Why did
men whose support of Bell and Douglas suggests that expansion was
not one of their central concerns suddenly become preoccupied with
the necessity of expansion and become secessionists to achieve it?
While the expansion interpretation may help explain the Breckinridge
supporters among secessionists, it seems to imply that the social
thought of conservative Bell and Douglas men underwent a drastic
reorientation after Lincoln's election. It seems unlikely that their orien-
tation toward the Union was reversed because they were suddenly
persuaded of the social necessity of the expansion of slave territory. In
sum, the recognition that slaveholders dominated the South must be
carefully qualified if we are to account for what secessionists said and
for what both their newly won conservatives allies and their opponents
did.

None of the interpretations of the Old South satisfactorily accounts
for the results of the secession election in Georgia. Each interpretation
contains compelling arguments for certain events but none of the interpretations offers a coherent explanation of the social and ideological
disunity in Georgia and the movement of voters both toward and away
from secession. Our task is to integrate the promising arguments from

each interpretation into a new interpretation that makes the outcome of the secession election comprehensible.

The Internal Crisis of the South

The divisions revealed by the secession election were the political manifestations of the long-developing internal crisis of the South. At bottom, the internal crisis challenged the social and political dominance of slaveholders. The ideological roots of the challenge ran back to the American Revolution. Throughout the first sixty years of the nineteenth century the sons and grandsons of the generation of slaveholders who helped formulate the ideals of 1776 maintained their social, economic, and political preeminence by owning slaves and relying on their labor. The tension between revolutionary ideals and the institution of slavery was expressed early in the nineteenth century in the argument that slavery was a necessary evil. Even more important evidence of the tension were the thousands of slaves who were manumitted in the upper South in the years after the Revolution.[10] In the lower South, where there were more slaves and where planters were more powerful in relation to other social groups, manumissions were rare. If one had an obvious and strong interest in slavery, it was not especially difficult to accommodate the practice of slavery to the ideals of the Revolution. The internal crisis of the South in 1860 did not arise simply because slaveholders confronted an ideological challenge.

More important, the ideology of the American Revolution was translated into a set of political institutions which, by the 1840s, roughly paralleled revolutionary ideals. The increasingly democratic political institutions generated political conflict and ideological ferment

---

10. In many ways, the secession election was for slaveholders what the election of 1896 was for the industrial elite. For discussion of the significance of the 1896 election, see Walter Dean Burnham, "The Changing Shape of the American Political Universe," *American Political Science Review,* LIX (1965), 7–28. For a thorough and sophisticated discussion of the relation between slavery and revolutionary ideals see David Brion Davis, *The Problem of Slavery in the Age of Revolution, 1770–1823* (Ithaca: Cornell University Press, 1975), and Edmund S. Morgan, *American Slavery, American Freedom: The Ordeal of Colonial Virginia* (New York: Norton, 1975). On the post-Revolutionary manumissions, see Ira Berlin, *Slaves Without Masters: The Free Negro in the Antebellum South* (New York: Pantheon, 1974), 30–31, and in general, 15–50.

within the South in the antebellum years, but they did not lead inevitably to the internal crisis of 1860. Indeed, democratic politics and slavery expanded together as the area of the South itself expanded during the first half of the nineteenth century. Up to 1860 manhood suffrage had not threatened the rights of slaveholders, even though most voters owned no slaves. Of course, southerners were sharply divided on a host of political issues—taxation, internal improvements, banking, tariffs, and governmental organization and representation. But throughout these political struggles, slaveholders managed—by making concessions and by working toward consent—to preserve their dominance, or, as Eugene D. Genovese has put it, "to prevent the emergence of an effective challenge to the basis of society in slave property."[11]

Yet slaveholders confronted an internal crisis in 1860 precisely because neither their political concessions nor their attempts at consent had been successful enough to guarantee that nonslaveholders would not become Republicans, if given the opportunity. The internal crisis of the South occurred because the democratic political institutions that were an inheritance of the Revolution had a large and powerful social base in nonslaveholders, who represented a potential electoral majority. Many nonslaveholders were relatively independent of slaveholder influence since they lived in the upcountry, remote from the rich soil that attracted concentrations of staple-crop-producing planters.[12]

11. Eugene D. Genovese, *Roll, Jordan, Roll: The World the Slaves Made* (New York: Pantheon, 1974), 658. For an elaboration of this point, see Eugene D. Genovese, "Yeomen Farmers in a Slaveholders' Democracy," *Agricultural History*, XLIX (1975), 331–42. On southern opposition to slavery, see Carl N. Degler, *The Other South: Southern Dissenters in the Nineteenth Century* (New York: Harper and Row, 1974), 12–96.

12. The degree of independence of nonslaveholders is disputed. Recent studies of the cotton South have accumulated very strong evidence that plantations were virtually self-sufficient, thus tending to undermine the old view that nonslaveholders depended on planters for a market for their food crops. There is probably some truth to the view that there was a degree of mutual dependence between planters and nonslaveholders who lived in plantation districts. But the degree of mutual dependence between planters and the many nonslaveholders who lived remote from plantation districts is likely to have been quite small. While economic factors by no means exhaust the matters one should consider in determining the degree of dependence of one group on another (family and church ties are also of obvious importance), is not exactly clear what difference the actual degree of dependence makes. Dependence, after all, can lead to distrust and mutual suspicion as well as to harmony and mutual support. In any case, the important question here is whether non-slaveholding areas acted independently in politics, a question I discuss

Southern climate, soil, and topography combined with the evolution of slavery, the increasing political self-consciousness of slaveholders and nonslaveholders, and the development of democratic political institutions to make many slaveholders fear nonslaveholders so intensely that, in their view, secession was essential to the protection of slavery. When " 'we have been driven to the wall,' and the option is given us of Abolition or War," one South Carolinian rhetorically asked another in 1859, "think you that 360,000 slaveholders will dictate terms for 3,000,000 of non-slaveholders at the South—I fear not," he answered. "I mistrust our own people more than I fear all of the efforts of the Abolitionists." The internal crisis of the South necessitated secession. Otherwise, secessionists foresaw all too clearly "the emergence of an effective challenge to the basis of society in slave property."[13]

These fears, which were widely shared in Georgia, were intensified when secession was sought by having voters elect delegates to a state convention. It is ironic and telling that secessionists sought protection for slavery with a procedure which was at the root of the very danger they sought protection from—the danger of a genuine political choice on the question of slavery. By consenting to the secession election, secessionists revealed that they could not escape the internal crisis of the South. Instead, by secession, they hoped to overcome it.

POLITICAL INSTITUTIONS AND CONFLICT

In Georgia, political institutions developed within the framework of the constitution of 1798, which endured until 1861. Compared to other southern constitutions of the time, Georgia's was democratic. It provided that adult white males would elect legislators who would, in turn, elect a governor and various judicial officers. Subsequent amendments gave voters a still larger role. In 1812 the voters were

---

below. See Robert E. Gallman, "Self-Sufficiency in the Cotton Economy of the Antebellum South," and Eugene D. Genovese, "Commentary: A Historian's View," *Agricultural History*, XLIV (1970), 5–23, 143–47; George M. Fredrickson, *The Black Image in the White Mind: The Debate on Afro-American Character and Destiny, 1817–1914* (New York: Harper and Row, 1971), 66–67; William W. Freehling, "The Founding Fathers and Slavery," *American Historical Review*, LXXXVII (1972), 81–93; Genovese, "Yeoman Farmers in a Slaveholders' Democracy," 331–42.

13. Daniel Hamilton, quoted in Channing, *Crisis of Fear*, 255–56; Genovese, *Roll, Jordan, Roll,* 658.

authorized to elect justices of the inferior courts, which were, in the opinion of a modern expert, "the most powerful organ of county government." In 1824 voters were allowed to choose the governor, and, in 1843 general officers of the militia were made subject to election by those under their command. Even the judges of the nine superior courts—except for the supreme court, the highest judicial bodies in the state—were popularly elected beginning in 1852. Added to these reforms in 1847 was the abolition of any property qualification for candidates for governor or for the legislature, thereby making government potentially both *by* and *of* the people. The policy of giving away farm-sized lots of state lands to citizens chosen by lottery showed that the government was also *for* the people, at least in this important way.[14]

But the constitution was by no means thoroughly democratic. It provided for a system of representation that favored the wealthier, more settled, planter-dominated counties.[15] As settlers moved west and south across the fertile expanse of central Georgia, as they filtered along water-courses into the valleys of north Georgia and edged into the sandy wiregrass and pine barrens region of southeast Georgia, the unequal apportionment of the legislature became more and more intolerable. Since the constitution could only be amended by the legislature, reform seemed impossible. In 1832 an extralegal convention assembled and gave every indication of taking things into its own hands and rewriting the constitution from scratch. Under pressure, the legislature defused the rebellion by calling for a convention of its own to devise a plan to equalize representation and reduce the number of

14. For the 1798 constitution and some of the subsequent amendments, see Francis Newton Thorpe (ed.), *The Federal and State Constitutions* (7 vols.; Washington: Government Printing Office, 1909), II, 791–809. For a discussion of the constitution, see Albert Berry Saye, *A Constitutional History of Georgia, 1732–1945* (Athens, Georgia: University of Georgia Press, 1948), 155–95; Walter McElreath, *A Treatise on the Constitution of Georgia* (Atlanta: The Harrison Co., 1912); Ellen Kime Ware, *A Constitutional History of Georgia* (New York: Columbia University Press, 1947); Fletcher M. Green, *Constitutional Development in the South Atlantic States,* 99–14; Melvin Clyde Hughes, *County Government in Georgia* (Athens: University of Georgia Press, 1944), 14. For laws governing the election of superior court judges, see Howell Cobb, *Compilation of the General and Public Statutes of the State of Georgia* (New York: Edward O. Jenkins, 1859), 58–60. James C. Bonner, *A History of Georgia Agriculture, 1732–1860* (Athens: University of Georgia Press, 1964), 38–40.

15. James C. Bonner, "Legislative Apportionment and County Unit Voting in Georgia Since 1777," *Georgia Historical Quarterly,* XLVII (1963), 354.

legislators. Although the plan adopted by the convention when it met in 1833 abolished the federal ratio—which counted slaves as three-fifths of a person for representational purposes—and substituted a free white basis of representation, reformers were dissatisfied, arguing that the plan still left a majority of the legislature elected by a minority of the population. In a subsequent referendum, the plan was soundly defeated. Similarly rebellious moves in 1837 and 1838 led to a similar legislative response and, similarly, to no change. In 1843 the legislature itself devised a new system of apportionment which, as revised in 1851 and 1852, provided for one senator and one representative from each county and for an additional representative from the thirty-seven largest counties.[16]

Since representation was still determined by the federal ratio, this plan continued to favor areas of concentrated slaveholding at the expense of towns and northwest Georgia. Furthermore, representation from an area could be increased simply by carving one county into two new smaller counties. In exactly this way, representation from the newer cottonlands of southwest Georgia was greatly increased during the 1850s when the legislature created twenty-one new counties in the area. Although slave-poor north Georgia gained thirteen new counties in the same period, the region remained underrepresented.

Still, the dominance of the slaveholding counties had been sharply contested throughout the antebellum period in these conflicts over representation. Although the federal ratio was not abolished, enough concessions in representation were won to overcome slaveholder opposition in the legislature on certain important issues. In 1852, for example, Georgia slaveholders had their slaves taxed for the first time on an ad valorem basis, instead of on the long-standing per capita basis which they had stoutly but vainly defended.[17] But during the antebel-

16. Lucien E. Roberts, "Sectional Factors in the Movements for Legislative Reapportionment and Reduction in Georgia, 1777–1860," in James C. Bonner and Lucien E. Roberts (eds.), *Studies in Georgia History and Government* (Athens: University of Georgia Press, 1949), 94–122; Bonner, "Legislative Apportionment and County Unit Voting in Georgia," 354–56; Saye, *A Constitutional History of Georgia,* 174; Green, *Constitutional Development in the South Atlantic States,* 208–10, 233–39, 258–61.

17. George Ruble Woolfolk, "Taxes and Slavery in the Ante Bellum South," *Journal of Southern History,* XXVI (1960), 195–98; Lawrence Frederick Schmeckbier, "Taxation in Georgia," in Jacob Harvey Hollander (ed.), *Studies in State Taxation with Particular Reference to the Southern States* (Baltimore: Johns Hopkins Press, 1900), 220–22.

lum period slaveholders were more frequently divided by party differences than they were united behind their common interest. Thus the occasional victory over the interests of slaveholders was probably less important than the clear demonstration to slaveholders of both parties that the nonslaveholders who were concentrated in low slaveholding areas could and occasionally did practice a disquieting degree of political independence. Perhaps even more disquieting, the political self-confidence of voters in low slaveholding areas seemed to be growing.

POLITICAL IDEOLOGY AND THE DEFENSE OF SLAVERY

The political causes supported by the low slaveholding areas seemed to conform to the public consensus on democratic political rhetoric. In contrast, slaveholders faced the problem of casting the defense of their interests into suitably democratic terms. The racial defense of slavery was the most common method of squaring the practice of slavery with the theory of equality.[18] If slaveholders had made it a common practice to insist in public that white men were not equal, they were certain to commit political suicide. Instead, they conformed to the prevailing democratic tone of political rhetoric and argued that all whites were equal and all blacks were immutably inferior.

Some apologists for slavery went further to argue that democracy could be maintained only in a society based on slavery. Slavery, the argument went, gave slaveowners the leisure to study public affairs and the experience of being a responsible ruler, concerned with the welfare of many others. On the other hand, the slaves who performed the menial labor of the society were political eunuchs who could never revolt and demand a larger share of the fruits of their labor, which, ran a corollary argument, would be the inevitable fate of the northern free-labor system.[19] Such an argument grandly overlooked several facts. For one thing, many white nonslaveholders did work that was comparable to slave labor, and *they* voted. Furthermore, nonslaveholders voted in a society where the richest 10 percent of families owned three-quarters of all the wealth, much of it in the highly visible, so-

18. Fredrickson, *The Black Image in the White Mind,* 43–70; Degler, *The Other South,* 47–96.

19. See for example, Thomas R. R. Cobb, *An Inquiry into the Law of Negro Slavery in the United States of America* (Philadelphia: T. & J. W. Johnson, 1858), ccxii.

cially ostentatious form of large numbers of slaves. And, unlike poor northern laborers—whose rootlessness and foreignness were formidable barriers to the articulation of grievances through political action—many southern nonslaveholders were potent political threats precisely because they were southern, relatively settled, and politically independent.[20]

Thus, when apologists for slavery offered racial status to white nonslaveholders in exchange for deference to the interests of slaveholders, high-pressure salesmanship was necessary, as the secession campaign rhetoric demonstrated. It required only a little reflection to understand that the states' rights argument of the secessionists was a doublebitted ideological axe. If the state could protect slavery, it could also endanger it. Realizing this, perhaps the secessionists emphasized the bloodiness of the emancipation they foresaw if they stayed in the Union precisely because they feared that emancipation might be a bloodless political act. In any case, when the defenders of slavery swam with the rhetorical currents within the South, they implicitly acknowledged the strength of those democratic currents and their own inability to swim against them.

A convincing defense of slavery cast in democratic terms also seemed to promise the benefit of a South that was united against its sectional enemy. But party politics in Georgia and elsewhere in the South since nullification had suggested that the promise was nearly empty. In one sectional crisis after another, large segments of Georgia voters and important political leaders lined up with the Union against the numerous, more extreme southern rights spokesmen.

In 1833 President Andrew Jackson's Force Bill, which threatened

20. For evidence on the distribution of wealth, see Lee Soltow, *Men and Wealth in the United States, 1850–1870* (New Haven: Yale University Press, 1975), 99, 101, 124–46; Gavin Wright, "'Economic Democracy' and the Concentration of Agricultural Wealth in the Cotton South, 1850," *Agricultural History*, XLIV (1970), 63–93. We have only begun to learn about the remarkable geographical mobility of many nineteenth-century Americans. The best study of social and geographical mobility in the South, which provides evidence that the southern planters were less mobile than comparable groups in the North, is Jonathan M. Wiener, *Social Origins of the New South: Alabama, 1865–1885* (forthcoming). For evidence of the importance of geographical stability for political awareness and organization, see Wiener, "Planter-Merchant Conflict in Reconstruction Alabama," *Past and Present*, LXVIII (1975), 79–94, and Joan W. Scott, "The Glassworkers of Carmaux, 1850–1900," in Stephan Thernstrom and Richard Sennett (eds.), *Nineteenth Century Cities: Essays in the New Urban History* (New Haven: Yale University Press, 1969), 3–48.

South Carolina nullifiers with military retaliation, created enough discontent in Georgia for a state convention to be called to consider Georgia's response. At the convention, only a minority led by John M. Berrien denounced the bill. Most of the delegates walked out, organized the Union party, openly endorsed the Force Bill, and easily defeated the anti-Jackson, pronullification States' Rights party in the gubernatorial election. The latter party did not come to power in Georgia until 1843, when it changed its name to the Whig party, three years after it had associated with the national Whig ticket. The price of the following six years of power for the Whigs, that "company of gentlemen, politically inclined," was the sacrifice of exclusively states' rights doctrines and acquiescence to the national Whig program.[21]

The Compromise of 1850 shattered these political accomodations. A group of fire-eaters and moderate Democrats organized the anticompromise Southern Rights party which contested unsuccessfully with the procompromise Constitutional Union party, composed of both Democrats and Whigs, including such prominent Georgians as Howell Cobb, Robert Toombs, and Alexander Stephens. The views of the procompromise men prevailed since a comfortable majority of the convention of 1850 preferred the Union, with the compromise.[22] But, as the Georgia platform of 1850 suggested, a public commitment to the protection of southern rights became a requirement for political success in the 1850s.

Constitutional Unionists were unable to find a national party with such a commitment, and they tended to drift rudderless in the swirls of national politics. Some, like Toombs and Stephens, became Democrats. Others supported the Know-Nothing movement in the middle

21. Ulrich Bonnell Phillips, *Georgia and State Rights: A Study of the Political History of Georgia from the Revolution to the Civil War, with Particular Regard to Federal Relations* (Washington: Government Printing Office, 1902; reprinted by the Antioch Press, 1968), 132; Richard P. McCormick, *The Second American Party System: Party Formation in the Jacksonian Era* (Chapel Hill: University of North Carolina Press, 1966), 241–45; Arthur Charles Cole, *The Whig Party in the South* (Washington: American Historical Association, 1913), 39–43; Ulrich Bonnell Phillips, "The Southern Whigs, 1834–1854," in *Essays in American History, Dedicated to Frederick Jackson Turner* (New York: Henry Holt, 1910), 228.

22. Horace Montgomery, *Cracker Parties,* (Baton Rouge: Louisiana State University Press, 1950), 17–42; Phillips, *Georgia and States Rights,* 163–66; Richard Harrison Shryock, *Georgia and the Union in 1850* (Philadelphia, n.p., 1926).

fifties and the Constitutional Union and national Democratic tickets in 1860.[23] The Southern Rights party, on the other hand, affiliated with the national Democratic party in 1852 and participated in the "Calhounization" of the party of Jackson. Democrats increasingly argued that the protection of southern rights—a necessity few disputed—could only be achieved by such extreme measures as secession. Such arguments made many of the unionist Jacksonian elements of the party, centered in north Georgia, increasingly restive. They continued to believe that the preservation of the Union and the protection of southern rights were not incompatible. The enthusiasm of these voters was reserved for those Democratic candidates within the state who had the appropriate Jacksonian appeal. These voters were brought back into the Democratic fold in large measure by the antibank, Jacksonian stance of Joseph E. Brown in his successful campaign for the governorship in 1857 and by his subsequent actions in office. In fact, Brown's views were closer to Calhoun's than to Jackson's, as his actions in the secession crisis disclosed.[24] But the secession election returns revealed that his north Georgia supporters could tell the difference, for the bulk of them refused to share his enthusiasm for secession.

The history of a generation of Georgia politics had shown secessionists that democratic political practices did not lead to unity vis-á-vis the North. Instead, such practices disclosed the divisions within the state on the questions of what southern rights were and how they should be protected. The independence of the nonslaveholding Jacksonian elements of the Democratic party gave slaveholders ample reason to assume little about the ultimate loyalties of these elements and to fear the worst. The fears generated by the protracted political conflict, by Lincoln's election, and by the campaign for secession not only caused some men to question in public the value of self-government, as we have seen, but they also reenforced the long-

23. Paul Murray, *The Whig Party in Georgia, 1825–1853* (Chapel Hill: University of North Carolina, 1948), 201–202; Ulrich Bonnell Phillips, *Life of Robert Toombs* (New York: Macmillan, 1913), 55–71; W. Darrell Overdyke, *The Know-Nothing Party in the South* (Baton Rouge: Louisiana State University Press, 1950).

24. Montgomery, *Cracker Parties,* viii, 29–91, 126, 195–211, 234–35.

submerged private doubts of many conservatives that self-government was compatible with social and economic security and political stability.

Conservatives and the Secession Election

Conservatives who harbored nagging doubts about the wisdom of manhood suffrage were acutely sensitive to the fears generated by the internal crisis of the South. Their doubts led them to suspect both the voters and their leaders. They suspected that there was a large measure of expediency in the commitment of political leaders to democratic rhetoric and practices, as indeed there had been from the very beginning. They recognized the democratic bombast of Whig candidates as the necessary window dressing for conservatives in a democratic political culture. The secession crisis caused them to wonder, "Have not the people too much power and what is the exact line of demarcation between Republican and mobocratic institutions?" Conservatives diagnosed "the *great causes* of the trouble among us" as the "frequency of elections, and the universality of suffrage, with the attendant arousing of the people's passions, and the necessary sequence of demagogues being elevated to high station." Indeed, according to one editor, "very many wise, thinking men" said that "the whole Republican system [of government is] a failure" because, as "history proves," a constitution was no ultimate safeguard for minority rights since "no Constitution ever stood in the way of either real or apparent majorities."[25] Whether conservatives translated these political insights into support for secession or opposition to it depended largely on their immediate environment.

If we accept a vote for Bell or Douglas in 1860 as a roughly accurate identifying mark of conservatives, then it appears that conservatives

---

25. Lisle A. Rose, *Prologue to Democracy: The Federalists in the South, 1789–1800* (Lexington: University of Kentucky Press, 1968), xvi, 286; Norman K. Risjord, *The Old Republicans: Southern Conservatism in the Age of Jefferson* (New York: Columbia University Press, 1965); Phillips, "The Southern Whigs," 204–206; Chilton Williamson, *American Suffrage: From Property to Democracy, 1760–1860* (Princeton: Princeton University Press, 1960), 287; H. C. Massburgale to Alexander H. Stephens, December 2, 1860, in Stephens Papers, Library of Congress Collection, on microfilm, University of Georgia; Augusta *Chronicle and Sentinel*, December 8, 1860.

generally opposed secession in country Democratic counties and increasingly favored it in high slaveholding country Whig counties and in both Whig and Democratic town counties. Since voters were electing *county* delegates in 1861, it is not surprising that conservatives behaved differently in different counties. In consistently Democratic country counties, conservatives were most likely to have something approaching a siege mentality. They had opposed and lost to Democratic voters at the local level for a long time. In high slaveholding Democratic areas, these conservatives probably counted on their Democratic neighbors to vote for secession in 1861 as they had for Breckinridge in 1860. Consequently, these conservatives were likely to let their fears for the future outside the Union outweigh their fears for the future within the Union. That is, they voted according to their most salient fears, the fears created by their neighboring political opponents. In high slaveholding country Whig counties, on the other hand, conservatives were in the majority. Since it was quite uncertain and somewhat unlikely that secession would muster a majority in these counties, conservatives were more free to overcome the fears which held them in the Union and to succumb to the fears which impelled them from it.

In the countryside in general, conservative social ideas restrained Breckinridge opponents from embracing secession. But that restraint was eroded in a Whig political environment while it remained more or less firm in Democratic areas. When the low turnouts and the erosion of conservative opposition to secession in these high slaveholding areas are compared to the high turnouts and solid antisecession majorities in low slaveholding areas, it is clear that it was more difficult for conservatives to resolve their conflicting loyalties than it was for the poorer, more democratic cooperationists in low slaveholding areas. In the upcountry, few voters found it so difficult to make a choice between opposition to secession and their traditional political loyalties that they stayed away from the polls. In high slaveholding areas, on the other hand, many conservatives were apparently undecided enough to skip voting and allow others to make their decision for them. The secessionist votes of many of their fellow conservatives indicated that, in general, conservatives in high slaveholding areas were more inclined toward support for secession than opposition to it. To many conservatives in these social environments where it was difficult to forget the importance of slavery, it became clear that they could abandon the Union without abandoning their conservatism. Curiously, a high slaveholding environment which embodied conservative principles operated to undermine those very principles to the degree that conservatives dropped their opposition to disunion.

In all the country counties the pace of life was measured, time was marked by the growth of plants, and men knew their neighbors. In contrast to the stable countryside, towns were nodes of motion. Crops, credit, commerce, news, and people moved through towns managed by merchants, bankers, lawyers, and planters—"our great interests," a Savannah editor called them.[26] The functional importance and social prominence of such men tended to create a town elite, open to entry by properly mannered country planters, but closed to the bulk of townsmen. Many townsmen were on rising career trajectories, were eager to adopt the proper "natural" manners and attitudes of dirt-street-town aristocrats, and worked hard at it.[27] Thus the views of the town elite and those who aspired to it tended toward uniformity. Mechanics, for example, were looked upon as "sometimes a great annoyance," although they were acknowledged as "a necessary evil," for without them "cities, towns and villages could not be built up." Still, many townsmen apparently regarded them as socially undesirable. "Some people are inclined to turn up their noses at the appearance of a mechanic in their parlors," and, an editor continued, "we have

---

26. Savannah *Republican,* January 1, 1861. This contrast between town and country draws upon the concepts developed in Samuel P. Hays, "Political Parties and the Community-Society Continuum," in Walter Nisbet Chambers and Walter Dean Burnham (eds.), *The American Party System: Stages of Political Development* (New York: Oxford University Press, 1967), 152–81, and Darrett B. Rutman, "The Social Web: A Prospectus for the Study of the Early American Community," in William L. O'Neill (ed.), *Insights and Parallels: Problems and Issues of American Social History* (Minneapolis: Burgess, 1973), 57–89.

27. David Brion Davis has suggested (in *The Slave Power Conspiracy and the Paranoid Style* [Baton Rouge: Louisiana State University Press, 1969], 26–29, 49–51) that the rapid mobility of American society necessitated self-conscious role-playing as men assumed new social positions, and that this led these men to be susceptible to conspiratorial imagery, since they had come to believe that deception was a large part of reality. To follow the rapid rise of Charles Colcock Jones, Jr. from prosperous planter's son to mayor of secessionist Savannah, see Meyers (ed.), *Children of Pride,* 33–776.

known many a young lady who would turn the cold shoulder to an honest mechanic, because he has a hard hand." Mechanics not only lacked soft hands and social graces, but they also lacked complete dependence on town society. Although they depended on town society for jobs, they could always move on and seek jobs elsewhere, since their livelihood lay not in land but in their hands and tools. Thus their presence in town and their loyalty to town society were conditioned by a cash nexus and by fastidiously maintained social distance. Conservatives in towns had reason to wonder, then, whether the loyalties of these men to the "great interests" was as negotiable as their rate of hire.[28]

Secessionists realized the dangers that such slaveless whites posed to slavery in the Union under a Republican president, a realization that was sharpened in the recent presidential election when many Irish townsmen rebuffed their Democratic leaders and voted for the hated Douglas.[29] Conservative townsmen saw the dangers represented by such men as endemic in the political culture rather than unique to the secession crisis. It was not simply that the slaveless majority was a potential threat to slaveholders, but rather, conservatives believed, the stability of any society and the security of propertied minorities were always threatened if the less propertied majority were enfranchised.

Town conservatives were especially sensitive to the dangers of an enfranchised laboring population. Not only were there more free laborers in towns than in the country, but also the laborers were personally less well known to members of the town elite and more independent of them than were laborers in the country. Indeed, conservatives' fears in the secession crisis were refracted by locale until, for many, the operative fear was of their neighbors. Yet the country environment attenuated this fear while in towns it was intensified. In a town environment, it

---

28. Atlanta *Daily Intelligencer,* February 13, 1861. Edmund S. Morgan has argued (in "Slavery and Freedom: The American Paradox," *Journal of American History,* LIX (1972), 5–29) that similar fears were crucial to the development of slavery in the seventeenth century.
29. For evidence of Irish support of Douglas, see Savannah *Republican,* July 7, 28, September 24, 1860; Atlanta *Daily Intelligencer,* September 10, October 3, 23, 1860; A. R. Lawton to Howell Cobb, November 5, 1860, in Howell Cobb Papers, University of Georgia; E. A. Southland to Alexander H. Stephens, November 7, 1860, in Stephens Papers, Library of Congress Collection on microfilm, University of Georgia.

was more apparent to conservatives that their political ideas necessitated secession. It did not require much imagination for them to identify fellow townsmen who were potential recruits for a southern Republican party. Thus conservatives' support for secession in town counties seems to have been less in spite of their conservatism than because of it.

Almost as important as prosecession voters in creating the large secessionist majorities in town counties were the 20 to 30 percent of the electorate who failed to vote. The town environment facilitated the organization and exertion of social pressure to bring deviants into conformity. In Democratic counties, most of those who failed to vote apparently opposed secession while in Whig counties prosecessionists stayed away from the polls. In each case, the nonvoters were different from what was the predictable majority—in the case of Whig counties, the nonvoters may have been surprised to learn from the outcome of the election that their views were more orthodox than they had thought. Conformity fostered by the town environment restrained townsmen from expressing views which they feared might be considered wrong by people who mattered. These social pressures could be direct as well as subtle. For example, before Eugenius A. Nisbet announced that he would be a candidate for a seat in the state convention, a small group of secessionists met with him and he was "made to confess his *true* sentiments." Minute Men in the towns were not reluctant to use intimidation, especially in the name of eternal vigilance. But probably more common than outright threats was a more subtle form of intimidation: "those who favor moderation are branded as cowards or traitors." These brands were not only humiliating to receive but they were also dangerous to carry around, for the distance between opposition to secession and betrayal of the South was small and getting smaller. Several men went to the length of writing public letters denying rumors of their disloyalty.[30] In such an atmosphere, it is not surprising that

30. Mary Ann Cobb to Howell Cobb, December 10, 1860, in Howell Cobb Papers; A. J. Fisher to Herschel V. Johnson, November 14, 1860, in Johnson Papers, Duke University; A Farmer to Alexander H. Stephens, December 1, 1860, C. R. Hanleiter to Stephens, December 1, 1860, in Stephens Papers, Library of Congress Collection; James Atkins to Alexander H. Stephens, December 10, 1860, in Stephens Papers, Duke University; Poor Jim to editor, Macon *Telegraph,* November 15, 1860, Thomas C. Nisbet to editor, Macon *Telegraph,* November 24.

cooperationists claimed to differ with secessionists only about means, not ends.

Of course these social pressures in towns affected both conservative and not so conservative opponents of secession. It is likely that in town counties, just as in low slaveholding Democratic counties, there were Breckinridge voters who were opposed to secession. Yet the social environment of the town probably made it more risky and more difficult for such voters to express their sentiments at the ballot box. Similar pressures also may have kept such voters at home in high slaveholding country counties. In any case, it is clear that the town environment not only increased the number of conservative supporters of secession, but it also decreased the voting of many whose fears of expressing a minority position outweighed the personal consequences of silent acquiescence. "I did not have a chance to vote," Richard Malcolm Johnston wrote Alexander Stephens from Athens. "If I had," he added, "I should have voted for your policy and that most heartily; but if Georgia secedes must we not all regard Georgia as our country, and our only country, and all other countries as foreign nations? So it seems to me," he concluded, striking the note of acquiescence that was probably common to many nonvoters.[31]

Yet, instead of being acquiescent, many town conservatives were active proponents of secession. They were propelled not just by their conservative ideas but also by their social experience. The merchants, lawyers, and bankers among the town elite were men whose professional activities transcended the confines of their towns and counties and whose economic interests depended on the vitality and security of southern society. Of course, these men were anxious to protect the social and economic status quo. For nearly two generations the Union had been part of the status quo they defended. Above all, the Union had provided political stability as well as a degree of economic predictability. Lincoln's election threatened both.

The mood of fearful uncertainty that gripped Georgia during the

---

1860; Wm. Stewart to Public, Albany *Patriot,* December 6, 1860; Wm. Samford to editor, Rome *Weekly Courier,* January 11, 1861.

31. Johnston to Stephens, January 10, 1861, in Stephens Papers, Library of Congress Collection.

secession winter created a severe financial crisis. From Savannah, Augusta, Macon, and throughout the state came reports that the crisis had "utterly destroyed confidence in money matters, and the wealthiest of men cannot raise a dollar." "Business is literally at a stand still ... hundreds are being thrown out of employment, and the merchants are living, it may be said, from hand to mouth." Not only merchants, mechanics, and laborers but also bankers and "the planting interests" suffered from the financial paralysis. Since the banks would "do literally nothing," Savannah was "absolutely burdened with cotton, but there is no money to buy, and therefore it cannot move." Most Georgians would have agreed with one man's conclusion that "It is by far the worst times here that I have ever seen anywhere." [32]

The economic paralysis did not make it any easier for conservatives to decide whether to continue their support for the Union or to become secessionists. It was by no means clear that the southern economy would be healthier out of the Union than in it. But the financial crisis did press conservatives to make some decision, to do something to restabilize things, to bring things back to normal, to resecure the status quo. It appears that town conservatives chose to embrace secession less because of an anticipated financial gain than because secession presented an opportunity to achieve the political stability which the Union had formerly provided but which, under a Republican president, it threatened. Indeed, the actions of the state convention suggest that conservatives abandoned their commitment to the Union as it became clear that the social and economic status quo could be secured outside the Union in a way that was impossible within the Union—by changing the political status quo.

If the people are "incapable of self-government, why not then set about some other plan of government?" an Augusta editor asked. He outlined some of the alternatives that were being discussed:

> Some of the wisest and best citizens propose a hereditary Constitutional monarchy but however good that may be in itself, the most important point to discover is, whether or not the people are prepared for it. It is thought

32. [?] McIntosh to John M. Kell, November 26, unsigned letter, December 11, 1860, in John McIntosh Kell Papers, Duke University. See also Joseph J. Bradford to Col. David C. Barrow, November 12, 1860, in Barrow Papers, University of Georgia; H. J. Wayne to Mama H., December 3, 1860, March 10, 1861, in Edward Harden Papers; Solomon Cohen to Joseph E.

again by others that we shall be able to go on for a generation or two, in a new Confederacy, with additional safeguards—such for instance as an *Executive for life, a vastly restricted suffrage,* Senators elected *for life,* or for a long period, say *twenty-one years,* and the most popular branch of the assembly elected for *seven* years, the Judiciary absolutely independent and for life, or good behavior.[33]

Such alternatives began to appeal to slaveholding secessionists of narrower views and interests when, after the secession election, they had new and convincing reasons to question the value of democratic political practices as bulwarks of a slaveholding society. The outcome of the secession election pushed many Democratic secessionists toward conservative ideas about the dangers of democracy while conservative town voters were pulled toward secession by perceptions of the threats to the organic unity of southern society and by the emerging consensus among secessionist leaders that "when Georgia dissolves her connection with the other States, and with the Federal Government . . . it will become her wisely and soberly to consider whether the present mode of State Government will suit her people and the exigencies of the times."[34]

The electoral success of secession depended on town conservatives who, instead of being subservient to country planters, acted upon experiences, interests, and social values which transcended the plantation and embraced the plantation society from which townsmen and planters mutually benefited. The conservatism of the townsmen had sensitized them to the dangers in southern society and propelled them into the secessionist vanguard while many planters held back. The conservatives who converted to secession acted not simply to protect slavery but to protect the security and stability of the society they lived in and prospered from. These men and their ideas were increasingly important as secessionists prepared to make a "double revolution."[35]

Brown, November 12, C. G. Baylor to Brown, December 19, 1860, James A. Nisbet to Brown, January 25, 1861, in Telamon Cuyler Papers, University of Georgia; Wm. H. Prtichard to Alexander H. Stephens, November 20, 1860, in Stephens Papers, Library of Congress; John S. Dobbins to Wm. H. Dobbins, December 14, 1860, John S. Dobbins Papers, Emory University.

33. Augusta *Chronicle and Sentinel,* December 8, 12, 1860.

34. *Ibid.,* December 2, 1860.

35. Savannah *Morning News,* March 25, 1861. The ideas and role of conservatives in political crises are cogently discussed by Arno J. Mayer, *Dynamics of Counterrevolution in Europe, 1870–1956: An Analytical Framework* (New York: Harper and Row, 1971), 49–55.

PART THREE

The Double Revolution

The Double Revolution

The state convention had achieved a "double revolution" a Savannah editor observed late in March, 1861. The convention had not only taken the state from the Union and aligned it with the Confederacy, but it had also written a new state constitution "with all the amendments and improvements that experience has suggested."[1] The revolution in the external relations of the state had been matched by an internal constitutional revolution.

The editor's observation was accurate and his terminology apt. An opinion that was widely shared during the secession winter was that, "now that we are about to break up the present form of government, it is well that we look to the future, and commence now to make arrangements for some other form."[2] Shortly after the secession election one editor commented that since it was likely that the state convention would vote to secede, then "the delegates should begin at once the study of Constitutional law."[3] Opinions differed on the goals of such a study. Some thought that "a Republican form of Government—just such a one as our fathers of the Revolution gave us" was "good enough for us."[4] Others sought simply "a better government than has ever heretofore been instituted."[5] Some were determined "to uphold, with all the power in us, the majesty of Law, and the sacred rights of property," and for that purpose "a bad government is better than no government at all"; but "above all things," they sought "*a* government."[6] Still others thought that the "necessity for a modification of

---

1. Savannah *Morning News,* March 25, 1861.
2. Augusta *Chronicle and Sentinel,* December 8, 1860.
3. Augusta *Daily Constitutionalist,* January 3, 1861.
4. Atlanta *Daily Intelligencer,* January 28, 1861.
5. Rome *Weekly Courier,* February 7, 1861.
6. Milledgeville *Federal Union,* January 29, 1861.

105

our political institutions *has been* fully demonstrated," and that "call it by what name you please, some stronger and more efficient government must be adopted."[7]

Although these views differed sharply, taken together they demonstrated that the double revolution was no coincidence. The internal changes that accompanied secession were actively sought and widely discussed throughout the state. In fact, they consumed more of the time and attention of the state convention than did the act of secession itself. The character of the internal changes is corroborating evidence that conservatives and conservatism were as important as the secession election results have suggested. The actions and ideas of the state convention delegates and their constitutents revealed that secession was a revolution both for home rule and for those who ruled at home. Without the second half of the revolution, the first had little meaning, as some conservatives had long understood and as some enthusiastic secessionists were beginning to recognize. The same political dangers which necessitated home rule likewise necessitated the institutionalization and solidification of the authority of those who ruled at home, those who defended the status quo and, thereby, their manifold special interests in slavery and southern society.

Although secessionists revolted in the name of the Declaration of Independence and its assertion of the right of self-rule, they came to realize that the right of self-rule had to be limited if independence was to be safer than union. While secessionists claimed, in some ways rightly, to be the heirs of 1776, they were in other ways counter-revolutionaries. When they insisted that there was no ambiguity in the revolutionary ideals of liberty and equality and that those ideals were embodied in Southern society, they explicitly denied that the revolutionary ideals could be potent weapons for social change. On the other hand, by supporting secession, they implicitly contradicted that denial and affirmed their recognition that the ideals had been operating as corrosives, slowly eroding the political foundation of the existing order. By using the revolutionary legacy of self-government to retreat from a confrontation with the political consequences of that legacy, the

7. Augusta *Chronicle and Sentinel,* January 31, 1861.

secessionists tried to make certain that any ambiguity which did exist in the revolutionary ideals would be resolved in ways that did not threaten the social and economic status quo. One way to insure against an unsatisfactory resolution of the ambiguity was to change Georgia's basic governmental institutions, to carry through the second half of the double revolution. But to provide positive insurance that revolutionary ideals would be interpreted in a satisfactory fashion, secessionists had to make certain that the seats of power were filled by the right men, by Georgia's social and economic leaders, men whose interests and ideas were so closely tied to the status quo that a threat to it was a threat to them, and vice versa. Although the act of secession was primarily a move toward the achievement of political independence—the first half of the revolution—it was, in this latter sense, an example of what the results of the second half of the revolution should be—the best men doing what they thought was best for their society. Thus the first half of the double revolution began the second, while the second completed the first.

6

Secession: The First Revolution

Election Postmortem and Convention Prelude

In the two weeks before the state convention met on January 16, Georgians tried to piece together the results of the January 2 election. "The *people have* spoken . . . and their voice must be respected," an Atlanta editor wrote, confident that the secessionists would be "the dominant party" in the convention. Cooperation, he crowed, *"was voted down because it did not mean secession."* In general, secessionists claimed that there was not "even a shadow of a doubt . . . that the people of Georgia have deliberately and solemnly decided in favor of immediate and unconditional secession." Privately, secessionists rested their confidence less on the popular vote than on the convention delegates. "We have every reason to hope that the convention will be much better than the list [of delegates] as it now appears," one ardent secessionist wrote shortly after the election. His hope rested on his belief that "some of those who were elected as coo-men may turn out very good secessionists."[1]

While secessionists were confident, clouds of doubt hung over cooperationists. They distrusted the secessionists' addition of the popular vote. They were even more suspicious of the convention itself. Since convention delegates were apportioned on the basis of representation in the legislature, which was based on the federal ratio,

1. Atlanta *Daily Intelligencer,* January 11, 15, 1861; Milledgeville *Federal Union,* January 8, 15, 1861; James Mercer Green to Robert N. Gourdin, January 4, 5, 1861, in Robert Newman Gourdin Papers, Emory University.

slaveholding counties were favored at the expense of counties with many voters but few slaves, one cooperationist complained.[2] Others doubted that the delegates had been nominated in a truly representative fashion. According to one correspondent, "The delegates appear to be nominated by mass conventions assembled at the county sites; and it is plain that not half of the citizens attend these nominations. But few men living ten or fifteen miles from [the] county-site, go to such conventions . . . and as it is an admitted fact, that the secession sentiment is much stronger in and around the cities, than it is among the common people in the country, it is easy to see the advantage the "immediate secessionist[s]" will have in the Convention."[3]

Other cooperationists were troubled not only by townsmen's secessionism, but also by their social and political views. Late in November a co-operationist editor had urged that the convention be "composed principally of the Farmers, Manufacturers and Mechanics of the Country who in case of war, will pay the taxes and do the fighting," rather than of "the perfumed carpet knights who can '*caper nimbly in a Ladies* [sic] *chamber*' but whose white hands are unfit to be soiled by the blood and smoke of battle." "The people of the 'crossroads and groceries' should see to it," wrote another cooperationist, that those "who would like to be called Lord so and so," those who had a "hankering after nobility, and would like an aristocracy established in this land of freemen," would be "left in private life." Instead, "the destiny of Georgia" should be entrusted to the "honest, cool and reliable planter of the country [who] is our only hope in this crisis." These cooperationists' distrust of the social pretensions of townsmen was returned in kind by some secessionists. "Many . . . are opposed to waiting to hear from the grog-shops and cross-roads" because, one editor reported, "they believe [that] the people have not sufficient virtue and intelligence to do that which is best for *their own interests.*" Such observations reinforced the conclusion of many cooperationists that, as one wrote, "we do not believe that the charac-

2. Columbus *Daily Enquirer*, January 10, 1861. The thirty-seven largest counties received three convention delegates; all other counties received two.
3. L. F. to editor, *Upson Pilot*, December 22, 1860.

ter of the sentiments of a majority of the Convention, will represent the wishes of a majority of the people."[4]

Significantly, these cooperationist comments raised doubts about the democratic legitimacy of secession and played upon suspicions about the aristocratic hankering of some secessionists, particularly the "perfumed carpet knights" in towns. The implicit democratic values in these comments suggest that they probably expressed the views of the democratically inclined opponents of secession. Many conservative cooperationists, far from faulting secession for being antidemocratic, were coming to embrace secession in the hope that the comments of their former cooperationist colleagues might be correct, that secession might provide an opportunity to turn away from a full commitment to democratic values, or at least to control and limit the political expression of those values. Thus the plea, made by some cooperationists, that any action taken by the upcoming convention should be submitted directly to the voters for ratification failed to rally the vigorous support of all cooperationists.[5]

Secessionists vehemently opposed any referendum on secession. "The effect of such a course," they claimed, "would only be to produce *delay,* and enable Abe Lincoln to get into office and rivet the fetters which bind us as slaves for all coming time." Secessionists argued that the idea of a referendum on secession was merely the "last dying struggle of a defeated party."[6] In this way, secessionists tried to discredit the charges that a majority of Georgians did not support their plan and to point out the absolute necessity of immediate action.

Secessionists were also aware that many of their conservative opponents were beginning to desert their commitment to cooperation, following the lead of the many conservative union men who, as we have seen, had come to embrace secession by the time of the January 2 election. A cooperationist who spoke "in behalf of the capital and industrial interests of the state" was willing to embrace secession if it

4. Upson *Pilot,* November 24, 1860; Earl to editor, Augusta *Chronicle and Sentinel,* December 12, 20, 1860, January 8, 10, 1861; L. F. to editor, Upson *Pilot,* December 22, 1860. See also George A. Hall to Herschel V. Johnson, January 7, 1861, in Herschel V. Johnson Papers, Duke University.

5. Caution to editor, Augusta *Chronicle and Sentinel,* January 3, 8, 1861.

would be safe, if it could be "bloodless" and "done in a way that shall not destroy her [Georgia's] commerce and break down the fortunes of her people." But the stance of cooperationist delegates was even more important than that of their constituents. "Many [delegates] who were elected as Co-operationists, will doubtless in the Convention, go . . . for immediate secession," secessionists predicted.[7] By the time of the convention, cooperationist delegates were faced with the problem of cooperating with states which had already seceded unilaterally. Herschel V. Johnson asked Alexander Stephens if he thought it was "possible to obtain cooperative action, in the face of several separate state secessions." Although cooperationists' position was embarrassing, Johnson admitted, he had not changed his mind about opposing secession. "How," he asked Stephens, "can we escape the difficulties which have been heaped over and around?"[8] While Johnson held firm, other cooperationists concluded that since South Carolina, Mississippi, Florida and Alabama *"have* already seceded . . . in order to *act* with them, we must secede with them."[9]

Secessionists did not rely on the pressure of events alone to convince cooperationists of the error of their ways. They also did some politicking. One secessionist wrote Howell Cobb that the delegates from his county "if properly tutored will vote for secession;" he recommended they be "flattered and nursed." Another county was sending "two Baptist Preachers [,] submissionists . . . [who] can be (perhaps) made do right," he wrote, urging that they be "attended to." Cobb himself did not stand for election to the convention but he did go, he wrote his wife, "because my presence there might be of some service in persuading the delegates from this section of the State [north Georgia] on the true line."[10] As the day for the convention approached, the relative

6. Macon *Telegraph*, January 9, 1861; Atlanta *Daily Intelligencer*, January 11, 15, 19, 1861; Milledgeville *Federal Union*, January 15, 1861.

7. Savannah *Republican*, January 14, 19, 1861; Atlanta *Daily Intelligencer*, January 11, 1861. See also Augusta *Daily Constitutionalist*, January 5, 1861.

8. Johnson to Stephens, January 9, 1861, in Johnson Papers. This situation was accurately predicted by J. Henly Smith in his letter to Stephens, December 20, 1860, in Stephens Papers, Library of Congress Collection on microfilm, University of Georgia.

9. Rome *Weekly Courier*, January 17, 1861.

10. Andrew Young to Howell Cobb, January 4, 1861, Cobb to Mary Ann Cobb, December 26, 1860, in Howell Cobb Papers, University of Georgia.

disarray among cooperationists caused secessionists' confidence to soar.

The Secession Convention

At ten-thirty in the morning on Wednesday, January 16, 1861, the delegates to the state convention assembled in the statehouse. After the roll call and an opening prayer, George W. Crawford, a prominent politician and wealthy lawyer from Richmond County and a secessionist, was chosen president by acclamation. Other officers were selected, a committee was appointed to invite the commissioners of South Carolina and Alabama to take seats in the convention and address it, and "it was unanimously resolved, that one of the standing rules of this Convention shall be the suppression of all applause or other noisy demonstration during, or following the remarks of any delegate." [11] Then the convention adjourned until the following day.

The tone of the convention in that first day characterized the rest of its meetings. A convention of gentlemen was deciding the fate of Georgia, and even, in some measure, "the fate of the South, for weal or woe." Disagreements would be tempered by gentlemanly courtesy and respect. Divisive parliamentary maneuvers would be obviated by the mutual trust between gentlemen and by their desire for harmony. "Joining in the general opinion," President Crawford told the convention at the end of its last meeting in late March, "and referring to my own observation of other large deliberative bodies, I venture to say, that I have seen none, which surpasses this Convention in general decorum and all the amenities of social life." Coming from a former congressman and cabinet member, Crawford's observation was all the more impressive, and with good reason. [12]

Among the delegates were many of the state's prominent political leaders: Crawford himself, former United States senators Robert Toombs and Herschel V. Johnson, Alexander H. Stephens and six

11. *Journal of the Convention*, 3–9.

12. Atlanta *Daily Intelligencer*, January 16, 1861; *Journal of the Convention*, 302. Crawford was Zachary Taylor's secretary of war. This information and much of that which follows is from the invaluable, painstaking research of Ralph A. Wooster, as reported in "The Georgia Secession Convention," *Georgia Historical Quarterly*, XL (1956), 21–55.

other former United States congressmen, and a host of state leaders. Although three important politicians—Governor Brown, Howell Cobb, and Charles J. Jenkins—were not delegates, they were nevertheless seated by the convention, along with the judges of the supreme and superior courts.[13]

The political distinction of these leading delegates was matched by the social and economic distinction of the delegates as a group. The median wealth of the delegates was more than half again as large as that of the 1860 state legislature and more than twenty-four times as large as the per capita wealth in the county of median wealth. Not only were there more slaveholders in the convention than in the state legislature, but also the proportion of delegates who owned fewer than twenty slaves was a third less than in the legislature, while the proportion of delegates owning fifty or more slaves was twice that in the legislature. Further, half of the slaveholding delegates owned twenty or more slaves, which was more than three times the proportion of those owning twenty or more slaves among all slaveholders in the state. And while nearly two out of three Georgia voters owned no slaves at all, fewer than two out of ten convention delegates were slaveless.[14] In short, the convention was an unusually concentrated assemblage of men who were part of a wealthy slaveholding elite. Their display of "general decorum and all the amenities of social life" was perfectly in character.

Secession

After spending a day agreeing to the rules of the convention and listening to the speeches of James L. Orr and John G. Shorter, the commissioners from the newly independent states of South Carolina

13. *Ibid.*, 24; *Journal of the Convention*, 14.
14. The median wealth of the convention delegates was $24,000 versus $15,000 for state legislators in 1860. When the per capita white wealth is calculated for each of the state's counties, median county per capita white wealth is less than one thousand dollars. Seventy-two percent of the state legislators were slaveholders compared to 87 percent of the delegates. While 71 percent of the legislators held fewer than twenty slaves, 53 percent of the delegates did. At the other end of the scale, 9 percent of the legislators and 18 percent of the delegates owned fifty or more slaves. The data on state legislators are from Ralph A. Wooster, "Notes on the Georgia Legislature of 1860," *Georgia Historical Quarterly*, XLV (1961), 22–36, while those on the delegates are from Wooster, "The Georgia Secession Convention." 28–29.

and Alabama, the convention went straight to work. On Friday, January 18, the convention voted to go into secret secession "admitting no one but the members and officers of the Convention, and those gentlemen who have been invited to seats on the floor," an action which prevented a full recording of the convention debates and which newspapers promptly criticized.[15] After the statehouse doors were closed, Eugenius A. Nisbet, who, according to Alexander Stephens, was "regarded as the embodiment of conservatism," proposed "That in the opinion of this Convention, it is the right and duty of Georgia to secede from the present Union, and to co-operate with such of the other States as have or shall do the same, for the purpose of forming a Southern Confederacy upon the basis of the Constitution of the United States."[16]

Nisbet's resolution was immediately countered by a substitute cooperationist resolution offered by Herschel V. Johnson. Johnson's resolution in contrast to Nisbet's concise proposal for secession first and then cooperation, was an assortment of proposals which even other cooperationists found eminently arguable. Johnson proposed that "whilst the State of Georgia will not and cannot, compatibly with her safety, abide permanently in the Union, without new and ample security for future safety, still she is not disposed to sever her connection with it precipitately, nor without respectful consultation with her Southern confederates. She invokes the aid of their counsel and co-operation, to secure our rights in the Union, if possible, or to protect them out of the Union if necessary."[17] To that end, Johnson advocated: a meeting of the slaveholding states and "independent Republics" in Atlanta in mid-February; a series of "indispensable amendments to the Constitution of the United States" prohibiting Congress from the abolition or prohibition of slavery in the territories and tight-

15. *Journal of the Convention.* 9–14, 15; Augusta *Chronicle and Sentinel,* January 19, 1861; Milledgeville *Southern Federal Union,* January 29, 1861. *The Journal of the Convention* does not record the debates. However, the daily newspapers printed full reports of the debates in the public sessions of the convention.

16. Nisbet had been a congressman, a Georgia Supreme Court justice, and a Whig who had supported the Georgia platform in 1850, the American party in 1856, and Douglas in 1860. Alexander H. Stephens, *A Constitutional View of the Late War Between the States* (Atlanta: National Publishing Co., 1868), II, 313–14.

17. *Journal of the Convention,* 16.

ening the enforcement of the fugitive slave law; threats to separate from any states refusing to repeal personal liberty laws and to join in common cause with the seceded states if the federal government "should attempt to coerce" them; a resolution to continue the occupation of Fort Pulaski and other federal property pending Georgia's final decision; the appointment of commissioners to the other slaveholding states to inform them of Georgia's action and to urge them to attend the Atlanta meeting; a promise to cooperate with the other southern states in "the formation of a Southern Confederacy upon the basis of the present Constitution of the United States; and, finally, the adjournment of the convention until late in February when it could "take such action . . . as may be required by the proceedings of the Congress at Atlanta, and the development of intervening events."[18]

After the war, Johnson wrote that he had "included [in his resolution] every proposition which the most ultra of the delegates could contend for, hoping thereby to cut off such opposition as I knew extremists would make against every and anything short of actual secession." Johnson personally "was prepared to accept terms far more moderate" than the ones he offered. But, "in my propositions," he wrote, "I went as far as I could to stop short of actual secession, with the view of obtaining a majority of the Convention." Johnson had apparently been requested by the other leading cooperationists "to draw up something expressive of the[ir] views" and the others saw and "approved" his proposals before they were presented on the convention floor.[19] But the very logic of Johnson's resolution destined it for the fate of the wonderful one-hoss shay.

In the "elaborate discussion" that ensued, Alexander Stephens, who had shunned Johnson's request to lead the cooperationist delegates, announced that although his opposition to secession was "unshaken," he did "not now intend to go into any argument on the subject." "No good could be effected by it," he added, since it "was fully considered in the late canvass and I doubt not [that] every delegate's mind is made

18. *Ibid.*, 16–20.

19. [Herschel V. Johnson], "Historic Notes Touching the Purpose I had in Offering the Preamble and Ordinances in Favor of Cooperation in the Secession Convention, Jany. 18, 1861" (MS, n.d.) in Johnson Papers, Duke University.

up on the question.'' Johnson wrote later that Stephens' speech "amounted to a surrender of the contest . . . [and] was so interpreted by many who heard it."[20] What the secessionists said went unrecorded. Whatever was said in the debate probably did little to influence the delegates, as Stephens observed in his speech. The crucial test came when Nisbet's resolution was called.

In the Senate chamber, the impromptu, "funny convention" of the spectators and reporters who had been excluded by the convention was "unanimous for immediate secession." But the delegates in the convention hall were much more evenly divided on Nisbet's resolution. The vote was 166 to 130 in favor of immediate secession.[21] The shift of nineteen voters into the cooperationist column would have defeated Nisbet's proposal. But many delegates were shifting in the opposite direction, away from cooperation, not toward it. Such shifts were encouraged when a committee of seventeen—which included the leading cooperationists—was promptly appointed and asked to draft an ordinance of secession.

Although the cooperationists were defeated, they were not yet dead. Just before the convention adjourned for the day, cooperationist William Martin of Lumpkin County proposed "That the Governor be requested to furnish this Convention with a statement of the result of the election of delegates for this Convention, specifying the whole number of votes polled in each county, and the number received by each candidate."[22] The next day, Saturday, January 19, by a division nearly identical to the one on Nisbet's resolution, the convention approved a motion for "indefinite postponement" of Martin's resolution. Cooperationist strength was tested a third time when, after Nisbet introduced the secession ordinance, Benjamin Hill proposed Johnson's resolutions of the day before as a substitute, and they were defeated again, this time 164 to 133.[23]

20. Stephens, *A Constitutional View of the Late War Between the States*, II, 305; Herschel V. Johnson, "From the Autobiography of Herschel V. Johnson," *American Historical Review*, XXX (1925), 323.

21. Georgia to editor, January 18, 1861, Augusta *Daily Constitutionalist*, January 20, 1861; *Journal of the Convention*, 20–23.

22. *Ibid.*, 26–27.

23. The vote postponing Martin's resolution was 168 to 127. The majority included six who had opposed Nisbet's resolution and all but three who had favored it. *Journal of the Convention*, 27–31, 32–35.

While the convention was still in secret session, the ordinance "To dissolve the Union between the State of Georgia and other States united with her under a compact Government entitled 'the Constitution of the United States of America'" was taken up, an amendment to delay the operation of the ordinance until March 3—the day before Lincoln's inauguration—was avoided by moving the previous question, and the vote was taken. The convention adopted the secession ordinance by a vote of 208 to 89.[24] Georgia had seceded.

The Response to Secession

The report from the cannon on Capitol Square about two o'clock in the afternoon signaled the secession of Georgia. Booms echoed across the state as the news spread. "About sun-down this evening the news reached here," wrote a man from Campbellton, a village slightly less than twenty miles southwest of Atlanta on the Chattahoochee River. "In one hour, which brought night, the boys had two anvils on the public Square near the Courthouse and fired fifteen rounds in honor of the fifteen southern states . . . [and] in a few minutes time nearly every house in town was illuminated."[25] The volunteer company formed, marched to the homes of prominent citizens, and fired salutes. "While we were thus rejoicing, we could hear the guns on the west side of the river, at Bullard's and Holloman's, and other places, in answer to our fires (the river being up at the time, and almost impassable). Upon the whole," the correspondent concluded, "such rejoicing was never before seen in this village."

Similar celebration occurred in towns and villages throughout the state.[26] But jubilation was not universal, even among secessionists. Emotions that were vented in celebration by some were turned inward by others. "An indescribable sadness weighs down my soul as I think of our once glorious but now dissolving Union!" Mrs. Mary Jones, a

24. *Ibid.*, 31–39.
25. William E. Bates, "The Last Stand for Union in Georgia," *Georgia Review*, VI (1953), 464; letter to editor, Campbellton, Ga., January 19, 1861, Rome *Weekly Courier*, January 22, 1861.
26. See for example, Augusta *Chronicle and Sentinel*, January 20, 1861; Rome *Weekly Courier*, January 22, 1861; Columbus *Daily Enquirer*, January 21, 1861; T. Conn Bryan, "The Secession of Georgia," *Georgia Historical Quarterly*, XXXI (1947), 102; T. Conn Bryan, *Confederate Georgia* (Athens: University of Georgia Press, 1953), 11–12; Kenneth Coleman, *Confederate Athens* (Athens: University of Georgia Press, 1967), 31.

secessionist, wrote her son, the mayor of Savannah. "My heart aches," wrote a Savannah woman. The *"expediency* of secession, though *absolute,* calls in my mind, for any other emotion than *joy* . . . gladly," she added, "thankfully would I wake up, and find it all a dream, and Black Republicanism a horrible nightmare." To many cooperationists, secession seemed a nightmare. "I never felt so sad before," Herschel V. Johnson remembered after the war. Judge Garnett Andrews of the northern circuit of Georgia "shut himself up in his house, darkened the windows, and paced up and down the room in the greatest agitation," his daughter remembered, while outside "the people of the village were celebrating the event with bonfires and bell ringing and speech making." Doubt-racked contemplation in darkened rooms was probably common since, as one cooperationist editor observed, "many men . . . have not got the light-heartedness to rejoice at the consummation of an act involving such stupenduous consequences." "To say that we *rejoice,"* wrote another cooperationist, "would be simple hypocrisy—we can not, and do not, rejoice."[27]

Far from rejoicing, some Georgians were defiant. "What is to be done with those Georgians who unfurled the Stars and Stripes when the news reached them?" Mrs. Mary S. Mallard asked her mother. From north Georgia came reports of a meeting in Pickens County that resolved continued allegiance to the Union, of someone in Walker County shooting holes through the state flag during the night, and of a threat to seize the federal mint at Dahlonega and hold it for the federal government.[28] In sum, Georgians were no more united in greeting secession than they were in voting for it.[29]

27. Mrs. Mary Jones to Hon. Charles C. Jones, Jr., January 3, 1861, in Charles Colcock Jones, Jr. Papers, University of Georgia; Sophie H. Clinch to Robert N. Gourdin, Christmas, 1860, in Gourdin Papers; Johnson, "Autobiography," 327; Eliza Frances Andrews, quoted in Bryan, "The Secession of Georgia," 103–104; Rome *Weekly Courier,* January 22, 1861.

28. Mrs. Mary S. Mallard to Mrs. Mary Jones, January 25, 1861, in Robert Manson Meyers (ed.), *Children of Pride* (New Haven: Yale University Press, 1972), 646; Athens *Southern Banner,* January 30, 1861; George Kellog to Gov. Joseph E. Brown, January 12, 1861, in Telamon Cuyler Papers, University of Georgia.

29. My conclusion that Georgians were deeply divided in their responses to the news of secession is at odds with the view of Ralph A. Wooster who (in "The Secession of the Lower South: An Examination of Changing Interpretations," *Civil War History* VII (1961), 117–27) declares, "Insofar as public display of enthusiasm and zeal can be taken as a true measure of the feelings of a people, southerners in 1860–61 favored the ordinances of secession" (p. 126). In

In contrast to the varied responses to secession throughout the state, the responses of the convention delegates were more uniform. The deep division about the wisdom of secession that still existed among the delegates when they reconvened on Monday, January 22, was demonstrated by William Martin's unsuccessful motion to submit the ordinance of secession to the voters for ratification.[30] But a brilliant secessionist tactic exposed the substratum of uniformity among the delegates. Eugenius A. Nisbet introduced the resolution which defined the common ground on which the delegates took their stand:

Whereas, the lack of unanimity in the action of this Convention, in the passage of the Ordinance of Secession, indicates a difference of opinion amongst the members of the Convention, not so much as to the rights which Georgia claims, or the wrongs of which she complains, as to the remedy and its application before a resort to other means of redress:

And whereas, it is desirable to give expression to that intention which really exists among all the members of this Convention, to sustain the State in the course of action which she has pronounced to be proper for the occasion, therefore:

Resolved: That all members of this Convention, including those who voted against the said ordinance, as well as those who voted for it, will sign the same as a pledge of the unanimous determination of this Convention to sustain and defend the State, in this her chosen remedy, with all its responsibilities and consequences, without regard to individual approval or disapproval of its adoption.[31]

Nisbet's resolution, which was adopted by an unrecorded margin, redefined the question facing cooperationists. It transformed opposition to secession into opposition to the state, partisanship into near treason. At the same time, it tapped one of the deepest public loyalties Georgians felt, loyalty to their state. The tactical genius of immediate secession was that, unlike cooperation, it did not require Georgians to weigh their present loyalty to one federation against their potential loyalty to another. Instead, immediate secession required Georgians to decide only whether they were indeed Georgians. Secessionists counted on the fundamental emotional soundness of Supreme Court

---

Georgia, the zeal and enthusiasm of some persons was matched by the despair and defiance of others.

30. The vote was not recorded. *Journal of the Convention,* 46.

31. *Ibid.,* 45.

Justice Roger B. Taney's legal definition of national citizenship as an outgrowth of state citizenship. And, for all the convention delegates and many other Georgians, the secessionists were dead right. "From youth to old age all my attachments have been to Georgia's honor and her welfare," wrote "An Old Man." "In her has been my pride and my hope. For her have I lived, and for her would I be willing to die." [32]

Although there were "many good men who greatly deplore the seeming necessity for secession and who look upon the act as a *painful duty,*" nonetheless, it *was* a duty for loyal Georgians, many felt. "[B]elieving that my primary allegiance was to Georgia, I felt bound to obey her mandate," Herschel V. Johnson wrote later. Even the six cooperationist delegates who formally declared that they "most solemnly protest[ed] against the action of the majority in adopting an Ordinance for the immediate and separate secession of this State" signed the secession ordinance because, as they said in terms perfectly compatible with Nisbet's resolution, "as good citizens, we yield to the will of a majority of her people as expressed by their representatives, and we hereby pledge 'our lives, our fortunes, and our sacred honor,' to the defense of Georgia, if necessary, against hostile invasion from any source whatever." [33]

As all the delegates lined up to sign the ordinance of secession at noon on Monday, January 21, it became clear that the tactic of immediate secession had deftly eviscerated any organized resistance. Who would resist when "the evidence of the popular voice became so clear and overwhelming that all the minority delegates gave way ... before it"? [34] Where was the man who was disloyal to Georgia, his home? Asking these questions allowed secessionists to avoid the disturbing question of who was disloyal to slaveholders. Immediate secession had smoothly translated the defense of slavery into the defense of the state.

Outmaneuvered and outnumbered, the cooperationist delegates were also outclassed. When the vote on the secession ordinance was

32. An Old Man to editor, Columbus *Daily Enquirer,* January 2, 1861.

33. Rome *Weekly Courier,* January 22, 1861; Johnson, "Historic Notes," 5; *Journal of the Convention,* 51.

34. Macon *Telegraph,* February 2, 1861.

taken—when the issue was still support for secession rather than loyalty to the state—the social distance between cooperationists was exposed. More than eight out of ten of the cooperationists who broke ranks and voted for the secession ordinance represented high slaveholding cotton belt counties, nearly all of them Whig counties. In contrast, the counties whose delegates remained solidly in the cooperationist column were nearly all located in north Georgia and the pine barrens of southeast Georgia. Two-thirds of the counties represented by these hard-core cooperationists were Democratic, more than half of them were low slaveholding.[35] Although an important contingent of delegates from high slaveholding Whig counties remained in the cooperationist camp, the movement of many of their conservative political kinsmen into the secessionist column indicated the importance of conservatives to secession and of secession to conservatives.[36] For without the shift of these conservative cooperationist delegates into the secessionist ranks, the vote on the secession ordinance might have been much closer than 208 to 89, just as the popular vote for secession would have been reduced, as we have seen, if conservative voters in Whig counties and town counties had not made a corresponding shift toward secession. But the margin of victory these delegates provided on the secession ordinance was probably less important than the legitimacy their social and political status lent to the decision to secede. When cooperationist ranks broke along social and political lines on the secession ordinance, it showed that secession was selectively attractive to delegates from counties which were noted for their conservatism. It was a hint of the role conservatives and their ideas would play in the subsequent actions of the convention.

Although the divisions within the convention on the secession ordinance revealed the social and ideological disunity in Georgia, the cooperationist opponents of the ordinance were not irreconcilable.

---

35. Forty-one cooperationist delegates voted for the secession ordinance. Thirty-four (83%) represented high slaveholding counties. Of these, five delegates (12%) were from Democratic counties and twenty-nine (71%) were from Whig counties. The other seven cooperationists who voted for the ordinance represented low slaveholding Democratic counties (17%). Of the thirty-one counties all of whose delegates voted against the secession ordinance, twenty-one (68%) were Democratic, ten (32%) were Whig, seventeen (55%) were low slaveholding, and fourteen (45%) were high slaveholding.

After all, they, like the other delegates, were both Georgians and gentlemen. "When our common patroness spoke," President Craw-ford told them, "her sons, less from opinion than instinct, forgetful of the past and mindful of the future, rallied to the rescue." Alexander Stephens, who had voted against the secession ordinance, wrote later that the "great object" of the cooperationist delegates was "har-mony." Cooperationist Alexander Means recorded in his diary that he voted for the secession ordinance "to show no signs of serious internal feuds or distractions, which the coercionists at the North might seek to turn to their advantage."[37] "I came here opposed to secession," William Martin reminded the convention several days after the ordi-nance was signed. "My people were opposed to it," he continued. "But the people of Georgia, in convention assembled, have decided that I was wrong and my people were mistaken. We bow with filial obedience to the behest of that sovereignty which holds our undivided allegiance, and are ready to act upon the supposition that Georgia is right and all else is wrong." Alexander Stephens probably expressed the sentiments of many cooperationist delegates when he wrote a few weeks later that it was "a fixed irrevocable fact" that "we are now in the midst of revolution." "It is bootless to argue the causes that pro-duced it or whether it be a good or a bad thing in itself," he advised. Instead, the "wise man—the patriot and statesman in either

36. Ralph A. Wooster (in "The Georgia Secession Convention," 37) overlooks the character of the cooperationists who voted for the secession ordinance and emphasizes that delegates from Whig counties tended to favor cooperation. Yet, according to the definitions used here, which are different from Wooster's and therefore not directly comparable, thirty-seven of the fifty-six Whig counties (66%) voted solidly for the secession ordinance, ten Whig counties (18%) voted solidly for cooperation, and the vote was split in nine counties (16%). On the other hand, delegates from forty-two of the seventy-six Democratic counties (55%) were solidly for the secession ordinance, twenty-one counties (28%) were solidly for cooperation, and in thirteen counties (17%) the vote was split. Thus the proportion of Whig counties in favor of the secession ordinance was in fact larger than the proportion of Democratic counties. Ulrich Bonnell Phillips was right, then, when he wrote (in *Georgia and States Rights,* 206) that "delegates sent by Whig or Constitutional Union counties were inclined to vote for secession," although he was wrong when he contended that "those from counties which had given Breckinridge majorities tended to vote against im-mediate secession." For other discussions of voting in the convention, see Bryan, "The Seces-sion of Georgia," 101–102, and Bryan, *Confederate Georgia,* 10.

37. *Journal of the Convention,* 302–303; Stephens, *A Constitutional View of the Late War Between the States,* II, 321; Alexander Means, *Diary for 1861,* ed. Ross H. McLean, *Emory University Publications* (Atlanta: Emory University, 1941, Ser. VI, n. 1.), entry for January 19, 1861.

section—will take the fact as it exists, and do the best he can under the circumstances as he finds them for the good, the peace, welfare and happiness of his own country."[38]

Georgia was thus led out of the Union in the wake of the convention delegates—cooperationists and secessionists alike—rather than being swept out on a wave of popular approval. When all the delegates signed the secession ordinance, the first revolution had been achieved in fine style. Georgia had claimed its independence. All that remained was to secure it and to defend it. As the convention delegates turned to those tasks, they revealed the importance of conservative ideas. Just as the first revolution received vital electoral impetus from conservatives, the second revolution was nourished by conservatism. The prospects for the second revolution had provided part of the impetus for the first, while the electoral contribution of conservatives made the second revolution possible. The achievement of secession did not mean, then, that the convention delegates could go home. Their work was just beginning.

38. Report of convention debates, January 29, 1861, Savannah *Morning News,* February 2, 1861; Stephens to Samuel R. Glenn, February 8, 1861, in Stephens Papers, Library of Congress.

7

Toward
a Southern Utopia:
The Second Revolution

He had been away from home too long, Thomas R. R. Cobb wrote his wife Marion again and again during the early months of 1861. He left Athens in January to serve as a delegate from Clarke County to the Georgia convention in Milledgeville. During much of February he was in Montgomery, Alabama, representing Georgia in the Confederate convention. And for most of March he was in Savannah for the second session of the Georgia convention. When the state convention finally adjourned on March 23, Cobb went back home to Athens in time to celebrate his thirty-eighth birthday with his family. During the three months of "exciting anxiety," his hair had become "sprinkled" with gray. It must have been good to be home and to reflect on all that had been accomplished in the new year. On April 6, six days before the firing on Fort Sumter, Cobb told an audience in Athens that "a great Revolution [has been] accomplished, and not a Sabbath violated or a church-going bell silenced, nor the most timid woman alarmed—not a life sacrificed nor one drop of blood shed."[1]

Cobb himself was probably more responsible for the form the second revolution took in Georgia than any of the "other noble and patriotic Georgians" at the convention.[2] The intelligence he had demonstrated in his thoughtful *Inquiry into the Law of Negro Slavery in the*

1. T. R. R. Cobb, "The Correspondence of Thomas Reade Rootes Cobb 1860–1861," *Publications of the Southern History Association,* XI (1907), 147–85, 233–60, 312–28; T. R. R. Cobb to Marion Cobb, February 7, 1861, in Thomas Reade Rootes Cobb Papers, University of Georgia; T. R. R. Cobb, speech to citizens of Athens, April 6, 1861, Athens *Southern Banner,* April 10, 1861.

2. The quoted passage is from T. R. R. Cobb, speech to citizens of Athens, April 6, 1861, Athens *Southern Banner,* April 10, 1861.

United States, the industry he had exhibited in his *Digest of the Statute Laws of the State of Georgia,* and the knowledge he had gained in his researches, his law practice, and his eight-year tenure as reporter of the state supreme court were energetically applied to achieving and consolidating the secession of Georgia. Until November, 1860, Cobb had spent his time and talents on his profession, his family—which he began by marrying the eldest daughter of state supreme court justice Joseph H. Lumpkin—and his religion. But Lincoln's election necessitated secession, he told the Georgia legislature in his first political speech, and he campaigned vigorously to insure that he and other secessionists would be elected delegates to the state convention. When the standing committees of the convention were appointed, Cobb was chosen for the Committee on the Constitution of the State and the Constitutions and Laws of the United States.[3] Under his leadership, the Committee on the Constitution became the primary vehicle of the second revolution in Georgia. The work of the committee corroborated the "conviction" of one Georgian that Cobb was "as much of a Federalist today as John Adams or Alexander Hamilton . . . that in a struggle between power and liberty, Mr. Cobb may *always* be *looked for* on the side of *power.*"[4]

"[N]o credit was reflected on our State" by the state constitution, Cobb told his Athens audience in April. "Its construction was awkward; its taste horrible; its very grammar disgraceful. And upon this original very poor groundwork, successive legislatures, swayed by temporary popular prejudices, had inlaid a patchwork of amendments."[5] Mindful that "No government should be changed for light or transient causes; nor unless upon reasonable assurance that a better will

3. Cobb was an elder in the Athens Presbyterian church, superintendent of the Sunday school, and active in the temperance society. He also served on the committee of seventeen which drafted the ordinance of secession. In Montgomery, he was instrumental in the drafting of the Confederate Constitution. See the biographical sketches in T. R. R. Cobb, "Correspondence," 148–52 and in *Dictionary of American Biography,* II, 246–47; Charles Robert Lee, Jr., *The Confederate Constitutions* (Chapel Hill: University of North Carolina Press, 1963), 87–88, 113–16, 120, 121, 148; *Journal of the Convention,* 49.

4. Willis Strickland to Alexander H. Stephens, February 4, 1861, in Stephens Papers, Library of Congress Collection on microfilm, University of Georgia.

5. Cobb, speech to citizens of Athens, April 6, 1861, Athens *Southern Banner,* April 10, 1861.

be established," Cobb's committee completely rewrote the state constitution and, thereby, created the institutional form of the second revolution.[6] The committee designed a government which they and most of the other delegates hoped would preserve the social order and, in that way, make the act of secession worthwhile. The committee's success was attested to by a courtesy of the convention which no other committee received, a formal resolution of thanks for the "untiring zeal and signal ability displayed, in their Reports to this Convention, and especially in their Report on the Revision of the Constitution of the State."[7]

As Cobb surveyed what had been done from his April vantage point, he was pleased. "When did you ever see so harmonious, so united a people," he asked his Athens townsmen. "Whence comes this harmony? To what can it be referred but to the common satisfaction of our entire people?" Europe, Cobb continued, revealing his own vision of the emergent southern utopia, was beginning to see the South as "a people with the most liberal political institutions, the most patriarchal and perfect social polity and the most pure unadulterated simple Christian Faith, that the world now contains."[8] A southern utopia was almost at hand.

What Cobb said, in other words, was that the internal crisis of the South had been resolved. Within two months after the passage of the secession ordinance, the state convention agreed upon a plan which promised to reconcile slaveholding and democratic traditions. The plan was the tangible foundation for the ideal, truly southern society which Cobb and many other Georgians believed was within their grasp. But when the state convention reconvened on Monday, January 21, for their first meeting since the passage of the secession ordinance, it was not at all clear what the plan would be. Many secessionists clearly understood that the protection from external threats that secession had

6. The quoted passage is from the Declaration of Fundamental Principles that Cobb's committee drafted and affixed to the new state constitution. Art. 1, paragraph 2, *Journal of the Convention,* 285.
7. The resolution was proposed and passed just before final adjournment on the evening of Saturday, March 23, 1861.
8. Cobb, speech to citizens of Athens, April 6, 1861, Athens *Southern Banner,* April 10, 1861.

provided needed to be matched by additional protection from political threats within the state. Yet it was also clear that any steps to protect against internal threats had to observe a healthy respect for established democratic ideals and practices, unless, that is, secessionists were willing to make the foolish move of increasing the danger from within by blatantly ignoring and alienating the many Georgians who revered those democratic traditions.

The convention had to find a way to resolve the internal crisis of the South. To leave the task to any other group, especially the state legislature, was to court danger rather than to reduce it. "I hesitate not to say," T. R. R. Cobb observed in April, that the state convention "combined more talent and patriotism than has ever assembled in your state before or will again soon assemble." With such safe hands on the levers of sovereignty, the convention was not about to let go. If the right adjustments were made, many believed, independence could bring perfection. Above all, the adjustments had to be conservative, to go as far as necessary but no farther, to recognize the short but dangerous distance that separated the southern society that was from the perfect one that might be. "[O]ur ideal," an Augusta editor wrote, speaking for many other Georgians, "is a PRO-SLAVERY REPUBLIC." [9] The question facing the convention delegates was how to realize that ideal.

A Republic of Slaveholders

"Ours is a pro-slavery form of Government, and the pro-slavery element should be increased," an Atlanta editor recommended. "For our part," he continued, "we would like to see every white man at the South the owner of a family of negroes." Democracy and slaveholding should be reconciled, the editor proposed, by making all voters slaveholders. Then a threat to slaveholding would be a threat to all. All voters would be "linked together by the chain of interest, which, after all that may be said," Governor Brown noted, "is the great motive power in government." One convention delegate—a secessionist like Brown and the Atlanta editor—wanted *every* Southerner bound by an

9. *Ibid.;* Augusta *Daily Constitutionalist,* January 17, 1861.

interest in slaveholding. "[E]very man, woman and child in the Southern States should own a slave," he told the convention.[10]

Some secessionists, then, wanted to resolve the internal crisis of the South by radically changing Southern society. More like the abolitionists than they would have cared to admit, they wanted to derive their society from their principles, rather than their principles from their society, as they claimed. Their support of secession showed that they believed there was a gap between their principles and their society. When they proposed to close that gap by democratizing slaveholding, by changing their society rather than their ideas, they revealed a romantic radicalism in the guise of a sober, conservative organicism. By recommending that "the pro-slavery element should be increased," they implied that they believed that many of those who did not own slaves were not proslavery. The second revolution which these secessionists proposed, then, was an attempt to create the community of interest that their ideology had posited as a given, but which, in fact, did not exist, as they knew. They wanted to transmute ideology into sociology. But, like earlier alchemists, they were unsuccessful.

THE SLAVE TRADE AND THE SOCIAL ORDER

One reason the convention delegates did not devise a plan to make slaveholders of all Georgians was that the most practical step in that direction—opening the African slave trade—was strongly opposed. "[I]t would be better to open the African slave trade, until a negro would be imported and given to every nigerless [*sic*] voter," one slaveholder wrote, "than [that] this all important interest [of slavery] should be at the mercy of a majority that might think itself having no interest in the institution." But when a convention delegate announced that the "best plan" for expanding slave ownership was "to open the African slave trade" there was an unseemly "slight sensation in the Galleries."[11] And on January 23, the convention unanimously re-

---

10. Atlanta *Daily Intelligencer*, June 23, 1861; Brown to David Walker, April 19, 1861, Milledgeville *Southern Federal Union*, April 30, 1861. The delegate was E. W. Chastain of Fannin County. Report of convention debates, January 22, 1861, Macon *Telegraph*, January 24, 1861.

11. Georgia to editor, Augusta *Chronicle and Sentinel*, February 9, 1861; E. W. Chastain of Fannin County in Report of convention debates, January 22, 1861, Macon *Telegraph*, January 24, 1861.

solved to continue to uphold the laws of the United States prohibiting the African slave trade.[12] The convention also resolved, by an unrecorded margin, to maintain all laws allowing and regulating the interstate slave trade that had been in effect before the secession ordinance was passed.[13]

There were many reasons why the interstate slave trade was acceptable to the delegates while the African trade was not. Opening the African trade might turn potential foreign friends, like England, into actual enemies; it would upset the racial balance of the state by bringing in large numbers of black persons; it would bring more rebellious foreign slaves into the more docile "southernized" slave force; and the conditions of the African trade might offend the moral principles of some Georgians.[14] But perhaps the overriding reason for the convention's opposition to the African trade was that it threatened to destroy the established hierarchy of slaveholding by bringing in low-priced foreign slaves. The African trade threatened to do for slaves what Henry Ford was to do for automobiles: make them available to nearly

12. Except for a few minor amendments, the convention resolved to uphold all laws of the United States regarding the African slave trade; *Journal of the Convention,* 59–60. For the prohibition of the foreign slave trade in the new state constitution, see Art. II, Sec. 7, paragraph 1, *ibid,* 293. For the provision in the Confederate Constitution, see Art. I, Sec. 9, paragraph 1, *ibid.,* 168.

13. *Journal of the Convention,* 59–63. The new state constitution allowed the legislature to "prohibit the introduction of negroes from any state" but not "to prevent immigrants from bringing their slaves with them." This provision was probably intended to conform to the provision in the Confederate Constitution (which the state convention had ratified before writing the state constitution) which prohibited the importation of slaves from any state not in the Confederacy. Most historians interpret this as an economic stick which the lower South waved threateningly at the upper South to encourage them to join the Confederacy. For our purposes, it is important that the convention was willing to allow the legislature some leeway with the interstate slave trade, but not with the African trade. For the provision in the new Georgia Constitution, see Art. II, Sec. 7, paragraph 2, *ibid.,* 293. For the provision in the Confederate Constitution, see Art. I, Sec. 9, paragraph 1, *ibid.,* 168.

14. For a good discussion of the African slave trade controversy, see Ronald T. Takaki, *A Pro-Slavery Crusade: The Agitation to Reopen the African Slave Trade* (New York: Free Press, 1971), Takaki emphasizes the controlling influence of morality in the opposition to the trade. Although moral scruples undoubtedly influenced some Georgians, it should be noted that they were part of a moral code which did not threaten the existing social order, but which conformed to it and justified it. Moral opposition to the slave trade threatened slavery only if the morality of slavery could not be distinguished from the morality of the slave trade. Even for such a religious man as T. R. R. Cobb, the distinction was easily made. Although the African trade raised moral qualms for Cobb, domestic slavery was entirely another matter. It was a "mild" bondage in which slaves advanced mentally, physically, and above all, morally. Far from being a moral curse, slavery was a moral blessing. See T. R. R. Cobb, *An Inquiry into the Law of Negro Slavery in the United States of America* (Philadelphia: T. & J. W. Johnson, 1858), clii-ccxxviii.

everyone. The delegates eschewed that sensational prospect. They opposed allowing "the men of Georgia [to] buy their slaves as cheap as Africa can afford them."[15] They favored the continuation of the interstate trade apparently because it would continue to funnel relatively expensive domestic slaves into the existing social mold. At least, they favored the kind of slave trade which would preserve the social order as they knew it.

Most of the delegates acted as if they believed that a southern utopia should preserve and protect the established social hierarchy rather than radically alter it. Plans for democratizing slaveholding were doomed, then, by the conservatism of most of the delegates. For them, the important persons were those who already owned slaves. The convention protected these present owners' rights by actions, both direct and indirect, which were thoroughly conservative. Just as the convention refused to change the society drastically by increasing the number of slaveholders, so it refused to protect slavery as obtrusively as some desired.

THE NECESSITY OF CONSERVATIVE ACTION

One slaveholder put the issue all too clearly. "In forming a new government," he wrote, "the first and most important thing to be secured is the protection of slavery. It is of more importance than the form of government itself." The "security [of slavery] requires defence against domestic and foreign foes—yes domestic foes," he continued, "for in the formation of the Constitution of the U.S., there was less danger from domestic foes than [there] will be in the Southern Confederacy, supposing it formed of all, or nearly all, the slave states." He predicted that "all this ultra pro-slavery feeling will, in a few years, give way to the excitement of some other interest" and that meanwhile the "disproportion between slave- and non-slave-holders under the present order of things, will continue till soon it will be as twenty to one and over." He suggested that the "all important and minority interest [might] be protected" from domestic foes in two ways: "The first," he

15. S. M. Carrolton to Gov. Joseph E. Brown, March 12, 1861, in Telamon Cuyler Papers, University of Georgia.

wrote, "is that one slave of a debtor shall be exempt from levy and sale for debts, and that no one be entitled to vote who shall not be the owner of slaves." Such a plan guaranteed the vote to all present slaveholders and left the door to slaveholding, and therefore to voting, slightly ajar for the "industrious and prudent." The second "or perhaps most practicable plan, would be to have one body of the legislative department of the Government to represent the slave interest," he suggested. Such action would merely be adapting "that conservative idea of a dual executive of Mr. Calhoun's [*sic*]" to the legislative branch, he believed. If this were not feasible, he thought it "would be better to have even another department [of government], based purely on slave representation, than [that] it should go unprotected."[16]

Such direct proposals and candid reasoning were shunned by the convention delegates. They acted as if they believed that the best way to protect existing slaveholders was to take cautious, unobtrusive steps which would neither depart drastically from tradition nor be likely to stimulate prolonged, active opposition. Even the only direct step the convention took to limit the political threat to slaveholding was a quiet one. When the delegates adopted the new state constitution, they struck out a clause from the old constitution which had allowed the legislature to emancipate slaves with the prior consent of each affected owner.[17] The new constitution read, "The General Assembly shall have no power to pass laws for the emancipation of slaves." An amendment to add "except by the unanimous consent of the General Assembly" failed to pass.[18] The change was small, but appropriately absolute and appropriately conservative.

The other changes that the convention made were less explicitly related to their actual purpose: reducing the internal threats to slaveholders and the social order. Most of the convention delegates

16. Georgia to editor, Augusta *Chronicle and Sentinel,* February 9, 1861. He proposed to deal with foreign enemies by making the government "emphatically a military government, as strong as our means can make it."

17. Unfortunately, this took place while the convention was in secret session on March 22, and therefore the debate went unrecorded. *Journal of the Convention,* 259. See Art. IV, Sec. 11 in the Constitution of 1798 in Francis Newton Thorpe (ed.), *The Federal and State Constitutions,* (7 vols.; Washington: Government Printing Office, 1909), II, 801.

18. Art. II, Sec. 7, paragraph 3, *Journal of the Convention,* 259, 293.

realized that any actions which would boldly and overtly protect the rights of slaveholders at the expense of democratic traditions would be likely to excite opposition. The convention proceeded with calm, indirect, conservative actions because the delegates recognized the internal threats to southern society and sought to protect against them without exacerbating them. Few doubted that dangers existed. There was too much evidence to the contrary.

Although "we should have but one mind now," an Athens editor wrote in mid-March, "[w]e are forced to believe that there are yet some traitors and tories among us." Noting that he had "seen no resignation of any of the Judges [,] Marshalls[,] or Collectors in Georgia," one man was "rather inclined to the opinion that the hangman will have to perform his duties in Georgia before we have a united people." From Hall County in north Georgia a secessionist wrote Howell Cobb that there "seems to be still some among us disposed to act with The Black Republican party. It is uncertain which has the power in our county," he observed, using an ironic anachronism, "the Black Republicans or the true American people." Who held the power in Hall County was demonstrated when the Confederate flag was hoisted over the Gainesville Light Infantry during court week in late March. But when the flag raising stimulated a public demonstration of "considerable feeling" of dissatisfaction, it showed that the symbols of those in power provoked public opposition rather than automatic respect.[19]

If the actions of some of the people of Hall County were unsettling to secessionists, the ideas of an Atlantan, J. A. Stewart, were worse; "incendiary and treasonable" an Atlanta editor called them. Stewart wrote to the editor of the Nashville *Democrat* in early March that, "If let alone, I think the Union men, at the *ballot box,* will effectually put down the revolution." Union men should unite, he wrote, "in opposition to Disunionists—North and South—to abolition fanatics North, and aristocracy, monarchy, and despotism South." A "more danger-

---

19. Athens *Southern Banner*, March 13, April 3, 1861; John B. Cobb to Howell Cobb, January 28, 1861, in Howell Cobb Papers; A. M. Evans to Howell Cobb, March 20, 1861, in Ulrich Bonnell Phillips (ed.), *The Correspondence of Robert Toombs, Alexander H. Stephens, and Howell Cobb* (Washington: Government Printing Office, 1913), 551.

ous man never lived in a slaveholding community," the Atlanta editor observed, perhaps fearing Stewart's confidence as much as his ideas. If Stewart was "fit" to live in Georgia, the editor concluded, "then we must prepare for a revolution in our very midst."[20]

Another Georgian reportedly had even more dangerous ideas which he shared not with unionists in Tennessee, but with black Georgians. Osborne Burson, who lived outside Atlanta in Fulton County, was overheard by "responsible men" saying "that the negroes were as free as he was and that he would have voted for Lincoln had he a chance to do so, and if he had a chance he would assist in freeing them." Observations made in the summer and fall of 1860 that "there certainly are mean white men endeavoring to render them [the slaves] discontented with their lot and prepare them for insurrection" still seemed to be alarmingly true. To prevent slave rebellions "all we have to provide against are the machinations of white enemies," one editor wrote just after Lincoln's election.[21] His advice still made sense to many Georgians, including some convention delegates.

Five days after the passage of the secession ordinance, J. L. Singleton, a secessionist delegate from Screven County on the South Carolina border, confronted the danger squarely and offered the convention a plan to prepare for it:

> *Whereas,* war may be one of the consequences of secession, and whereas, the recent outrage upon the state of Virginia, admonishes us that in the event of such war, attempts will be made to incite our slaves to insurrection, and whereas, the vicious and unprincipled, during the absence of many of the true men from their respective counties in the defence of the State, may be disposed to seize upon such opportunity, to commit wrongs and outrages upon the then defenceless wives and children of the absent, as well as upon the other good people of the State,

Singleton proposed that the governor accept the service of between fifteen and fifty men in each county and commission them as a

---

20. Atlanta *Daily Intelligencer,* March 9, 1861; J. A. Stewart to editor, Nashville *Democrat,* March 2, 1861, reprinted *ibid.,* March 9, 1861. The editor recommended that Stewart leave town.

21. Although the men "let Burson go free, attributing his language to ignorance," the *Daily Intelligencer* (March 14, 1861) recommended that the matter be "investigated immediately, and if this account of the language of Burson be true he should be dealt with in a summary manner." Rome *Weekly Courier,* August 28, 1860; Macon *Telegraph,* November 9, 1860.

"Mounted Military Police" for their respective counties. Singleton made certain that the "vicious and unprincipled" John Browns in each county would have no influence over the mounted police by recommending that the police "constitute a distinct and independent arm of the military of the State, not subject to the orders of any officers of any army having authority in the State, nor of any officer of militia, thereof," who, after all, had been elected by the men under his command. Although Singleton's version of a prewar slaveholders' Klan for regulating whites failed to gain the approval of the Committee on Military Affairs and subsequently of the convention, the resolution demonstrated that the delegates were aware of the internal dangers and that at least one of them was prepared to meet them head-on.[22]

Most of the convention delegates found Singleton's plan too bold. They preferred publicly to deny admitted dangers and quietly to take steps to prevent them. A resolution probably more to the convention's taste provided for independence from northern textbooks and "their absurd theories and dogmas upon the subject of African equality and the sinfulness of African slavery" by having the governor and the Senate appoint commissioners to write "a complete series of textbooks" which, upon the approval of the governor and two-thirds of the Senate, would be required in all schools.[23] Although this resolution died in committee, it was probably more palatable to the convention than Singleton's plan since it only implied that there was trouble at home.

The convention tried to avoid even implying the existence of internal threats. But the very caution with which the delegates acted demonstrated that they believed that genuine dangers existed and that only conservative actions might avoid them. Like the secessionists during the secession campaign, the convention delegates chose to take actions which, if their public rhetoric was taken at face value, were unneces-

---

22. *Journal of the Convention,* 64–66; 99. Mrs. Augusta J. Evans, a Georgian living in Alabama wrote a friend that she "would infinitely prefer to perish" at Fort Morgan where her father and two brothers were stationed, "rather than endure the horrors which hundreds of John Browns would inevitably stir up in our midst; seltered [*sic*] by the protecting mantle of Lincoln's Administration." Evans to L. Virginia French, January 13, 1861, *Alabama Historical Quarterly,* III (1941), 65–67.

23. *Journal of the Convention,* 135–36, 142–43.

sary. But, as the conservative actions of the convention demonstrated, their words were merely another way of showing respect for the internal political threats they sought to avoid.

A Republic of White Men

"We will have a Republic of white men," purred an editor in Macon, happy to be free of the North. The racial theory for such a southern republic was spelled out in detail when Alexander H. Stephens, the new vice-president of the Confederacy, addressed an audience in Savannah in late March, 1861. "Our new Government['s] . . . foundations are laid, its cornerstone rests, upon the great truth, that the negro is not equal to the white man; that slavery—subordination to the superior race—is his natural and normal condition," Stephens announced to resounding applause. "This, our new Government, is the first, in the history of the world," he notified the audience and posterity, "based upon this great physical, philosophical, and moral truth."[24]

By asserting that the "primary law of our social organization is DISTINCTION OF RACE," Stephens and other Georgians tried to resolve the internal crisis of the South by offering whites a democracy of racial status.[25] By reminding nonslaveholders of the racial benefits of slavery, they hoped to preserve slavery's social and economic benefits for slaveholders. Emphasis on what was commonly accepted as an obvious truth—the yawning racial chasm that separated whites from blacks—allowed Stephens and many convention delegates to ignore, and thereby to protect, the social hierarchy among whites that they treasured. A shared white racial status was a perfectly conservative concession to democratic traditions. For if the necessary obeisance could be paid to democratic traditions by giving white men equal shares of racial status rather than political power, then the southern social order could be protected without explicitly sacrificing traditional ideals. The internal crisis of the South could be resolved by the rhetorical democracy of racial status and by the more substantial institutional

---

24. Macon *Telegraph,* February 15, 1861; Stephens, speech to citizens of Savannah, March 21, 1861, Augusta *Daily Constitutionalist,* March 30, 1861.
25. Atlanta *Daily Intelligencer,* June 23, 1861.

changes which were designed to protect slaveholders in case the racial cornerstone was not truly laid.

RACE AND AMBIGUOUS IDEALS

Squaring white racial superiority with traditional ideals was not easy. Since the Declaration of Independence had not said that only white men were created equal, conservative apologists for the second revolution in Georgia needed to show that, nevertheless, that was what it meant. The great "truth" of white superiority "has been slow in the process of its development . . . even amongst us," Alexander Stephens acknowledged in his "cornerstone" address. "Many who hear me," he said, "perhaps can recollect well, that this truth was not generally admitted, even within their day. The errors of the past generation still clung to many as late as twenty years ago."[26] Many Southerners had foolishly believed, Stephens, implied, that the revolutionaries of 1776 had meant what they said and that their opinions were right. But the revolutionary pronouncement that *"all* men were created *free* and equal," T. R. R. Cobb wrote, was "the natural result of the excited state of the public mind." The Founding Fathers had meant what they said, but were wrong.[27]

Were they, then, all wrong? Were there mudsill whites too? Unless such questions were forestalled, they might become the ideological center around which might crystallize the political opposition that Stephens, Cobb, and other Georgians feared. The ideals of the Declaration of Independence could not be scrapped altogether. Instead, they had to be reinterpreted. Confederate racial theorists had to find ambiguity in the Declaration of Independence—to show that when it spoke of the inalienable rights of men, it grasped a partial truth, but failed to make the essential racial distinction. Having located the ambiguity, theorists then had to expunge it from their own position—to explain that, appearances to the contrary notwithstanding, *all* whites were "of a superior race and a higher civilization."[28]

26. Stephens, speech to citizens of Savannah, March 21, 1861, Augusta *Daily Constitutionalist*, March 30, 1861.
27. Cobb, *An Inquiry into the Law of Negro Slavery*, clxix–clxx, clxxii–clxxiii.
28. Atlanta *Daily Intelligencer*, June 23, 1861.

By expurgating traditional ideals, Stephens and other Georgians revealed their reluctance to depart from traditional forms at the same time that they disclosed their readiness to abandon traditional principles. They showed that they intended to conserve the social and political status quo rather than traditional ideals. They sought once and for all to molt their old ideological skin and to grow a new one which conformed perfectly to the environment. Their environment determined their principles. The only principle that was not mutable was a commitment to the survival of the existing society. Perhaps they spoke so often of the principles on which they acted to reassure themselves and others that the obvious was not true. In any case, they had to be careful to prevent the clarity with which they insisted on the inequality of blacks from slipping into a politically dangerous ambiguity about the equality of whites. The error was made by the Columbus editor who wrote that "the great principle[s] which we think the founders of the new republic ought to have kept steadily in view [are] the vindication and strengthening of African slavery on this continent, and the recognition of the master's or white citizen's 'divine right' to rule in our whole economy."[29] Did only the minority of white citizens who were masters possess the divine right to rule the whole economy? Did the right extend, as it seemed, to ruling white citizens who were not masters? Apologists for the social order had to be very careful with their ambiguities.

UTOPIAN ASSERTIONS

The safest way for Georgia's leaders to avoid embarrassing misstatements was to assert that what should be was. "Now our people are perfectly homogeneous. Their interests are identical," T. R. R. Cobb told his fellow Athenians in April. Such uniformity meant that "all classes of society are harmonized with each other and linked together by the chain of interest," Governor Brown wrote. The "desire [for] unanimity of sentiment and action among our people" that an Atlanta editor felt seemed eminently realizable to some Georgians and already achieved by others. Since there was no clash of interests to energize

29. Columbus *Daily Enquirer*, March 15, 1861.

political contests, political parties were withering away, many claimed. "We have now no political parties in the South," it was commonly observed; "we are united as a band of brothers—former political asperities are forgiven and forgotten—and a glorious career of unity, harmony, prosperity, and renown awaits us." [30]

Political liberty would not shrivel in the absence of political parties because, as one Georgian wrote, "We have amongst us an agent... that is the great bulwark of popular liberty—I mean African slavery." Indeed, "African slavery and political liberty are inseparable," Governor Brown asserted. The North, he predicted, "cannot maintain republican institutions," while the South "can, and will maintain and perpetuate the institutions of our fathers to the latest generation." "The great political point," Brown explained, "is, that in the South, there is no alarming conflict between Capital and Labor ... each is vitally interested in maintaining and upholding the other." [31]

Secession had proved the truth of these theories, many believed. To the crowd that had assembled outside his home with a band and welcomed him back from the first session of the Georgia convention with three cheers, T. R. R. Cobb said that secession was "the crowning evidence of the capacity of this people for self-government." "Here was a great people," he said, "deliberately voting a revolution— overturning a government which the world envied, and seeking calmly and firmly to uprear another and a better." Meanwhile, "all is peace" in the Confederacy, wrote an Augusta editor. "Our State Governments maintain law and order," another Georgian observed from Montgomery in mid-February: "Social life moves in its accustomed channels, property has encountered no disastrous depreciation, and business no fatal revulsion. The people have felt no revolutionary shock, and the transition from the old Government to the new, has been almost insensible. Co-operation leaders and the co-operation press, with few exceptions, affirm the revolution. Moderate men hold

30. Cobb, speech to citizens of Athens, April 6, 1861, Athens *Southern Banner,* April 10, 1861; Brown to David Walker, April 19, 1861, Milledgeville *Southern Federal Union,* April 30, 1861; Atlanta *Daily Intelligencer,* March 27, 1861; Augusta *Daily Constitutionalist,* March 20, 1861.

31. Letter to Jared I. Whittaker, Atlanta *Daily Intelligencer,* February 26, 1861; Brown to David Walker, April 19, 1861, Milledgeville *Southern Federal Union,* April 30, 1861.

in check ambitious rival aspirants." [32] The basis for these sober judgments brought an Athens editor to proclaim that, "The people of the South are today the masters of the universe, in their hands rests the destiny of all governments—the combined powers of the world is [*sic*] at her bidding, and the edict is but to be sent forth to be obeyed." Many who would have found this statement too hyperbolic did seem to believe that the South had turned the corner and was closing on the millenium. Even Alexander Stephens, who possessed an unfathomed reservoir of despair, told his Savannah audience that since the new government was organized "upon principles of perfect justice and right—seeking amity and friendship with all other powers—I see no obstacle in the way of our upward and onward progress." [33]

CONSERVATIVE IDEAS

These images of a southern utopia were visible in the placid surface of Georgia's society when viewed from the angle of Georgia's leaders. Social, economic, and political leaders were finding new unity in secession. "Within the comparatively small circle of our personal intercourse," a Macon editor noted in mid-February, "many who have strongly opposed the secession movement are now fully reconciled to it and oppose all reconstruction, and this feeling is daily gathering strength." [34] Secession had not resulted in anarchy as conservative cooperationists had feared. Instead, the opposite was more nearly true. Life moved in its "accustomed channels," wearing them smoother, deeper, and safer. In place of social and political nightmares, secession had brought conservative cooperationists pleasant dreams of realizing the organic society they had long hypothesized. By embracing secession, they had created the unity among Georgia's leaders that their social theory posited as a characteristic of a social organism. The empirical evidence of unity among Georgia's leaders led many to conclude that Georgia was likewise unified. Conservatives could then

32. Report of Cobb's speech, Athens *Southern Banner,* February 6, 1861; Augusta *Daily Constitutionalist,* February 13, 1861; Macon *Telegraph,* February 22, 1861.
33. Albany *Patriot,* February 28, 1861; Stephens, speech to citizens of Savannah, March 21, 1861, Augusta *Daily Constitutionalist,* March 30, 1861.
34. Macon *Telegraph,* February 15, 1861.

reaffirm the organic nature of southern society. And what they had earlier portrayed as threats to the Union, they could now portray as threats to Georgia.

In his "cornerstone" address, Alexander Stephens warned, "If we become divided—if schisms arise—if dissensions spring up—if factions are engendered—if party spirit, nourished by unholy personal ambition, shall rear its hydra head, I have no good to prophesy for you." In short, Stephens and others who echoed his opinions denied that opposition to the policies of the newly independent state could be legitimate. In their view, parties could not be based on conflicting social goals and interests because a healthy organic society was harmonious and interdependent rather than conflict-ridden. "[I]n the absence of any real necessity or basis for [party] organization," a Milledgeville editor wrote in mid-April, some Georgians were "endeavoring to create artificial ones." Whether or not such observations disarmed critics, they certainly strengthened the commitment of Georgia's leaders to the unassailable legitimacy of their own ideas and observations. An opponent was either written off as "no true friend to the peace and prosperity of the Confederate States" or urged to seek a more hospitable climate for his ideas: "If they do not like the new order of things," one editor wrote of some critics, "let them go to some place where they will be better satisfied."[35]

Instead of criticism, Georgia's leaders needed loyalty from their followers, they said. "With wisdom, prudence and statesmanship on the part of our public men, and intelligence, virtue and patriotism on the part of the people, success, to the full measure of our most sanguine hopes, may be looked for," Alexander Stephens predicted. Each Georgian had a part to play, especially suited to his talents. "Public men" should lead, the "people" should follow. Social change should be avoided because it would upset the delicate balance of social interdependence. "We have intelligence, and virtue, and patriotism," Stephens continued. "All that is required," he said, "is to cultivate and perpetuate them."[36]

35. Stephens, speech to citizens of Savannah, March 21, 1861, Augusta *Daily Constitutionalist*, March 30, 1861; Milledgeville *Southern Federal Union*, April 16, 1861.

36. Stephens, speech to citizens of Savannah, March 21, 1861, Augusta *Daily Constitutionalist*, March 30, 1861.

Once conservatives had become secessionists, then, their social views provided a rhetorical defense of the established social hierarchy.[37] The rhetoric was necessary for a viable republic of white men, where, as T. R. R. Cobb wrote, "every citizen feels that he belongs to an elevated class." That all-important feeling could be cultivated by actions, of course, and it was. "The poorest meets the richest as an equal," Cobb continued; "[he] sits at his table with him; salutes him as a neighbor; meets him in every public assembly, and stands on the same social platform." But these actions might seem to be assertions of equality on the part of the poor and to hint of paternalism and even condescension on the part of the wealthy. Rhetoric was needed not only to dispel these interpretations but also to demonstrate that slavery was the key to white equality. For unless it was emphasized that slavery elevated whites to "republican equality in the ruling class," it might seem that democratic ideals, not slavery, were responsible for the degree of white equality that existed.[38] This was a dangerous idea for Georgia's leaders. It suggested that a republic of white men might be achieved not by racial elevation but by social leveling. Conservative social ideas were of central importance, then, because, on the one hand, they carefully avoided the suggestion that just *any* republic of white men was acceptable, and, on the other hand, they justified and defended the republic that already existed.

CONSERVATIVE GUARANTEES

The actions of the state convention guaranteed that Georgia would be a republic of white men only. The citizenship ordinance which the convention adopted provided "that in no case, shall citizenship extend to any person, who is not a free white person." The new state constitution institutionalized the guarantee by making explicit that only "free white male citizens" could vote. But these guarantees were nothing more than formal recognitions of established practices. The convention did not act as if it thought, as one Georgian did, "that the constitution

---

37. The Atlanta *Daily Intelligencer*'s complaint (April 1, 1861) that the "papers that are so solicitous in argueing [*sic*] against the formation of political parties, were the very last to come into the new order of things" was accurate. The editor wrote that such men represented "Federalism, Whiggism, Know-Nothingism, Squatterism, and anti-Secessionism... which [had] bitterly opposed States Rights Democracy for the last seventy years "
38. T. R. R. Cobb, *An Inquiry into the Law of Negro Slavery,* ccxiii.

would best vindicate the supremacy of the white race, and most certainly reconcile all sections and classes, by treating slaves consistently as mere property and apportioning representatives, as most of the States do in their systems, without computing them."[39] Although such a scheme would have been consistent with a republic of white men— since it would shift the political center of gravity away from slave-rich counties toward more exclusively white counties—it was anathema to the convention delegates and to many other influential Georgians, as subsequent events would show. The convention delegates were willing to distribute equal shares of the racial status which the presence of blacks conferred upon all whites. But they were unwilling to tamper with the unequal distribution of political power that some whites enjoyed because they and many blacks lived in the same county. The republic of white men that the convention delegates had in mind was nothing more nor less than the one that existed when Georgia seceded.

But the present republic could be guaranteed neither by enacting citizenship ordinances nor by doing nothing. To maintain and protect the established social, economic, and political hierarchy, the convention rewrote the state constitution. Thereby, they demonstrated that, ultimately, they did not trust the rhetoric of racial status to protect what they had seceded to maintain. Rhetoric alone, their actions implied, might not preserve a republic of white men with a properly spacious and honored place for gentlemen and their slaves. Only a patriarchal republic could provide that guarantee.

---

39. *Journal of the Convention,* 72–73, 88. The suffrage requirement in the new constitution was in Art. V, paragraph 1, *Journal of the Convention,* 299. For the corresponding provision in the old constitution, see Art. IV, Sec. 1, in Thorpe (ed.), *Federal and State Constitutions,* II, 800. Columbus *Daily Enquirer,* March 14, 1861.

8

A
Patriarchal
Republic

The way to resolve the internal crisis of the South, many Georgians believed, was neither to democratize slaveholding nor to depend on a democracy of racial status, but instead to circumscribe democratic practices with institutional reforms. The convention delegates should "go to work in earnest, and reform all abuses," one Georgian urged. "Let them check the radical tendencies of the age," he wrote: "Reduce the Legislature—organize Senatorial Districts—change the Constitution and give the selection of Supreme and Superior Court Judges to the Governor; subject to confirmation by two-thirds of the Senate . . . [and thus] take the election [of these judges] from the people, or in the transitive state through which we are now passing, anarchy and mobs may rule."[1]

If the actions of the convention delegates indicated their ideas, then a majority of the delegates agreed not only with this Georgian, but also with another, who urged them to consider "the many other incubuses around us which our present condition and circumstances loudly demand that we should throw off." For when the state convention finally adjourned, Saturday night, March 23, it had accomplished a "double revolution"—as a Savannah editor noted—by rewriting the state constitution and including "all the amendments and improvements that experience has suggested." The constitutional changes that the delegates made demonstrated that their experience suggested that they had less to fear from extralegal mob rule and anarchy than from perfectly legal political challenges to the southern social order. Experience

1. Georgia to editor, Macon *Telegraph,* January 24, 1861.

143

suggested that "the radical tendencies of the age" on the one hand could become dangerously manifest through the existing government institutions—as Lincoln's election had shown—and, on the other hand, could be effectively checked only by institutional changes that were not drastic departures from tradition. The words that President Crawford used to summarize the change the convention had made in Georgia's external relations might equally well have been applied to the internal half of the double revolution. "You have retained ancestral wisdom in the formation of your government, separated only from those abuses which experience has developed," Crawford told the delegates just before they adjourned for the last time. "In short," he said, "you have effected a political reformation." The nature of the reformation allowed T. R. R. Cobb, its principal architect, to boast to his fellow townsmen that the South had both "the most liberal political institutions" and "the most patriarchal and perfect social polity . . . that the world now contains." [2]

Liberal political institutions and a patriarchal social polity were compatible in Georgia largely because of the work of Cobb and the convention. They sought, above all, to preserve their patriarchal social polity. But a republic that would conserve the social order had to incorporate liberal political institutions. Thus the constitutional changes made by the convention created a governmental structure that did not sacrifice liberal political institutions. Instead, it was more responsive than its predecessor to the social, economic, and political leaders in Georgia and more insulated from any effects of electoral politics that might seriously threaten their interests in the status quo. Acting as if they had, indeed, "raised [the plantation] to a political principle," the convention delegates tried to insure that Georgia would have conservative political masters whose prerogatives, responsibilities, and limitations were duly recognized in the fundamental law. [3] To guarantee that properly conservative men of quality governed

2. Romulus to editor, Rome *Weekly Courier,* March 1, 1861; Savannah *Morning News,* March 25, 1861; *Journal of the Public and Secret Proceedings of the Convention of the People of Georgia, Held in Milledgeville and Savannah in 1861* (Milledgeville, Ga.: Boughton, Nisbet, and Barnes, 1861), 303; Cobb, speech to citizens of Athens, April 6, 1861, Athens *Southern Banner,* April 10, 1861.
3. The quotation is from Eugene D. Genovese, *The Political Economy of Slavery: Studies in the Economy and Society of the Slave South* (New York: Random House, 1967), 31.

Georgia, the convention delegates turned, as had been traditional since the Federalists, to institutional reforms.

Conservative Proposals

"In the stir and excitement of the times, it is earnestly hoped that we may get back to conservatism," an Augusta editor wrote shortly after Lincoln's election. "The times portend great changes in our federal relations—[and] perhaps great changes in our internal management," he mused.[4] The actions of the state convention proved him right. The convention seemed to understand, as one Georgian put it, that the "security [of slavery] required defence against [both] domestic and foreign foes . . . and if guarantees are to be had they must be had now, while the public sentiment is ripe for it." If the second revolution were postponed, it might not be realized. The convention seemed to agree with the editor who wrote that the "much needed change can be easily effected" by acting "[n]ow, when our government is in a revolutionary state."[5]

Soon after the delegates convened, they began to consider proposals for the second revolution. On the third day of the convention, a day before the vote on the secession ordinance, the Committee on the Constitution—to be chaired by T. R. R. Cobb—was proposed, and, during the next two meetings of the convention, approved and appointed. During the first meeting after the passage of the secession ordinance, F. C. Shropshire, a secessionist from Floyd County in northwest Georgia, proposed another committee, which two days later had also been approved and appointed, "whose duty it shall be to inquire into the power of this Convention, to reduce the number of Senators and Representatives in the General Assembly of Georgia, and if the power to do so, exists in this body, to report an ordinance or such other measure as will effect this purpose, and on such basis as they may think best."[6] The Committee on Reduction, as it came to be called, and the Committee on the Constitution were both dominated by secessionist delegates who were elected in high slaveholding Whig cotton-belt counties. Both committees contained a disproportionately

---

4. Augusta *Chronicle and Sentinel,* November 24, 1861.
5. Georgia to editor, *ibid.,* February 9, 1861; Rome *Weekly Courier,* February 1, 1861.
6. *Journal of the Convention,* 26, 39–40, 45–46, 50, 55.

large number of delegates from town counties.[7] The fate of the second revolution was in reliable, conservative hands.

They understood, for example, that some proposals were too conservative. When a secessionist delegate proposed that the convention appoint a "Council of Safety" composed of citizens who would act as "counsellors and advisors" of the governor, the Committee on the Constitution recommended, and the convention approved, that "for the present, at least, such a Council is unnecessary and impolitic."[8] Another proposal approached the border between gentlemanliness and absurdity. "Georgia will demand, and enforce her rights, to her proportion of the public property, held by the General Government at the time of the dissolution of the partnership," in return for which, the delegate proposed, "Georgia will assume and guarantee the payment of her *pro rata* part of the public debt of the United States, existing at the time of her secession from the Union." Apparently the convention realized that there were limits beyond which courtesy and reciprocity could not go, and they allowed the proposal to die in committee.[9]

PROVISIONS FOR A SMOOTH TRANSITION

Some action was required, however, if only to bring Georgia's constitution into conformity with her independence. For example, the constitutional requirement that state legislators and the governor must be United States citizens had become obsolete.[10] But the convention

7. Of the thirteen members of the Committee on the Constitution, seven voted for secession on Nisbet's resolution, ten favored the secession ordinance, nine represented high slaveholding counties, eight represented Whig counties, ten were from cotton belt counties while the other three were from north Georgia, and the home counties of Athens, Rome, Milledgeville, Atlanta, Marietta, Columbus, and Albany were represented. The sixteen members of the Committee on Reduction had similar characteristics. Ten favored secession on Nisbet's resolution, eleven voted for the secession ordinance, eleven were from high slaveholding counties, ten were from Whig counties, twelve from cotton belt counties while the other four were from North Georgia, and the home counties of Augusta, Rome, Columbus, and Albany were represented. Over half (54%) of the delegates on the Committee on the Constitution and a fourth (25%) of the delegates on the Committee on Reduction were from town counties, while only 16 percent of all the convention delegates represented town counties.

8. The delegate was C. W. Styles of Ware County. *Journal of the Convention,* 51–52, 72–78.

9. The delegate was R. J. Cochran of Wilkinson County. *Ibid.,* 43. The proposal was referred to the Committee on Foreign Relations. *Ibid.,* 62.

10. See Art. I, Sec. 4 and 8, Art. II, Sec. 3, in Francis Newton Thorpe (ed.), *The Federal and State Constitutions* (7 vols.; Washington, Government Printing Office, 1909), 791, 792, 796, 805.

entertained and approved proposals that went far beyond removing such constitutional anachronisms in order to provide security and stability for Georgia's society. The delegates sought to change no less, and no more, that what, in their view, needed changing.

Soon after the passage of the secession ordinance, the convention approved provisions which insured, as an editor observed later, that Georgia "slid from one government into another without producing any sensible shock." The basic object of the convention's actions was, as the title of one ordinance stated, to "continue in force the Laws, and to preserve the order, peace, and convenience of the people of Georgia." On the recommendation of the Committee on the Constitution, the convention decided that all United States laws in force in Georgia before secession would continue to be binding after secession, with a few exceptions; that where the United States was mentioned in such laws, Georgia would be substituted; that the governor would take the place of the president in the laws, the attorney general that of the United States attorney, and the county sheriff that of the United States marshal; that the United States Circuit and District courts would be abolished and reconstituted as courts of Georgia with the same powers and jurisdictions; that sentences and punishments meted out before secession would continue in full force; and that criminals would be kept securely in jail. In addition to preserving these remnants of the federal structure, the convention voted to adopt federal personnel. United States postal and customs agents were simply accepted as agents of Georgia and United States military officers as officers of Georgia, with the same rank, grade, and pay. But the convention did not allow its firm commitment to the social order to overcome its mistrust of federal judges. It provided that United States judges in Georgia would lose their commissions and that new judges would be appointed by the governor.[11] Former army and navy officers could be trusted to shoot in the right direction, the convention's actions implied, but former federal judges could not be trusted to rule the right way.

By preserving the many components of the United States government in Georgia, the convention was not hedging against future reconstruction. A majority of the delegates opposed a cooperationist-

11. Milledgeville *Southern Federal Union,* March 5, 1861; *Journal of the Convention,* 44, 49, 52–53, 57–58, 69, 84–86, 88, 90, 92, 114–15, 126–29.

sponsored resolution that "the people of Georgia would be willing" to reconstruct the federal government whenever a basis was found that "would secure, permanently and unequivocally, the full measure of the rights and equality of the people of the slaveholding States," and it was buried in committee.[12] The convention also rejected the majority report of the Committee on Commercial and Postal Arrangements, which provided that federal customs agents be allowed "to continue to perform their functions under existing [federal] laws," and adopted a minority report which severed federal agents from "any further connection whatever with the Government of the United States."[13] The convention preserved nearly all of the federal structure in Georgia, then, because it was an integral part of the established order. Its continued existence would stabilize rather than threaten Georgia's society, the delegates decided.

THE APPROVAL OF GOD AND THE GODLY

Having severed their connection with one external power, the convention delegates reaffirmed their dependence on the Almighty. The same piety which was displayed on the transparency which hung on T. R. R. Cobb's residence in celebration of South Carolina's secession— "Resistance to Abolition is Obedience to God"—found its way into the proposed bill of rights that Cobb's Committee on the Constitution presented to the convention. The committee prefaced a guarantee of separation of church and state and a prohibition of religious tests with the observation that the "prevalence of the Christian Religion among the people, the basis of Christian principles underlying the laws, entitle this State to be ranked among the Christian nations of the earth." Although this preface was dropped in the new constitution, the "fundamental principle" that "God has ordained that all men shall live under government" was asserted.[14] The convention thus sought to invoke not only the aid but also the authority of God.

---

12. Cooperationist delegate P. W. Alexander of Upson County offered the resolution. *Journal of the Convention*, 40, 50.

13. The vote in favor of the minority report, taken on January 28, 1861, reflected the earlier vote on secession. Of the 130 delegates in favor of the minority report, 118 had voted for the secession ordinance, while of the 119 opposed to the minority report, 66 had opposed the secession ordinance, and 95 had voted against Nisbet's resolution. *Ibid.*, 62, 84, 91–96.

14. Athens *Southern Banner*, December 27, 1860; *Journal of the Convention*, 97, also Art. I,

From the godly came assurances that the separation of church and state should not strain the bonds of mutual interdependence. The "duty of Christians," a religious periodical noted, was "to recognize the government, and profess fealty to its constitution and law." "Neutrality now is moral treason," it continued; "for verily, the cause of the country is the cause of God." Once the "Christian denominations" had acted *"to consolidate the sentiment of the country,* in favor of the Government," they should go further, said the article, and "sanctify it, for the service of God." With such fealty from some Christians, it is perhaps not surprising that Georgia's new constitution did not include a clause guaranteeing freedom of religious belief.[15] The government, in a sense, ordained that Georgians lived under God.

PROTECTIONS FOR PROPERTY

The convention took other steps to insure that their new relations with God and the Yankees did not disturb those with Mammon. "In view of the present condition of the country, and the alleged apprehensions of foreign capitalists as to the scarcity of capital invested in this State," the convention resolved that "to encourage the manufacturing and mining and other permanent improvements of this State, this Convention does hereby declare it to be the fixed policy of Georgia to protect all investments already made, or which may be hereafter made by citizens of other States, in mines or manufacturing in this State, and capital invested in any other permanent improvement."[16]

Local as well as foreign economic interests were protected by adding to the new constitution prohibitions against "laws impairing the obligation of contracts" and the taking of private property for public use without just compensation, neither of which had been in the old constitution. The new constitution went beyond these prohibitions to state an ironclad obligation of government to property. "Protection to per-

---

paragraph 2, p. 285. The preamble to the Confederate Constitution also invoked "the favor and guidance of Almighty God." Art. 1, paragraph 2, p. 161.

15. Article from *Christian Index,* reprinted in Milledgeville *Southern Federal Union,* April 16, 1861. See also *ibid.,* May 21, 1861. Art. I, paragraph 7 of the new constitution read, "No religious test shall be required for the tenure of any office; and no religion shall be established by law; and no citizen shall be deprived of any right or privilege by reason of his religious belief." *Journal of the Convention,* 285.

16. The ordinance was offered by cooperationist Benjamin Hamilton of Lumpkin County. *Journal of the Convention,* 117.

son and property is the duty of Government," read one of the Fundamental Principles, adding that "a Government which knowingly and persistently denies, or withholds from the governed such protection, when within its power, releases them [its citizens] from the obligation of obedience."[17] Coupled with the denial of any legislative power to emancipate slaves, these provisions made clear that the convention intended to protect the means of the men who had them.

The convention also sought to continue economic development in the same direction and with the same directors. The new constitution allowed the state legislature "to grant corporate powers and privileges" to "banking, insurance, railroad, canal, plank road, navigation, mining, express, lumber, and telegraph companies" only. All other private groups seeking incorporation would have to go to court, where judges would grant corporate privileges under rules defined by the legislature. In effect, this provision allowed most of the established corporations in the state the opportunity to seek special privileges from the legislature, while new groups were prevented from jockeying for legislative favors and compelled to conform to general guidelines for incorporation which judges presumably would administer in a more uniform and predictable manner than the legislature.[18]

Banks received special attention. A constitutional requirement of a two-thirds vote of both houses of the legislature for the granting of a bank charter restricted the creation of new banks and may, in part, have represented the desire of established town banks to impede the proliferation of new country banks, which had accounted for more than half of the banks chartered during the last decade. Banks already chartered were required to receive the approval of two-thirds of both legislative branches for charter extension and for the suspension of specie payment.[19] These provisions not only reflected the antibank

17. These features were proposed by cooperationist Hiram Warner of Meriwether County and eventually found their way into Art. I, paragraphs 18 and 21, *ibid.*, 56–57, 286, 287. Art. I, paragraph 3, *ibid.*, 285.

18. Art. II, Sec. 6, paragraph 1, *ibid.*, 292. For an excellent discussion of economic policy in Georgia in the antebellum period, see Milton Sydney Heath, *Constructive Liberalism: The Role of the State in Economic Development in Georgia to 1860* (Cambridge, Mass.: Harvard University Press, 1954). For the numbers, types, and resources of Georgia's corporations, see the tables on pages 305 to 309 and on 311.

19. Art. II, Sec. 6, paragraph 1, *Journal of the Convention*, 292, Heath, *Constructive Liberalism*, 223–33.

sentiment that had been revitalized by the recent depression and specie suspension, but also they were warnings to bank officials to consider more than just their private interests when they decided bank policies.

Although the convention wanted bankers to act in the interests of the state, the delegates prohibited direct state involvement in a new internal improvements by providing that "No law shall be passed by which a citizen shall be compelled, directly or indirectly, to become a stockholder in, or contribute to a rail road or other work of internal improvement, without his consent." This foreclosed the manipulation of the legislature by profit-hungry railroad promoters—who in the past had sought to enhance the value of one region at the expense of another—and compelled them to seek private support.[20] In effect, given the difficulty of raising the necessary funds from private sources, existing railroads were insured against competition and their potential value and profitability were thereby increased.

Taken together, these various actions and proposals demonstrate the importance of conservative ideas in the second revolution. The delegates wanted both to protect slavery and to stabilize the entire society. To that end, they were willing to use many of the former officials and institutions of the United States, to invoke spiritual authority, and to extract some legal teeth with which an angry legislature might snap at property interests. But when judged by the length and intensity of the debate generated and by the number and scope of actions taken, the convention relied most heavily on conservative reforms of government institutions. These institutional reforms, together with the convention's other actions, disclosed that a majority of the delegates perceived and feared a political threat from below.

Sovereignty: The Convention and the People

The final form of the new state constitution was hammered out and agreed upon in secret sessions on March 21, 22, and 23, the last three days the convention met.[21] Most of the reforms incorporated in the new

20. The "inhabitants of a corporate town or city" were excepted and allowed to choose local ownership. The convention added, "This provision shall not be construed to deny the power of taxation for the purpose of making levees or dams to prevent the overflow of rivers." Art. II, Sec. 6, paragraph 4, *Journal of the Convention,* 292; *ibid.,* 81.

21. *Ibid.,* 218, 223–303.

constitution had been discussed since January, both in and out of the convention. The debate—which occurred during the January session of the convention, in the interim period between January 29 and March 7 while the convention was recessed awaiting the creation of the Confederacy, and during the March session of the convention—focused on the power of the convention to take actions not directly related to secession. The debate revealed the vitality of republican ideas. All spokesmen acknowledged the sovereignty of the people. But for a majority of the delegates—led by conservatives, both cooperationists and secessionists—professions of the sovereignty of the people were justifications for actions which implied that, instead, the convention was sovereign. These delegates realized, as the debates disclosed, that the sovereignty of the people made conservative reforms necessary and likewise gave the convention the power to effect them: for the necessity of conservative reforms *was* directly related to secession. The debate illustrated the conservative uses of republican rhetoric, reminded the convention of the institutional limits which confined reforms that would conserve both order and the social hierarchy, and helped develop a rhetorical defense of the convention's actions and an institutional mechanism for squaring the convention's actions with ideas of a sovereign people. In short, the debate was over the power of the convention to complete the double revolution.

THE PRELIMINARY DEBATE

The legislative act that authorized the governor to call the convention empowered the convention to "consider all grievances impairing or affecting the equality and rights of the State of Georgia as a member of the United States, and determine the mode, measure and time of redress . . . and to do all things needful to carry out the true intent and meaning of this Act." But were amending the state constitution and reducing the size of the legislature appropriately "needful" modes or measures of redress? The prolonged and heated debate on these questions first arose on January 24 when a delegate suggested that the great seal of the state might need to be changed.[22] This seemingly innocuous

22. Candler (ed.), *Confederate Records,* I, 206–208; *Journal of the Convention,* 63.

proposal provoked a discussion that, combined with a series of actions, led to a definition of the outer limits of the convention's powers. In the course of the preliminary debate, the convention confronted the question of the exact locus of sovereignty in Georgia.

The view of those who believed that the sovereignty of the people severely restricted the power of the convention was expressed by Linton Stephens. "We represent the people, and have only such powers as they have delegated to us," Stephens asserted during the preliminary debate. "We have assembled under a grant of power, and cannot exceed it," he cautioned. A minority of the Committee on Reduction, which had been appointed to report a plan for reducing the size of the legislature, agreed that the powers of the convention were limited, but not so limited as to preclude action. "[M]indful of the necessity of . . . reduction," the committee minority reported, "We think that if the plan adopted by this Convention is submitted to the people, and by them ratified, it will cure any want of power." Although the majority of the Committee on Reduction had no "doubt [about] the power of this Convention to make such reduction," they acknowledged that "there is great diversity of opinion as to the propriety of doing so, without submitting the action of the Convention to the people for ratification or rejection."[23]

Others thought that the sovereignty of the people did not require voter ratification of the convention's actions—either to "cure any want of power" or to observe political "propriety." They argued instead that the sovereignty of the people was embodied in the convention and gave the delegates virtually unlimited powers. "One million and four thousand people of Georgia are here by their delegates," Robert Toombs told the convention. He said that since the "power of the People is unlimited," then the delegates' powers as their "Representatives is [sic] the same as theirs." "We are only limited by God and Right," he proclaimed. "We are the People, owing no allegiance to any Prince, Potentate, Power, or anything under Heaven, but ourselves and our society."[24] In other words, *l'Etat, c'est nous.*

23. Report of convention debates, January 24, 1861, Macon *Telegraph,* January 26, 1861; *Journal of the Convention,* 79, 81.
24. Report of convention debates, January 24, 1861, Macon *Telegraph,* January 26, 1861.

Toombs's statement that the delegates' powers were limited only by an obligation to themselves and their society accurately described the power which the convention exercised. But when Toombs spoke during the preliminary debate, most of the convention's actions had not yet been taken. The debate about the powers of the convention, which continued for nearly two months, helped the delegates decide what their obligations to themselves and their society required them to do. It became clear to them that their self-interest required them to acknowledge the sovereignty of the people and to defer to it at the same time as they took steps to control it and to shape its expression. For the time being, President Crawford closed the formal debate by ruling from the chair that "the Convention was acting under limited powers" and thus had "No power to alter the great seal" or "to make the proposed alterations in the Constitution."[25] An appeal from Crawford's ruling was left pending when the convention recessed to await developments in Montgomery. The pending appeal gave the delegates time to think, to draft new amendments to the constitution—a series of which were proposed before the convention recessed, and an opportunity to take soundings in their home counties.[26] But the pending appeal did not prevent the delegates from taking actions which they believed were indisputably within their powers.

Sovereign Action: Joining the Confederacy

On the same day that the convention debated the extent of its power, it chose seven of its members and three other men to represent Georgia in the upcoming Confederate convention in Montgomery.[27] "They were not such men as revolutions or civil commotions usually bring to the surface," Alexander H. Stephens wrote of himself and the other nine. When the southern pot boiled, the scum did not rise. "They were men

25. Crawford used these words during the debates in March to describe his own actions in the January session. Report of convention debates, March 9, 1861, Augusta *Daily Constitutionalist,* March 12, 1861.

26. *Journal of the Convention,* 79–82, 115–17.

27. Robert Toombs and Howell Cobb were elected as at-large delegates, and the others were chosen from each of the eight congressional districts in Georgia: Francis S. Bartow (First District), Martin J. Crawford (Second), Eugenius A. Nisbet (Third), Benjamin H. Hill (Fourth), Augustus R. Wright (Fifth), Thomas R. R. Cobb (Sixth), Augustus H. Kenan (Seventh), and Alexander H. Stephens (Eighth). Wright, Crawford, and Howell Cobb were not delegates to the Georgia convention. *Ibid.,* 62–64.

of substance, as well as of solid character—men of education, of reading, of refinement, and well versed in the principles of Government," Stephens remembered. "Their object," he noted, accurately, "was not to tear down, so much as to build up with the greater security and permanency."[28]

On Stephens' suggestion, the convention clothed its Montgomery delegates with power befitting their character and intentions. They were given "full and plenary" power to agree upon both a provisional government "to be modeled as nearly as possible on the basis and principles of the late Government of the United States" and a permanent constitution for the Confederacy. The Confederate Constitution would then become "binding or obligatory upon the People of Georgia" by being "submitted to, approved, and ratified by" the state convention.[29]

When the convention delegates reassembled in Savannah in early March, the results of the Montgomery meeting gave them reason to believe that their trust in their delegates had been well placed. The Confederate Constitution was not only modeled after that of the United States, but it also seemed to provide the "greater security and permanency" that the Georgia delegates sought. Congress, for example, was prohibited from passing "laws denying or impairing the right of property in negro slaves." For the most part, the constitution put the primary responsibility for the security of slavery upon the states. The Confederate Supreme Court, for example, was not explicitly given the power of judicial review of state legislation.[30] Nor were states prohibited from abolishing slavery—indeed certain provisions suggested that

28. Alexander H. Stephens, *A Constitutional View of the Late War Between the States,* (2 vols: Atlanta: National Publishing Co., 1868), II, 325–26. During his stay in Montgomery, T. R. R. Cobb took quite a different view. He wrote his wife, "Marion, it is sickening, I had the folly to believe that there was great patriotism in this movement. God help us, it looks now as if it was nothing but office seeking." Cobb, "Correspondence," 234.

29. *Journal of the Convention,* 91. There was some opinion that although the provisional government should be republican in form, a number of changes were desirable to meet the "exigencies of the hour" which required, one editor wrote, "a government approaching a British Parliament in power and authority, but restricted by a district declaration of inherent and reserved rights." Augusta *Daily Constitutionalist,* February 7, 1861.

30. Art. I, Sec. 9, paragraph 4, *Journal of the Convention,* 168; Art. III, *ibid.,* 174–75. For the Confederate Constitution, see *ibid.,* 160–80. The standard study of the constitution is Charles Robert Lee, Jr., *The Confederate Constitutions* (Chapel Hill: University of North Carolina Press, 1963).

even states with laws hostile to slavery were eligible to join the Confederacy.[31] Overall, the Confederate Constitution was so satisfactory to the Georgia convention that it was ratified by a unanimous vote, 276 to 0.[32]

When the convention joined the Confederacy by its own action, without seeking popular consent, it effectively demonstrated that it was, as it said, the "State, acting in its sovereign and independent character."[33] All the convention delegates were satisfied that at least in the realm of federal relations they were sovereign. Many other Georgians did not agree.

REMINDERS OF THE SOVEREIGNTY OF THE PEOPLE

"Was ever Aristocracy—was ever Oligarchy—was ever Monarchy more insolently assuming?" wrote a Georgian who claimed to be one of the "country people who have never learned any other way to get our bread than in the sweat of the face, and who have never been so fortunate (or unfortunate) as to be fed and fattened, greased and pampered with pap from the public crib." The state convention had unjustly assumed the power "to self-constitute themselves our agents in a higher commission," he wrote, "and arrogate to themselves the sole right of ratifying or rejecting the acts of that higher commission, and prolonging the time at our cost, and all without a word of approbation or consent from us."[34] "If the Gulf States were a big plantation, and our present [Confederate] Congress its perpetual rulers," wrote another critic, "I can imagine nothing more wise and politically perfect

31. Art. IV, Sec. 2, paragraphs 1 and 3, and Sec. 3, *Journal of the Convention,* 176–77. Some Georgia delegates were willing to set absolute limits on states' rights. The Committee on Relations with Slaveholding States offered the Georgia convention a resolution requiring every Confederate state to "tolerate the existence of slavery as one of its domestic institutions" and requiring that if any state abolished slavery it would immediately thereupon cease to be a member of the Confederacy. The resolution was recommended for passage, discussed, and recommitted to the Committee, where it died. *Ibid.,* 67–68, 88–89.

32. The vote was taken on March 16, 1861. *Ibid.,* 187–91.

33. This phrase from the preamble to the Confederate Constitution was intentionally included in the Georgia convention's act of ratification to describe the nature of the Georgia convention. *Ibid.,* 161, 188.

34. Vox Populi to editor, Upson *Pilot,* March 9, 1861. See also Vox Populi to editor, Augusta *Chronicle and Sentinel,* February 15, 1861, and March 3, 1861; M. to editor, Upson *Pilot,* March 16, 30, 1861.

than their present enactments." He thought that the Confederate congressmen should be informed "that the people are entitled to a voice and a vote on many subjects which they are now so summarily disposing of over their heads."[35] An Atlanta editor agreed. "Our public servants, who are now in Montgomery, organizing a Government, should not lose sight of the great principle lying at the foundation of our Republican system, that the people are the source of all power," he wrote.[36] "If sovereignty does *not* reside in the people," another Georgian warned, "then it is to reside in an Oligarchy, or a military despotism; either of which will tend to make the rich richer, and the poor poorer."[37]

Such statements reminded the delegates that the sovereignty of the people which they had invoked could be a political weapon in the hands of others as well. The critics found political ammunition in the action which the convention delegates unanimously agreed was within their province. The critics were not merely "croakers by nature," as some newspapers claimed. The editor of the Atlanta *Daily Intelligencer,* for example, was a secessionist who favored the formation of the Confederacy, but he criticized the convention and the Montgomery Congress for its usurpation of power. The editor himself identified the critics correctly when he wrote, after the Georgia convention had finally adjourned, that "those persons who are now expressing dissatisfaction with our Government were opposed to the ordinance of secession." "For awhile they were disposed to acquiesce," he observed acutely, "but as the great principles of Government, which arise out of the secession movement is [*sic*] being gradually developed ... the muttering thunders of their indignation cannot be suppressed."[38]

---

35. Paul to editor, Columbus *Daily Enquirer,* March 15, 1861.

36. Among the actions which the editor thought were "not entirely according with the great principle upon which our Government rests" were that the Georgia convention had sent seven of its members to Montgomery, that the Confederate Congress seemed "to be perpetuating its existence with unlimited power, for the whole period of the Provisional Government, instead of allowing the people to elect members to the Congress," and that the Confederate Constitution omitted a prohibition against members of Congress holding other government positions. Atlanta *Daily Intelligencer,* February 19, 1861.

37. M. to editor, Upson *Pilot,* March 16, 1861.

38. Athens *Southern Banner,* March 27, 1861; Rome *Weekly Courier,* February 8, 1861; Atlanta *Daily Intelligencer,* February 19, March 27, 1861.

Some Georgians in the upcountry were less concerned about the convention's ratification of the Confederate Constitution than they were about the act of secession itself. James W. Ailer, who claimed to speak for the people of Walker, Dade, and DeKalb counties, wrote Governor Brown that "we do not in tend to submit to [the] desision of the sesession movement which has been taken out of the hands of the People and has fallon into the hands of Dimegougs and office seekers pick pockitts and vagrants about towns and cities and Raleroads and Depotes that has not got anything at Stake only a deck of cards a qt of rot gut Cigar stuck in their mouth." Ailer explained that "the people of Cherochee want to stay in the union so I hope you will let us go in peace and we will set up for our celves and still remain in the union." He warned Brown that he had the names of over twenty-five hundred volunteers who were "gest as willing as you ever seen montain boies" to use the "point of the bayonett and the musel of the musket" to stay in the Union. Characteristically, Ailer's terms for supporting secession referred to the sovereignty of the people. "[I]f the people of Georgia will vote to go out of the union we will submit to it as quick as ever you seen and if it is not brought back to the people we will fight it as long as there are men to fight." [39]

In short, many cooperationists who had feared the conservative, antidemocratic sympathies of some secessionists now had reason to believe that their fears had been prescient insights. And the reports of the constitutional amendments proposed during the January session of the convention seemed to confirm their fears. Although the reports came to one Georgian along with the rumor "that some of the leading members [of the convention] are in favor of restricting the right of suffrage," he was able to "hope [that] these are only rumors" because the convention had left the question of its power to revise the state constitution pending along with the various proposals. Thus, those who thought that the convention had "encroached upon the privileges of the people" in the process of joining the Confederacy eyed the proposed constitutional changes suspiciously, and waited. [40]

39. James W. Ailer to Gov. Joseph E. Brown, February 15, 1861, in Telamon Cuyler Papers, University of Georgia.
40. "We care little about the right of suffrage, and such small matters," admitted the editor of

Others waited with undisguised enthusiasm. Since conservative former cooperationists were eager to "check the radical tendencies of the age," they urged, as one wrote, that the convention should not "balk at such a *small matter as a change of the Constitution.*" After all, wrote another, the convention's "appropriate work is the revision of fundamental law." [41] A secessionist editor noted that some former cooperationists were now not only eager for Georgia to remain independent, but also, "some of them" he wrote, "have even squinted at a Monarchy." [42] The editor of the Augusta *Chronicle and Sentinel* had indeed written that "it seems [that this generation's] only resort must be a constitutional monarchy." [43] And if one took the view that the "Convention have whatever power the people of Georgia possesses, and can abolish the Legislature altogether," then a monarchy was a possibility. [44] But it was only a dim one, given the opposition within secessionist ranks to altering republican forms.

Some based their opposition to any form of monarchy on the strength and value of republican government, others on the belief that the social system was monarchical enough—"The slaveowner is the last man to desire a monarchy because he is himself truly sovereign," wrote one—and still others on the grounds that it would stimulate political turmoil at a time when calm was required. One secessionist editor who favored the proposed constitutional changes did not think the convention had the power to make them, much less to crown a king. He urged that the constitution be amended "properly, and in a constitutional way" by another convention "elected for this special purpose." Conservative former cooperationists, however, were reluctant to let the present state constitution stand in the way of their conservatism. One admitted that "strictly and legally" the convention probably did not have the authority to make the proposed changes. But he

---

the Augusta *Chronicle and Sentinel,* November 24, 1860. Sidney to editor, Milledgeville *Southern Federal Union,* January 29, 1861; Upson *Pilot,* March 9, 1861. See also, Augusta *Daily Constitutionalist,* January 23, 1861 and the report of the ratification meeting in Towns County, Athens *Southern Banner,* February 20, 1861.

41. Unsigned letter to editor, Macon *Telegraph,* January 24, 1861; Columbus *Daily Enquirer,* January 25, 1861.

42. The editor interpreted the discussion of a monarchy as an attempt to give Georgia something that its people would refuse to accept and, in that way, lead to eventual reunion. Athens *Southern Banner,* February 6, 1861.

argued that since the delegates were "the representatives of *the people*," they could do "whatever they choose, provided only [that] the people consent to their action."[45] With such reasoning, those who sought to make conservative reforms turned to their advantage both the ideas they doubted and the practices they sought to curb. Thus, talk of the sovereignty of the people reminded the convention delegates both that there were political limits on their actions and that the limits, properly used, could be sources of power for them to do as they wanted.

THE SOVEREIGN CONVENTION

Before the convention could decide what it wanted to do, it had to decide whether it had the power to do anything other than secede and join the Confederacy. The appeal from President Crawford's ruling that the convention's power did not embrace changing the state constitution was put to a vote soon after the delegates reassembled in Savannah for their March session. After several proposals for reducing the legislature were made during the first three meetings, A. H. Hansell from Thomas County along the Florida border moved that all such proposals be tabled until the next Christmas.[46] Hansell's motion provoked a long, elaborate debate about the power of the convention which revealed how the delegates reconciled the sovereignty of the people and the power of the convention.

Hansell made the motion to postpone indefinitely any plan for reducing the legislature not because he doubted the convention's power, although he thought the convention's claim of power "was certainly by a technical construction of the Act of the Legislature." Instead, he feared the reduction of the legislature would "excite sectional controversies and . . . jealousies" within the state and "create dissention

43. He wrote that he favored the continued "experiment" of republicanism until "the people" decided that it was "useless," when he would "acquiesce" but "in sorrow that the labors, perils, sacrifices and sufferings of our forefathers have all been in vain." Augusta *Chronicle and Sentinel,* January 26, 1861.

44. Macon *Telegraph,* January 23, 1861.

45. Augusta *Daily Constitutionalist,* January 30, February 15, 26, 1861; Atlanta *Daily Intelligencer,* February 9, June 23, 1861; Athens *Southern Banner,* February 6, March 27, 1861; Earl to editor, Augusta *Chronicle and Sentinel,* December 30, 1860.

46. *Journal of the Convention,* 132–34, 136–37, 143–49.

[*sic*]" at a time when "unity and harmony, among the people" were "of the very first importance." [47] As a secessionist, Hansell was worried that the convention's attempt to consummate the second revolution would cause many Georgians to question their commitment, or acquiesence, to the first revolution. As the debate on Hansell's motion continued, it brought to the surface the question of the relation between the first and second revolutions. Hansell's views demonstrated that some secessionists did not believe that the second revolution was necessary to complete the first.

Other delegates favored Hansell's motion for postponement because they believed the convention had "no power" to reduce the legislature. Respect for the sovereignty of the people underlay the beliefs of some, as the pointed hypothesis of one secessionist delegate demonstrated. Suppose that the legislature had called the convention to reduce the legislature, C. W. Styles of Ware County told the convention; "Why even I, sir, with all my fire-eating propensities, and red-hot secession proclivities, should not have voted to take Georgia out of the Union." Styles noted, as did many others, that the voters "went to the polls" to elect the convention delegates with the act of the legislature "in their hands," and thus they "had not delegated their whole powers." The convention had been delegated the power to act only for "a special purpose" and "what is not delegated," said Styles, "remains yet with the people." [48] These sentiments showed that some delegates, including some secessionists, respected the sovereignty of the people and the corollary doctrine of delegation of powers that had been integral to American political theory since 1787. Delegates with these views were unwilling to support actions which undermined the orthodox theory of republican government. If the debate on Hansell's motion did nothing else, it disclosed to them that many other delegates were not communicants in the orthodoxy.

Some delegates, for example, opposed what they called the conven-

47. Report of convention debates, March 11, 1861, Savannah *Morning News,* March 12, 1861; Atlanta *Daily Intelligencer,* March 15, 1861.

48. This was also the view of President Crawford which he reiterated in debate on March 9, See also the remarks of Hansell, Davis, and Saffold. Report of convention debates, March 11, 1861, Atlanta *Daily Intelligencer,* March 15, 1861; Augusta *Daily Constitutionalist,* March 12, 1861.

tion's "usurpation" not out of respect for the sovereignty of the people but out of fear of it. C. S. Gaulden of Brooks County reminded the delegates that the Georgia constitution required any constitutional amendment to be approved by a two-thirds majority of both houses of the legislature, to be published six months before the next election of legislators, and then repassed by the same margin in both houses after the election. "Neither the Legislature nor the people had any right to change the Constitution except in the manner prescribed by its framers" who, Gaulden said, sought "the protection of minorities" through the preservation of "the federal basis" of representation. If the "doctrine that the people can do what they please" did not have its limits, then he said he "was not in favor of popular government."[49]

The actions of the convention which Gaulden and others feared as a dangerous precedent were eagerly hoped for by others. W. A. Hawkins of Sumter County argued that the constitutional procedure for amendments was simply "a restriction upon the Legislature, who were only the Agents of the People." The convention, he implied and others said, had "the same power" as if the people "were here *en masse*." Indeed, F. G. Ramsey of Clinch County argued that his "theory of republican government" recognized "no limitations to the power of the people, save those self-imposed, and they [are] subject to removal at will, when in solemn convention assembled."[50]

These secessionist proponents of the second revolution saw no conflict between their plans and the sovereignty of the people, since, as convention delegates rather than mere legislators, they spoke with the voice of the people. From their point of view, an oligarchy was a legitimate instrument of republican government if it could be called a convention. It would be foolish for the convention to adhere rigidly to the notion that the convention had been delegated only limited powers. Indeed, many delegates had already exceeded their instructions. "Now, if we can exercise no powers but those specifically conferred,"

49. See Art. IV, Sec. 15, Thorpe (ed.), *Federal and State Constitutions*, 801; Report of convention debates, March 9, 1861; Savannah *Morning News*, March 11, 1861; Augusta *Daily Constitutionalist*, March 12, 1861.

50. Report of convention debates, March 9, 11, 1861, Savannah *Morning News*, March 12, 1861; Report of convention debates, March 11, 1861, Atlanta *Daily Intelligencer*, March 15, 1861. The quotation is from the remarks of W. B. Fleming of Liberty County.

F. C. Shropshire of Floyd County jibed, then "those delegates elected as co-operationists had no right to enter into the secession matter, and should have withdrawn from the convention." Cooperationists had not only exceeded their popular mandate but they also had joined secessionists in going "further than the powers delegated" in the act of the legislature, Hawkins added.[51]

These arguments provided a defense for the second revolution, but they did not provide a rationale. As in the rhetoric of the secession campaign, the rationale for the second revolution was usually left implicit, to be glimpsed more in the actions of the delegates than in their words. But in the debate on Hansell's motion, secessionist Henry L. Benning of Muscogee County put the rationale in a nutshell. The "power to 'determine the mode' of redress" given the convention by the act of the legislature was "absolutely unlimited," Benning said.

> Therefore, whatever thing the Convention may deem a mode of redress, it has the power to adopt. If the Convention can deem the formation of a General Government a mode of redress for grievances, why can it not deem the improvement of its own State Government a mode of redress for the same grievances? The main value of the new General Government is that it augments our strength to resist the North. But an improvement of our State Government would also augment our strength to resist the North.[52]

It was probably unnecessary, and even potentially inflammatory, to spell out exactly how improvements in the state government would protect Georgians from their sectional foes. The details were to be hammered out later. For the present, the debate on Hansell's motion helped the convention grope toward a mechanism to reconcile its commitment to the second revolution with the sovereignty of the people.

The way recommended by T. R. R. Cobb and other delegates was to refer the convention's actions to the voters for their approval.[53] This

---

51. *Ibid.*

52. Report of convention debates, March 9, 1861, Augusta *Daily Constitutionalist*, March 12, 1861.

53. Cobb explained that the referendum overcame the convention's admitted lack of power to change the constitution. Cobb, speech to citizens of Athens, April 6, 1861, Athens *Southern Banner*, April 10, 1861. Remarks of Asbury Hull of Clarke County. Report of convention debates, March 9, 1861, Savannah *Morning News*, March 11, 1861; and of S. B. Spencer of

would free the convention to define and shape the second revolution and, at the same time, allow the voters to approve or reject the convention's actions. Hansell replied that he thought this was "one of the very worst features" of the argument against his motion. Not only did "this ratification business . . . open an excuse for discussion among the people, and at this time [when] all discussions should be avoided," but also it "treat[ed] the people unfairly," he said. The voters would "have no opportunity for discussing the various measures proposed . . . [or] of instructing their representatives," but instead "they would be reduced to the necessity of saying either yes or no." [54] The mechanism of voter ratification of the convention's actions, Hansell argued, reduced the sovereignty of the people to mere consent. That was probably why Cobb and many others favored it. The ratification scheme promised to provide the substance of the second revolution by preserving the traditional form of deference to the sovereignty of the people.

The vote on Hansell's motion showed that most delegates believed that consent was sufficient sovereignty for the voters. The convention refused to postpone the reduction of the legislature as Hansell's motion went down to a stinging defeat, 54 to 206. [55] Many delegates probably opposed the motion because it threatened to abort the second revolution. Most of the delegates were unwilling to pass up what one referred to as "our last opportunity to correct the evil [of a large legislature]." [56] Their negative votes implied that they feared the consequences of what some of Hansell's supporters wanted, namely for a reduction of the legislature to "start down with the people and come up, not be started up here, and go down to the people." [57]

Thomas County, Report of convention debates, March 11, 1861, Atlanta *Daily Intelligencer,* March 15, 1861.

54. However, at least one delegate—Simpson Fouche of Floyd County—did take active measures to consult his constituency. He asked for the views of his constituents on the question of the power of the convention to reduce the legislature in a public letter published early in February, between the two sessions of the convention. Fouche to voters of Floyd County, Rome *Weekly Courier,* February 7, 1861. Report of convention debates, March 11, 1861, Savannah *Morning News,* March 12, 1861, Atlanta *Daily Intelligencer,* March 11, 1861.

55. *Journal of the Convention,* 146–49.

56. The delegate was Asbury Hull of Clarke County. Report of convention debates, March 9, 1861, Savannah *Morning News,* March 11, 1861.

57. Remarks of C. W. Styles of Ware County, Report of convention debates, March 11, 1861, Atlanta *Daily Intelligencer,* March 15, 1861.

By voting to carry out the double revolution, many of the delegates demonstrated that they believed liberal political institutions and a patriarchal social polity could coexist so long as the flow of political authority was from the patriarchy to the people. The subsequent actions of the convention best indicate the motives of most of those who opposed Hansell's motion. But the importance of conservative desires to establish and maintain a patriarchal relationship between Georgia's leaders and the rest of the citizens was hinted at in the vote on Hansell's motion. Conservative cooperationists who had voted for the secession ordinance were more strongly opposed to Hansell's motion than either secessionists or hard-core cooperationists.[58] But the vote on Hansell's motion cut across the division between secessionists and cooperationists. Many hard-core cooperationists opposed Hansell's motion probably because they hoped the convention would design a more equitable system of representation.[59] Likewise, many secessionists favored Hansell's motion less out of a principled adherence to ideals of popular sovereignty than out of a desire to forestall any reduction of the legislature which might decrease or abolish the representation of the large, thinly populated counties of south Georgia, the home counties of a large proportion of the delegates who voted with Hansell.[60]

But Hansell and his supporters were not simply defending the special representational privileges of south Georgia, nor were their opponents merely attacking those privileges. The immediate question was legislative reduction, but the much broader issue of the powers of the convention was addressed in the debate and resolved in the vote. The day after the vote, when C. W. Styles argued that the defeat of Hansell's motion did not settle the question of the powers of the convention, President Crawford, "with becoming gravity and dignity," said

---

58. For the tables which summarize the analysis of this vote and the votes discussed below, see the Appendix.

59. See for example, Columbus *Daily Enquirer,* January 25, 1861.

60. C. W. Styles charged that the proposals to reduce the legislature were intended "to weaken and break down" the representation of southwest Georgia, which, of course, was denied by the proponents of the measure. See the remarks of Styles and F. C. Shropshire, Report of convention debates, March 11, 1861, Savannah *Morning News,* March 12, 1861, Atlanta *Daily Intelligencer,* March 15, 1861.

that on the contrary, it did—whereupon the delegates burst into applause.[61] Having decided that it was sovereign, the convention proceeded to act accordingly. In the process, the convention began to act like the kind of government that many delegates hoped the second revolution would create: a patriarchal republic.

A Constitution for a Patriarchal Republic

Five days after the convention decided that it had the power to reduce the state legislature, T. R. R. Cobb asked the convention for a formal mandate for his Committee on the Constitution "to revise" the state constitution. The convention complied with Cobb's request, providing only that "the subject of reduction being now before the Convention is not submitted to said Committee until after final action of this Convention on that subject." Cobb claimed later, with a disingenuous innocence, that reduction of the legislature "required a change of the Constitution" and that when the convention "came to examine the instrument, they found other glaring defects upon its face."[62] It seems more likely that Cobb's explanation was an attempt to clothe the convention's unprecedented action of rewriting the state constitution with the mantle of respectability that earlier attempts to reduce the legislature lent to the convention's similar efforts. It would have been easy for the convention, had it so desired, to change only those parts of the constitution which dealt with the legislature. But since legislative reduction and other constitutional changes had been proposed and discussed before the convention first met in Milledgeville and during both the January session and the convention's February recess, it seems unlikely that rewriting the constitution had never occured to the delegates until they reduced the legislature. Given the thoroughness with which Cobb's committee revised the constitution, it is more likely that the reduction of the legislature was considered part of a general effort to design a state government that was less likely to threaten the social status quo than to protect and maintain it.

61. Report of convention debates, March 12, 1861, Atlanta *Daily Intelligencer,* March 16, 1861. *Journal of the Convention,* 151, 160.
62. *Journal of the Convention,* 187; Cobb, Speech to citizens of Athens, April 6, 1861, Athens *Southern Banner,* April 10, 1861.

Although the reasons for the delegates' actions must be inferred since the convention met in secret session—on Cobb's request—for the three days during which it agreed upon the new constitution, it appears that a majority of the delegates sought a government which would preserve the society that existed and would facilitate its development unhindered by political challenges. The delegates apparently wanted the government to be staffed by men whose social position and outlook qualified them to define what was good for the whole of Georgia's society. Proponents of the constitutional changes argued that "we are one people, now more than ever, with a community of interests" and therefore it was "time to discard the narrow unworthy notion that a member of the Legislature is the representative of a county" in favor of the view that a legislator "should be the representative of the honor and the interests of the State."[63] But the constitutional changes the convention approved showed that the delegates doubted that the present legislators would manifest Georgia's community of interests. Instead the delegates apparently thought that some other Georgians could better perceive and represent the community. In a sense, the delegates sought a state government manned by Georgians whose social standing, personal characteristics, and solicitude for the established order matched that of the convention delegates themselves, only seven of whom sat in the legislature in 1860.[64] The delegates' actions suggested that the voice of the people would have less potential for danger when the right people were listening to it and interpreting it. In the relation between citizen and government official, the delegates sought to decrease the dependence of the official on the citizen and, conversely, to increase the citizen's dependence on the official. In short, they sought a government whose relation to the present society was like husband to wife and whose relation to the future was like father to child: a protective, nurturing government, a patriarchal republic.

Not all the delegates wanted a patriarchal republic. Most of the

63. Troup to editor, Savannah *Morning News,* March 21, 1861.

64. Six delegates were state senators, one was a state representative. Ralph A. Wooster, "The Georgia Secession Convention," *Georgia Historical Quarterly,* XL (1956), 41–52, and Wooster, "Notes on the Georgia Legislature of 1860," *ibid.,* XLV (1961), 27–35.

proposed constitutional amendments were opposed by some delegates and on a few occasions the opposition prevailed. But, in general, a loose coalition of secessionists and conservative former cooperationists dominated the convention and forged the new constitution. By comparison, the hard-core cooperationists, who had voted against the secession ordinance, were strongly opposed to the proposed changes. Thus the proponents and opponents as well as the substance of the new state constitution reflected the importance of conservatives and conservatism in shaping Georgia's second revolution.

Looking backward to the Federalists, the delegates seem to have realized that it is sometimes necessary to make a revolution to preserve a society and a set of ideals. Although the delegates' society and ideals were quite different from the Federalists', they rewrote the Georgia constitution as if James Madison's Tenth Federalist was fresh in their minds. Thus the new state constitution was both traditional and, in a conservative way, revolutionary. The seeming contradiction between these adjectives bespeaks not the delegates' confusion but the dilemma of conservatives in the antebellum South: how both to be heirs of the American Revolution and to avoid its undesirable consequences. By rewriting the state constitution, the delegates affirmed certain of their ties to the past at the same time that they denied others. Perhaps, as men who sought to reshape their heritage, they deserve to be called Confederalists. At least they shared with their Federalist forebearers a desire to guarantee that republican government protected rather than subverted the society they knew.

A Smaller, Better Legislature

From the day the secession ordinance was signed the convention had had under consideration several plans for reducing the size of the state legislature. A plan acceptable to the delegates was finally worked out on March 20, just before the convention's final three days of secret meetings. Although the first reduction resolution that passed the convention cited the necessity of "an economical administration of Government" as the reason for the reduction, T. R. R. Cobb told an Athens audience afterward that the "great necessity [was] not simply on the picayune ground of saving a few dollars in annual expenses; but upon the higher basis of political necessity." Cobb explained that in "a republican government the true theory requires that the two branches of the Legislature should respectively represent, the one popular majorities, and the other territory and property." The problem with the old constitution, as Cobb saw it, was that *"neither population nor territory are represented truly* in either branch." The result, he pointed out, was that "as an attempt at Republican Government" the present legislature was "a *failure."* "A minority of the voters of Georgia can control both branches," he said, "and in the Senate much the smallest portion of the territory and wealth of the State can control the greater portion of each."[65] Cobb tried to bring the new state constitution into conformity with his ideas about republican government, but he was unsuccessful. The convention twice voted down his attempts to make the representation in the state house of representatives more closely reflect population.[66]

The delegates admitted "that population ought to be fairly represented," R. T. David of Putnam County observed. But, he said, "they refuse, in practical detail, what they admit in the abstract." Significantly, a majority of the delegates was not in favor of making the house of representatives more perfectly *"speak the voice of the popular majority of the State,"* as Cobb put it. Instead, their action showed that most of the delegates were more interested in "carry[ing] out the true idea of a Senate, as a permanent and conservative body, designed as a check upon the popular branch." The delegates' complaints about the existing Senate disclosed that what they sought was better senators, not reduction per se, as they claimed. Francis S. Bartow of Chatham County probably spoke for many other delegates when he told the convention, "Don't go into theories of representation, simply re-

65. *Journal of the Convention,* 45–46, 50, 79–82, 132–34, 136–37, 143–45, 151–53, 156–60, 211–13; Cobb, Speech to citizens of Athens, April 6, 1861, Athens *Southern Banner,* April 10, 1861.

66. Cobb actually proposed that the size of the house be increased from 132 to 200 members. Each county should have 1 representative and the remaining 68 representatives should be distributed in proportion to county population, he thought. When Cobb moved to reconsider the tabling of his plan, his motion lost on a roll call vote, 117 to 131. He said later that many delegates feared to increase the house "lest the popular cry for *Reduction* would be taken up by the 'Tupenny' newspapers, to bring condemnation upon our action." *Journal of the Convention,* 200–204. Cobb, speech to citizens of Athens, April 6, 1861, Athens *Southern Banner,* April 10, 1861.

duce." [67] But the method of reduction the convention chose revealed a desire for more than a simple decrease in the number of senators.

The "unwieldy size" of the legislature made it "too ponderous," inefficient, and "expensive," it was frequently observed. But the uniformly high opinion the convention delegates had of themselves and their work—an opinion widely shared outside the convention— suggests that it was not size alone, or even primarily, which caused these complaints, for the convention and the state legislature contained an identical number of members. Asbury Hull was probably more candid when he voiced a complaint about the senate that could not be made of the convention. "It is absurd . . . to associate [Georgia's Senate] with . . . the idea of deliberative dignity and conservatism," he told the delegates. [68]

Outside the convention the complaints about the legislators were less inhibited. The legislature contained too many "mere wrangling demagogues" and "county politicians" who could be excluded by reduction, some said. Reduction would produce "better legislators, better laws, and almost certainly . . . more capacity, integrity, and nerve in the Legislature," others argued. A group of citizens urged reduction because, as they wrote, "Local and class legislation is all wrong." In other words, what disturbed many Georgians and most convention delegates was that Georgia's legislators were too representative of their counties and not representative enough of the state. The delegates were fully aware that by "making small districts, you concentrate power in certain localities." What the convention had to decide was how large the senatorial districts had to be to guarantee that senators would be chosen who were "representative of the honor and the interests of the State." [69]

67. Report of convention debates, March 19, 1861, Atlanta *Daily Intelligencer,* March 22, 1861; Cobb, speech to citizens of Athens, April 6, 1861, Athens *Southern Banner,* April 10, 1861; Augusta *Chronicle and Sentinel,* March 7, 1861; Report of convention debates, March 13, 1861, Atlanta *Daily Intelligencer,* March 18, 1861.

68. See remarks of Alexander, Ramsey, and Bartow, Report of convention debates, March 9, 1861, Savannah *Morning News,* March 9, 11, 1861; March 11, 1861, Atlanta *Daily Intelligencer,* March 15, 1861; March 13, 1861, Atlanta *Daily Intelligencer,* March 18, 1861.

69. Clyde to editor, Augusta *Chronicle and Sentinel,* March 1, 1861; Macon *Telegraph,* January 23, 1861; J. M. Beall to editors, Milledgeville *Southern Federal Union,* February 19, 1861; Augusta *Chronicle and Sentinel,* February 15, 1861; Atlanta *Daily Intelligencer,* March 6,

Most of the proposals presented to the convention called for the eight congressional districts to become state senatorial districts. Within each district, voters would elect between four and eight senators, depending on the size of the senate provided for in the plan. Before the convention decided that "the popular branch" should be left unchanged "for the present," similar plans of at-large representation were presented for the house of representatives.[70] These proposals would have increased the constituency of a legislator from one county to at least eleven and as many as twenty-eight counties. After considering such drastically enlarged districts, the convention settled on a plan which increased senators' constituencies from one to three counties. Each of the forty-four districts of three contiguous counties would elect one senator, for a new senate one-third the size of the old one.[71]

President Crawford was undoubtedly correct when he told the delegates in his final speech that, "Reduction of the members of the Legislature may not have gone as far as many others have desired; still as a thing, *per se*, it cannot be otherwise than acceptable."[72] It would be better to have senators who were known throughout three counties rather than just one, although it might be better still to have even larger districts. The first draft of the new constitution tried to exaggerate the effect of the larger districts by permitting senators to reside outside their districts. But by a close vote of 116 to 112—with hard-core cooperationists providing the winning margin—the convention added a requirement that senators reside in their districts for at least one year.[73] Still, men elected from the larger districts were more likely to

---

1861; Remarks of J. P. Garvin of Richmond County, Report of convention debates, March 13, 1861, Atlanta *Daily Intelligencer,* March 18, 1861; Troup to editor, Savannah *Morning News,* March 21, 1861.

70. *Journal of the Convention,* 79–82, 132–34, 136–37, 152–53; Remarks of Francis S. Bartow, Report of convention debates, March 13, 1861, Atlanta *Daily Intelligencer,* March 18, 1861; *Journal of the Convention,* 82, 136–37, 143–45.

71. The plan provided that any new counties would simply be absorbed into the existing senatorial districts. The new constitution impeded the creation of new counties by requiring approval by a two-thirds vote of the General Assembly. *Journal of the Convention,* 156–60, 211–13, and Art. II, Sec. 2, paragraph 1, and Sec. 5, paragraph 2 of the new constitution, *ibid.,* 289, 291.

72. *Journal of the Convention,* 303.

73. The same amendment was added for representatives, who, in the first draft of the constitution, were not required to live in their counties. *Ibid.,* 251–53, 255; Art. II, Sec. 2, paragraph 2, *ibid.,* 289.

have personal qualities and experiences, as well as political constituencies, that inclined them to identify with the status quo.[74] The object of reduction, as one editor wrote, was "a body [of legislators] which would feel more personally and directly their responsibility."[75] The new senate, in contrast to the old, was designed to be more nearly a body of patriarchs.

But the patriarchal senators governed in a republic. The convention added to the new constitution the requirements that all elections of officials by the legislature be *viva voce,* rather than by secret ballot, and that the "yeas and nays" be recorded on all questions requiring a two-thirds majority for approval.[76] These provisions nicely demonstrated the limits that the tradition of republican government imposed on the patriarchal impulses of the delegates. On the one hand, these requirements permitted public scrutiny of certain important kinds of actions taken by the new legislators, reminding them of their responsibilities to their constituents. On the other hand, these provisions represented an attempt to guarantee that the new legislators would be the kind of men who could withstand the scrutiny of their constituents and their legislative colleagues.

The convention was not content merely to reduce the legislature. The new constitution explicitly denied certain powers which the legislature had exercised under the old constitution and circumscribed others, as we have seen. Although the new constitution gave the legislature the "power to make all laws and ordinances, consistent with this Constitution," the "Declaration of Fundamental Principles" in the new constitution included the provision that "Legislative Acts in violation of the fundamental law are void; and the Judiciary shall so declare them." By explicitly empowering the judiciary to review the constitutionality of legislation—in a part of the constitution which, it pro-

---

74. This concern to restructure the government to make it conform more to the needs and desires of dominant social groups is the antebellum southern counterpart of the later political reforms in city governments that Samuel P. Hays has examined in his article, "The Politics of Reform in Municipal Government in the Progressive Era," *Pacific Northwest Quarterly,* LV, (1964), 157–69.

75. Augusta *Chronicle and Sentinel,* February 15, 1861.

76. *Journal of the Convention,* 254–55, 268; Art. II, Sec. 4, paragraph 9, Art. V, paragraph 1, *ibid.,* 291, 299.

claimed, "shall never be violated on any pretence whatever"—the convention set up a definite and reliable institutional check on the legislature.[77] At the same time, the convention made it all the more vital that judges be men of proper character and standing.

AN INDEPENDENT JUDICIARY

If the courts were to be effective checks against the legislature, the old constitutional provisions had to be changed. The old requirements that the legislature elect supreme court judges and that the voters elect superior court judges and other court officers made the judges dependent on the groups they were supposed to check. Outside the convention, some Georgians complained that they were "thoroughly disgusted with so many, and such frequent, popular elections," and urged the convention to "take the election of Judges out of the hands of the people." A plan to do just that was presented to the convention before it recessed in January, and a revised form was eventually incorporated into the new constitution.[78] But since the debate on the judiciary question occurred while the convention was in secret session, the opinions of the delegates can only be surmised.

The provision in the new constitution that the supreme court "shall be appointed by the Governor with the advice and consent of two-thirds of the Senate, for such a term of years as shall be prescribed by law" disappointed some delegates because it did not give judges tenure for life or "good behavior." Others wanted to retain the provisions of the old constitution. but a proposal to substitute the old provisions for the new ones was defeated soundly, 63 to 151. Although the old provisions were favored by a larger proportion of hard-core cooperationists than of secessionists or of cooperationists who had voted for the secession ordinance, a majority of all groups were in

77. For the grant of power, see Art. II, Sec. 5, paragraph 1, *Journal of the Convention,* 291. Art. I, paragraph 17, *ibid.,* 286. Art. I, paragraph 28, *ibid.,* 287. The old constitution made clear that the Supreme Court was not given powers of judicial review. See Art. III, Sec. 1, as amended in 1835, Thorpe (ed.), *Federal and State Constitutions,* II, 806.

78. See the provisions in the old constitution, Art. III, Sec. 1, as amended in 1835, Thorpe (ed.), *Federal and State Constitutions,* II, 806–807. Augusta *Chronicle and Sentinel,* November 24, 1860, February 15, 1861; Georgia to editor, Macon *Telegraph,* January 24, 1861. The resolution was offered by W. B. Fleming of Liberty County, *Journal of the Convention,* 115–17.

favor of the new provisions. The bulk of the delegates agreed that the supreme court should be completely independent of the house of representatives and dependent on the senate only for "advise and consent" to their appointment, a provision which would "prevent the Governor from making Judicial honors the reward of demagogues, time-servers and party hacks," one Georgian pointed out.[79]

The new constitution provided that judges of the superior courts would no longer be elected by the voters but would be appointed in the same manner as supreme court judges, for a four-year term. These judges had exclusive jurisdiction in certain civil cases and all criminal cases—except those involving "people of color"—and had the power, on appeal, to review rulings by lower courts and to correct errors and grant new trials. Many delegates opposed taking the election of judges with such extensive powers away from the voters. A proposal to substitute the old constitutional provisions for electing superior court judges barely failed, 100 to 106.[80] Significantly, the conservative cooperationists who had voted for the secession ordinance voted three to two in favor of the appointment of superior court judges while the hard-core cooperationists voted better than three to two in favor of continued election of these judges. Those who had opposed secession partly out of fear of conservatives and their ideas were learning that their fears were well founded. Their conservative former colleagues in cooperation were in fact realizing some of the possibilities that had attracted them to secession.

The delegates sought to insulate judges from the "party bias" of the legislature and the opinion of the voters. "Judges ought not to be elected by the people over whom they preside," T. R. R. Cobb explained, "because it throws in the way of every Judge a temptation in *doubtful cases* to lean to the popular side." And the requirement that

79. The life tenure provision was included in the Fleming proposal. *Journal of the Convention*, 116. For the provision in the new constitution, see Art. IV, Sec. 1, paragraph 2, *ibid.*, 296. Herschel V. Johnson offered the substitute. *Ibid.*, 260–64; Georgia to editor, Macon *Telegraph*, January 24, 1861.

80. Art. IV, Sec. 2, paragraph 1, *Journal of the Convention*, 297. The constitution provided for the continued election of inferior court judges. Art. IV, Sec. 2, and Sec. 3, *ibid.*, 297–99, 264–67. On a separate motion, the state's attorney and solicitors were also made no longer elective, but appointive, in the same manner as supreme court judges. *Ibid.*, 268. Art. IV, Sec. 3, paragraph 2, *ibid.*, 298.

two-thirds of the senate approve judicial appointments would insure that *"politicians can never control the selection of judges,"* Cobb said. The judicial provisions would not only "encourage" judicial "independence and fearlessness" but they would also yield better judges. "Whatever may have been heretofore the high standard of your judges," President Crawford told the delegates, "that standard will be advanced still higher to independence and legal attainments."[81] The changes made by the delegates were thus implicit protests both about the degree of popular authority that judges had been subject to during the nineteenth century and about the quality of the judges on the bench. The "fearlessness" which the delegates sought in the judges was to be found not in dependence on the people but in independence of them and in reliance on the individual judge's strength of character. The majesty of the law would thus come less from the voters or their representatives than from the judges themselves. The delegates did not object to a higher law so long as they wrote it and fearless, independent judges administered it and interpreted it.

THE CONSTITUTION AND THE PEOPLE

The convention trusted the voters with the election of legislators whose powers were safely circumscribed and whose actions were subject to judicial review. But voters were cautioned to exercise their political privileges responsibly. To the guarantee of what had been First Amendment freedoms under the United States Constitution, the convention added the warning that "while every citizen may freely speak, write and print, on any subject, he shall be responsible for the abuse of the liberty."[82] Chastened, the voters were entrusted to continue to exercise their franchise as under the old constitution. But the convention was not willing to entrust them with the keeping of the fundamental law. The convention delegates acted as if they believed that the old constitution had been entirely too mutable.

Under the old constitution, the legislature proposed and approved constitutional amendments. A proposed amendment had to be ap-

81. Georgia to editor, Macon *Telegraph,* January 24, 1861; Cobb, speech to citizens of Athens, April 6, 1861, Athens *Southern Banner,* April 10, 1861; *Journal of the Convention,* 303.
82. Art. I, paragraph 8, *Journal of the Convention,* 286.

proved by a two-thirds majority of both houses, then published at least six months before the next election of legislators, and finally approved by being repassed by a two-thirds vote of the newly elected legislators.[83] Instead of allowing the power of amendment to continue to rest in the legislature, in spite of—and probably in part because of—the requirement for indirect voter approval of the legislators' actions, the convention provided that the new constitution "shall be amended only by a Convention of the people called for that purpose." The first draft of the new constitution even tried to guarantee that such a convention would be composed of a small group of men with reputations and social outlooks that were not confined by counties. It provided that a convention should consist of not more than 150 delegates, an equal number being chosen by and from each Congressional district existing at the time.[84] Although this restriction on the future was struck out in an unrecorded vote during the convention's secret session, the remaining amendment procedure tried to guarantee that no future convention would do what the present one had done.

It is hard to believe that the delegates were unaware that they were drafting a constitution in a way that was extraordinary and would have been unconstitutional under the provisions of both the old and the new constitutions. Their action was a measure of their confidence in themselves. As a group, the delegates would probably have agreed with T. R. R. Cobb's response to the charge of usurpation that was leveled against the convention. "I am not afraid of the popular judgment on a righteous act," Cobb announced. As the embodiment of the sovereignty of the people, the delegates apparently believed that their acts were righteous.[85] The assembled convention apparently saw itself as the only completely trustworthy repository of the sovereignty of the people.

The convention by no means ignored Georgia's voters. They simply bound the voters either to consent to what the convention had done or

83. See Art. IV, Sec. 15, Thorpe (ed.), *Federal and State Constitutions,* II, 801.

84. Art. V, paragraph 6, *Journal of the Convention,* 299, 249, 268.

85. Cobb, speech to citizens of Athens, April 6, 1861, Athens *Southern Banner,* April 10, 1861. See the remarks of Fouche and Bartow, Report of convention debates, March 9, 1861, Savannah *Morning News,* March 11, 13, 1861.

to reject it altogether. Proposals to allow voters to vote against portions of the constitution that they opposed or to vote separately on legislative reduction were defeated. Instead, the convention decided to submit the entire constitution to the voters to be ratified or rejected three months hence, on the second of July, 1861.[86] By rejecting proposals which would have allowed voters to exercise more choice than a single yes or no on the entire constitution, the convention delegates recognized the strength of democratic ideas and practices at the same time as they severely limited the range within which those established traditions could be expressed. In a sense, the delegates imposed upon the voters their images of the government of a southern utopia, a republic in which the voters spoke with one voice, yes or no.

On Saturday, March 23, 1861, the convention assembled for the last time. It adopted the new constitution as a whole, provided for the printing and general distribution of ten thousand copies, exempted the constitution and the ordinances of secession and ratification of the Confederate Constitution—among others—from "modification or repeal by the General Assembly," and then recessed until seven-thirty Saturday evening when they reconvened to receive the final copy of the new constitution, to extend their thanks to Cobb's committee for its "untiring zeal and signal ability," and to listen to President Crawford's closing remarks. "In the revision of your State Constitution," Crawford said, "you have, in my judgment, improved it by each alteration made in it. Nothing remains," he concluded, "after bidding you a cordial adieu, and wishing to each a safe return to his home, but to declare as I now do, that this Convention is finally adjourned."[87]

As the delegates went home, they had every reason to feel proud of themselves. They had made Georgia as they knew it more immune to

---

86. Again, the margin was not recorded nor was the debate, since it was during the secret session. *Journal of the Convention,* 268–71; Art. V, paragraph 7, *ibid.,* 300. Although it is true, as Ethel K. Ware has pointed out *(A Constitutional History of Georgia,* 122), that the 1861 constitution was the first to be submitted to the people for ratification, it is likewise true that it was the first constitution since 1798. Since the results of the conventions in the 1830s which attempted to equalize legislative representation were referred to the voters, it seems to me that the popular ratification provision of the new constitution was not a democratic innovation but a cautious deference to established democratic ideas and institutions.

87. *Journal of the Convention,* 272–302, 303.

political challenges than it had been in at least a generation. They had reduced the size of the senate and increased the size of the senatorial districts hoping thereby to filter into the senate men whose interests, outlook, and social standing inclined them to protect and maintain the status quo. They had denied the legislature the power to tamper with slavery or with other forms of property. They had entrusted the judiciary with the final word on the constitutionality of legislation and insulated the judges from shifting popular sentiments. And they had provided that any future constitutional changes would be made not by ordinary legislators but by convention delegates like themselves—men who stood above the hurly-burly, demagogic world of politics. They had done all this without changing the form of government or restricting the suffrage. It must have seemed to many that they had struck the proper balance, as T. R. R. Cobb put it, between "liberal political institutions," a "patriarchal and perfect social polity" and a "pure unadulterated simple Christian Faith." [88] They had designed a constitution for a patriarchal republic. The ensuing campaign for ratification reemphasized, in an unexpected way, the necessity of their efforts.

88. Cobb, speech to citizens of Athens, April 6, 1861, Athens *Southern Banner,* April 10, 1861.

9

Ratification:
The Second Revolution Completed

The Ratification Campaign

Soon after the convention adjourned, newspapers around the state published the complete text of the new constitution. Several editors noted that it contained "some radical changes from the old constitution." Before long, the changes were closely scrutinized and extensively discussed by the editors and some of their readers. Although the discussion was spirited and revealing, it was not part of a sustained, organized effort on the part of either proponents or opponents of the new constitution. Whatever the intentions of the leaders of either group may have been, the firing on Fort Sumter changed everything. When Major Robert Anderson surrendered the fort and marched his troops aboard the waiting federal ships, exactly three weeks after the Georgia convention had adjourned, the new Georgia constitution became much less important both to newspaper editors and to ordinary Georgians. Two days after Sumter was surrendered, on April 15, 1861, Lincoln declared that an insurrection existed and asked for 75,000 volunteers to put it down. Two days after that, Virginia seceded, to be followed into the Confederacy by Arkansas, Tennessee, and North Carolina. Newspaper columns brimmed with reports about war preparations, rumors of troop movements and minor skirmishes, and stories of the organization of local companies, of home defense units, and of ladies' aid societies. Troops marching in review, the presentation of hand-sewn colors by a local belle, emotion-choked farewells, and then waiting for letters and for news—time and again these scenes were reenacted in the towns and villages of Georgia during the late spring and early summer of 1861. The campaigns that Georgians thought about dealt with military not constitutional maneuvers. Four days before the ratification election, one editor noted that the war news had caused the new constitution to be "almost completely ignored." "The war sensation is so great," wrote another, "that we must remind our people [to vote]." [1]

It is somewhat surprising, then, that the new constitution elicited any discussion after the second week in April. But it did, and what was said was the best guide to the voters' actions on July 2. The results of the ratification election showed the voters' preoccupation both with the impending war and with the same problems that the convention delegates thought they had anticipated and, for the most part, resolved. Some of the delegates were probably shocked and distressed to learn that many Georgians thought the second revolution had not gone far enough. The delegates had expected to be "charged with usurpation" by those who tried, according to T. R. R. Cobb, to use "their feeble powers to bring the odium of our constituents upon the acts of our convention." [2] But it is most unlikely that the delegates had expected to be charged with creating a political threat to slavery. Instead, they had probably expected to be congratulated for protecting slavery and the social and political order.

Early in April, as the ratification campaign began, the convention delegates must have been gratified. Many newspapers noted that "the new Constitution is very decidedly preferable to the old," even though a few desirable reforms had not been included and a few included reforms were undesirable. The most extensive friendly analysis of the new constitution lamented that the membership of the house of representatives had not been reduced, thought that the appointment of superior court judges by the governor was "unnecessary" and "questionable" but not harmful, and doubted the wisdom of requiring a convention for any constitutional amendments. But most of the

1. Atlanta *Daily Intelligencer,* March 27, 1861. See also Augusta *Daily Constitutionalist,* March 26, 1861; Augusta *Chronicle and Sentinel,* March 26, 1861; Columbus *Daily Enquirer,* March 27, 1861; Athens *Southern Banner,* March 27, 1861; Rome *Weekly Courier,* March 28, June 28, 1861; Upson *Pilot,* June 22, 1861.
2. Cobb, speech to citizens of Athens, April 6, 1861, Athens *Southern Banner,* April 10, 1861.

changes were "valuable," the writer thought. "The excessive size of the Senate admitted into that body many persons, insignificant in character and intelligence," he wrote, pleased that the convention had reduced the senate and thereby ended "the reign of mice." On the whole, T. R. R. Cobb explained to his Athens townsmen, the changes were "good" ones.[3] In that faith, the proponents of the new constitution coasted through the three months before the election, confident of ratification, but more and more preoccupied with the developing war. Shortly before the July election, the favorable newspapers reminded their readers of the election and recommended a vote for ratification.[4]

Critics of the new constitution were almost equally becalmed by the war crisis. Soon after the convention adjourned, the editor of the Columbus *Daily Enquirer* pointed out that the new constitution did "not touch the radical evil," namely that the senate, though reduced, was "still the representative of counties . . . without respect to numbers, and THE PEOPLE as an element of political power are entirely ignored." And on the grounds that the constitution did not "reform the great and outrageous abuse of the principle of fair popular representation" and that the change in the amendment procedure "cuts off one of the existing modes by which this abuse may hereafter be corrected," the editor hoped the new constitution would be voted down. Another Georgian agreed with the editor's criticisms but thought they did not go far enough. He charged the convention with "acts of usurpation" and cited the changes in the method of selecting judges as proof. Why was the voice of the house of representatives excluded from the selection of supreme court judges, he asked, "unless it is for the purpose of inaugurating a policy of favoritism, or gradually to concentrate the elective franchise into the hands of the few." And since superior court judges and solicitors "are called to preside over affairs in which the people are immediately concerned . . . the people . . . should be the sole judges to

3. Ratification to editor, Augusta *Daily Constitutionalist,* April 3, 1861. See also, *ibid.,* March 26, 1861; Augusta *Chronicle and Sentinel,* March 26, 1861; Atlanta *Daily Intelligencer,* March 27, 1861; Rome *Weekly Courier,* March 28, 1861; Cobb, speech to citizens of Athens, April 6, 1861, Athens *Southern Banner,* April 10, 1861; Macon *Telegraph,* March 15, 20, 1861.

4. Rome *Weekly Courier,* June 18, 28, 1861; Albany *Patriot,* June 20, 1861; Upson *Pilot,* June 22, 1861; Milledgeville *Southern Federal Union,* June 25, 1861; Atlanta *Daily Intelligencer,* June 26, 1861.

determine who shall preside over them in the administration of justice," he argued. He appealed "to the voters of Georgia to suppress
every movement by your rulers to deprive you of your rights" and
urged them to seek their "remedy" at the ballot box by a vote against
ratification. But such criticisms failed to inflame men of similar views
to vocalize their opposition, probably because, as the critic noted,
"national troubles . . . [have] engaged our undivided attention."[5]

The most vocal opposition came from an unexpected quarter. Late in
June, the Savannah *Republican* warned "Middle and Southern Georgia" to beware of the new constitution. "[I]t is clear to our mind that
the intention of the framers of the new instrument was to alter radically
the system of representation . . . by substituting an exclusively white
for the old and well established mixed [or federal] basis," the editor
wrote. The result would be that three-fifths of the slaves would not be
counted, "thereby centering all power in the Legislature in the northern portion of the State!" If "the people of the large slave-holding
sections, Samson-like, quietly fall asleep . . . and allow this Delilah of
a convention thus to shear them of their power," the article said, it
"would be an act of suicide unparalleled in the history of a free
people."[6] The *Republican's* alarm sent shivers of fear through the
slaveholding population, converting friends of the new constitution
into foes.

The controversy centered on the new constitutional provision that
the "thirty-seven counties having the largest representative population" would get two representatives in the house, while all others
would get one. The old constitution made clear that "representative
population" was determined by "counting all free white persons, and
three-fifths of the people of color."[7] But the new constitution simply
used the term "representative population" without defining it. Many

5. Columbus *Daily Enquirer,* March 24, 27, 1861; Pitt to editor, Columbus *Daily Enquirer,*
April 26, June 17, 28, 1861.

6. The issue of the Savannah *Republican* containing this article was not available to me, and
therefore I do not know the exact date of publication. Judging from the responses to the article, it
must have been first published about June 25 or 26, 1861. The quotations are from a reprint of the
article which appeared in the Milledgeville Southern *Federal Union,* July 2, 1861 and Augusta
Daily Constitutionalist, July 2, 1861.

7. Art. II, Sec. 3, paragraph 1, *Journal of the Convention,* 289; Art. I, Sec. 7, as amended in
1843, Francis Newton Thorpe (ed.), *The Federal and State Constitutions* (7 vols., Washington:
Government Printing Office, 1909), II, 808.

believed the ambiguity was dangerous. Protests from convention delegates that they had assumed that "representative population" included
three-fifths of all slaves and reassurances that the Confederate Constitution used that definition failed to remove the unsettling ambiguity.[8] A detailed analysis of the new constitution trying to show that
the way the convention used the word "population" implied that
"slaves and free persons of color" were included was equally unavail-
ing. The editor of the Savannah *Republican* acknowledged that these
were good arguments, but thought that the effect they would have "on
the Legislature when it comes to apportion Representatives among the
counties, is altogether another question."[9]

At bottom, then this controversy was the resurgence of the fear
about internal enemies that the convention delegates thought they had
allayed. It seems probable that if the convention had specified that
three-fifths of black persons were to be counted, then the same fears
would have erupted in criticisms that the three-fifths clause was tainted
with implications of compromise with the enemies of slavery. These
fears were signs of a heightened, exaggerated awareness that a genuine
threat existed which was menacing enough to necessitate a double
revolution. What these Georgians feared, all professions of unity and
brotherhood aside, was the political challenge of slaveless Georgians.
While the ambiguity of "representative population" seemed harmless,
the danger lay in who would interpret the ambiguity. The constitution
"should be voted down for its ambiguity," one editor pointed out,
since the question would not be brought "before the Courts for adjudi-
cation" but would be settled "with a capricious or interested decision
by the Legislature."[10] The sovereignty of the people, that was the rub.

The Ratification Election

Governor Brown reported the results of the ratification election to the
legislature on November 6, 1861. "The vote cast was quite a small
one," he explained, "owing doubtless to the fact that the thoughts of

8. Augusta *Chronicle and Sentinel*, June 27, 1861; Pro-Slavery Man to editor, Macon *Telegraph*, June 29, 1861; Augusta *Daily Constitutionalist*, July 2, 1861; Milledgeville *Southern
Federal Union*, July 2, 1861; Old Constitution to editor and S. T. Bailey to editor, Macon
Telegraph, July 2, 1861.
9. Ratification to editor, Savannah *Republican*, July 2, 1861.
10. Augusta *Daily Constitutionalist*, July 2, 1861.

our people were so much engrossed with the war." But, he said, since "the Constitution had received the sanction of the Convention, composed as it was of so many of the brightest intellects and best men of the State, the people were, it would seem, generally willing to ratify their action without serious opposition." Apparently Brown defined "serious opposition" as something more than 48 percent of the voters, because that was the proportion of the voters who opposed ratification. The constitution was ratified by the bare margin of 795 votes out of 22,203: 11,499 in favor to 10,704 opposed.[11] It seems fair to question Brown's judgment about the seriousness of the opposition.

Although Brown was wrong about the magnitude of the opposition, he was right about the small turnout. Only one voter participated in the ratification election for every four who had voted for delegates to the secession convention. One editor wondered whether a constitution adoped by such a small vote should be the "fundamental law without another expression of the popular will." But newspapers across the state reported "little interest" in the July 2 election, and there was no effort to try again.[12]

Being "engrossed with the war" undoubtedly accounted for the apathy of some voters, as Governor Brown said. But the war also drew many men away from home, making it difficult if not impossible for them to vote, if they wanted to. For example, a Milledgeville editor reported that fewer than half of the eligible voters were present in his county at the time of the ratification election.[13] Still, many men who could have voted, did not. In town counties, where voting should have been easiest and voters most informed, the turnout was only 20 percent of that in the election of delegates to the secession convention. Indeed, in Fulton County, which included Atlanta, the turnout was a mere 6

---

11. Brown, message to legislature, in Allen D. Candler (ed.), *The Confederate Records of the State of Georgia* (Atlanta: Charles T. Byrd, 1909), II, 111–12. This total is corroborated (there was an insignificant difference of two votes) by a complete county-by-county tally that was published in the Augusta *Daily Constitutionalist,* August 17, 1861.

12. Columbus *Daily Enquirer,* July 9, 1861; Atlanta *Daily Intelligencer,* July 3, 4, 1861; Augusta *Daily Constitutionalist,* July 3, 4, 1861; Savannah *Republican,* July 3, 4, 6, 1861; Macon *Telegraph,* July 6, 1861; Milledgeville *Southern Federal Union,* July 9, 1861.

13. According to the editor (Milledgeville *Southern Federal Union,* July 9, 1861), only about 400 voters were in Baldwin County for the election; 219 actually voted. By comparison, 932 votes were cast in the 1860 presidential election and 568 for delegates to the secession convention.

percent. While the war was probably the major reason for voter apathy, the nature of the second revolution was probably a contributing factor. To a degree, voter apathy was a measure of the success of the second revolution. Voters who had gone to the polls at an earlier time were willing in July to trust their social and political leaders.

It is striking that as voter turnout increased, support for the new constitution decreased.[14] The counties with the highest turnout, 50 percent or more, voted two to one against the new constitution. At the other end of the turnout spectrum, in the counties where the turnout was less than 20 percent, two-thirds of the voters favored ratification. Likewise, the highest turnout, almost twice that in the rest of the state, was in the counties that most strongly opposed ratification. But as the support for ratification increased, the turnout remained about the same, between a third and a fourth of the voters who had voted in the January election. All this suggests that the overwhelming majority of the voters did not strongly oppose what their leaders had done for them. Only a small minority, although nearly half of those who actually voted, opposed the new constitution intensely enough to vote against it.

Almost half of the votes against ratification came from the Sixth Congressional District in northeast Georgia. This suggests that many of these voters were expressing once again their opposition to the antidemocratic tendencies in the secession movement. But if so, the intensity with which these sentiments were held was not shared by voters in the Fifth District in northwest Georgia, only 17 percent of whom turned out, 61 percent of them in favor of ratification. In the other Congressional Districts also, a majority of the few voters who turned out favored ratification. Clearly, the sectional division of the state that was exhibited in the secession election was not repeated in the ratification election.

However, the distribution of the ratification vote along the slaveholding, politics, and town-country axes was just what might be expected, given the results of the secession election. Low slaveholding Democratic country counties were the most pronounced opponents of ratification, just as they had been of secession. They gave the new constitution 39 percent of their votes. If the votes of the three low

14. For the tables that summarize the analysis of the ratification election, see Appendix.

slaveholding Whig counties—which were only 17 percent proratification—are included with the Democratic county votes, low slaveholding country counties gave 38 percent of their votes for ratification. In high slaveholding country counties, just as in the secession election, a majority—56 percent—was in favor of ratification. Also, parallel to the January election in these counties, Democratic counties were more strongly proratification than Whig counties, 77 percent to 46 percent. As we would expect, the strongest support for ratification was in town counties, where the new constitution received 69 percent of the vote, compared to 49 percent in the country counties. As in the secession election, Democratic town counties favored the new constitution with 77 percent of their vote, exceeding the 57 percent majority in Whig town counties.

Remarkably, the alignment of political forces that was disclosed by the secession election remained stable in the ratification election, in spite of the low turnout and the general preoccupation with the war. The support for ratification in town counties and high slaveholding country counties suggests that voters there were aware that their interests were better served by the new constitution. Likewise, the antiratification majority in low slaveholding counties suggests that those voters perceived the conservative innovations in the new constitution and expressed their preference for the more democratic old constitution. In short, the constituency of the second revolution was strikingly similar to that of the first revolution, as was the constituency of the opponents of the double revolution.

If there is a surprise in the ratification election results, it is that Whig counties did not favor ratification more strongly. Yet, it is likely that outside the low slaveholding counties the "representative population" controversy accounted for much of the opposition to the new constitution. Indeed, one editor speculated that if the question had not arisen, the vote in his county "would have been near unanimous for Ratification."[15] It is reasonable to suppose that many conservatives in Whig counties were particularly sensitive to the fears generated by the "representative population" question and opposed ratification for that rea-

15. Milledgeville *Southern Federal Union,* July 9, 1861. See also A Friend to editor, Savannah *Republican,* July 6, 1861; Columbus *Daily Enquirer,* July 9, 1861; Augusta *Daily Constitutionalist,* July 12, 1861.

son. The same fears that drove many conservatives toward secession might have brought them to oppose the new constitution, less because they opposed the conservative direction in which the new constitution moved than because they believed it had not gone far enough.

The old nightmares of internal subversion returned to haunt many Georgians, this time in the robes of the "representation population" question. These fears demonstrated that those who were afraid did not misread the degree of unity that Lincoln's military actions created among Georgians as anything more than a unity in defense. In fact, the unifying effect of military action was hoped for by some Georgians. Early in April one secessionist wrote that he hoped that reports of war were true, "for the longer we delay, the greater the division, which seems to be increasing among the people in this section, will grow, and I am in hopes that a brush or two will set them upon the proper basis."[16] Such comments made clear that although the immediate problem was in Washington, the final solution was at home, in Georgia.

The Second Revolution Completed

The second revolution, then, was successful. The new constitution failed to excite the determined opposition from democratically inclined opponents of secession that many delegates feared. And it weathered the active opposition of many Georgians who were expected to support it. But the plan for a patriarchal republic was slowly crushed by the impact of the war. The secession convention itself was thus both the beginning and the embodiment of the second revolution. The convention delegates and their actions stood as vivid reminders of what a patriarchal republic might have been. But they were just one of many memories of what might have been, except for the relentless military pressure from the North. On the eve of the ratification election "a magnificent comet" burst across the northwestern skies and it might well have been taken as an omen; "its nucleus was but a few degrees above the horizon, and its fiery tail reached nearly to the zenith."[17]

16. A. J. Hutchins to Dear Fritz, April 9, 1861, in Nathan L. Hutchins Papers, Duke University.
17. Savannah *Republican,* July 2, 1861.

Appendix

Some Precautions

Before beginning a detailed discussion of the quantitative results of this study, it is worth pointing out some potential pitfalls of an analytical approach that makes use of quantitative measures and methods. The ease with which numbers can be manipulated and the precision with which numerical results can be expressed can mislead us into thinking that our conclusions are as accurate and precise as our numbers. Certainly, it is possible to arrive at conclusions that are as firm and secure as that three is one more than two. We may strive for such solid conclusions, but we seldom achieve them. The basic reason is that while numbers are almost pure abstractions, persons and things are concrete and therefore, as good poets continually remind us, richly complex. The number one is a valid and useful abstraction whether or not it refers to one apple, one apple pandowdy, or one anything. When historians make generalizations about the complex reality of the past, the generalizations, like the number one, are abstractions. But unlike the number one, the historian's generalizations depend for their usefulness and validity upon the degree to which they accurately refer to a meaningful dimension of the actual past. While numbers are more or less independent of reality, historians are absolutely dependent upon it. As a result, historians must constantly be concerned with problems of evidence and problems of generalization, both of which mathematicians can legitimately ignore as colossal irrelevancies.

Historians use quantitative measures because they are convenient solutions to some of their problems of evidence and generalization.

189

Quantitative measures and methods of analysis can provide good answers to such questions as, "How many Georgians voted for secession?" or "How important was the influence of the 1860 Presidential vote on the vote for secession." But quantification by no means solves all historical problems, and if we fail to realize its limitations, it can cause problems of its own.

In this study, certain problems of evidence and generalization were particularly important. One of the basic pieces of evidence—the results of the election of delegates to the secession convention—is not known with absolute certainty.[1] Although the degree of uncertainty is quite limited, it is larger than was usual in elections in the nineteenth century. Given this uncertainty, our interpretation of the results of the election must be correspondingly cautious. A second problem of evidence raises not only the question of accuracy but also one of appropriateness. The census data which I used to analyze the voting returns was collected because it was important to the United States government at the time, and not because it was especially appropriate for subsequent analysis of the election returns. It is easy enough to imagine questions we might wish the census takers (or a pollster) had asked Georgians in the winter of 1860–1861. But such wishes are luxurious daydreams. Instead, we must dig into the evidence we do have: the census material, the election returns, and the records of what Georgians said and wrote which have survived the intervening century to be made available to interested scholars.

Closely related to these evidentiary problems are problems of generalization. These problems arise from the necessity of aggregation, of collecting individuals into groups of one sort or another. For example, when we speak of slaveholders or nonslaveholders, we have conceptually aggregated all persons who owned slaves into one group and all those who did not into another. While these rather routine mental exercises are legitimate, since they are absolutely necessary if we are to make generalizations, they are also somewhat dangerous. In this study, for example, the slaveholder group includes the many

1. For a discussion of the problem, see Michael P. Johnson, "A New Look at the Popular Vote for Delegates to the Georgia Secession Convention." *Georgia Historical Quarterly,* LVI (1972), 259–75.

Georgians who owned only one slave as well as the few who owned several hundred. And since we are especially concerned with the voting behavior of slaveholders, nonvoting slaveholders such as women and children are excluded from the group. This problem is magnified with the nonslaveholder group, which, by definition, includes only adult white males and excludes most actual nonslaveholders: women, children, and slaves. Although the definition is a sensible one—it is the behavior of adult white males we are interested in—it is sensible more because of our purpose than because it accurately reflects all kinds of nonslaveholders.

Aggregations also gloss over differences within groups and tend to suggest that the groups are more or less homogenous. The slaveholder and nonslaveholder groups, for example, suggest that a fundamental identity unites all those with slaves and divides them from those without, who are likewise united. Yet perhaps a man who was not a slaveholder but wanted to be was more like a slaveholder than a man who was a slaveholder but was somewhat indifferent about it. Or perhaps slaveholding planters and merchants were not united by their slaveholding but divided by their occupational identity, as nonslaveholding yeomen and mechanics might have been. Or perhaps small slaveholders were more like nonslaveholders than they were like large slaveholders. We may use quantitative measures, like other techniques, to try to test the degree to which these various possibilities are true. But the ambiguities that exist within the various categories we employ cannot be dissolved by quantitative or any other measures. The ambiguities are the price we pay for studying aggregates rather than individuals, for taking events rather than lives as our objects of investigation.

A special problem of aggregation is associated with the quantitative analysis of voting behavior. Most voting data was collected for some geographic unit; in Georgia in 1860 the unit was the county. We know much more about how counties voted than about how given individuals within a county voted. The problems which arise when what is true of counties is said to be true of individuals have themselves been aggregated under the umbrella of the "ecological fallacy." The ecological fallacy can be defined as the attribution of characteristics of an aggregate to the individuals who compose the aggregate. In this study, the ecological fallacy would be involved if one assumed either (1) that what is true of counties which are identifiable concentrations of social groups is also true of individuals in those social groups throughout the state; or (2) that what is true of a given county is also true of subgroups of individuals within that county. An example of the first error would be to argue that because counties with a high proportion of slaveholders favored secession, then most slaveholders favored secession. To argue that since a high slaveholding county favored secession by a two-to-one margin, then the slaveholders in the county did so too, would be an example of the second.

In many academic circles, the ecological fallacy is looked upon as something one commits, a kind of analytical sin. One path to righteousness is to interview individuals, as modern pollsters do.[2] Not only is this path closed to students of the nineteenth century, but also, like all righteous courses, it has its own dangerous passages, which its proponents sometimes ignore.[3] A second path around the ecological fallacy is to use multiple regression techniques to estimate the behavior of individuals given the behavior of larger aggregate units.[4] While this is a desirable path to follow in some circumstances, this is not one of them. The reason is that the method involves a fundamental assumption which we have good reason to believe is not true. The assumption, as an advocate of the method has recently put it, is "that a sub-group of the population will behave similarly no matter what percentage the

2. For a good discussion of the applicability of the findings of modern polling techniques to earlier periods, see Jerome M. Clubb and Howard W. Allen (eds.), *Electoral Change and Stability in American Political History* (New York: Free Press, 1971), vii–xix. For the views of an advocate of the use of votes to study past public opinion, see Lee Benson, "An Approach to the Scientific Study of Past Public Opinion," *Public Opinion Quarterly,* XXXI (1967–68), 522–67.

3. In general, problems arise from the interaction between the pollster and the person being polled. A lively discussion of the problem of interaction with some ingenious suggestions for avoiding it is Eugene J. Webb *et al., Unobtrusive Measures: Nonreactive Research in the Social Sciences* (Chicago: Rand McNally, 1966).

4. The following sequence of articles in the *Journal of Interdisciplinary History* is a good introduction to historical applications of the regression method: E. Terrence Jones, "Ecological Inference and Electoral Analysis," II (1972), 249–62; J. Morgan Kousser, "Ecological Regression and the Analysis of Past Politics," IV (1973), 237–62; Allan J. Lichtman, "Correlation, Regression, and the Ecological Fallacy: A Critique," IV (1974), 417–33; and Jones, "Using Ecological Regression," IV (1974), 593–96.

group forms of the total population of each county. Actually, it works out mathematically that we need not assume a sub-group behaves in *exactly* the same manner from county to county, but only that its behavior changes *randomly* when its proportion in the population varies."[5] In other words, we must assume that the vote of a nonslaveholder is the same whether he lives in a county whose population is 90 percent nonslaveholders or 90 percent slaveholders, with only random variations. Not only does this seem in fact to have been untrue in Georgia, but also it was widely acknowledged at the time that given groups behaved quite differently in different areas. Therefore I have not adopted this method of avoiding the ecological fallacy.

Instead, my route around the ecological fallacy is interpretive rather than analytical. In a sense, I have made a virtue out of a vice. That is, I have spoken of the behavior of geographic units rather than the behavior of individuals, except when I am reasonably certain of what individuals were doing. This approach assumes the importance of environmental influences on individual behavior.[6] As I have argued in the text, there is abundant evidence that different social environments were indeed associated with different political behaviors. Indeed, it seems odd to assume that individual behavior is independent of social context. Or perhaps it only seems odd to me because I live in Orange County, California. In any case, I have tipped my hat to the ecological fallacy and tried to pass by it quietly, respectfully keeping my distance.

These preliminary precautions about the problems of evidence and generalization will remind us, I hope, that with quantitative methods, as with any other, we should not relax our skeptical guard, but double it. As Alfred North Whitehead admonished, we must seek simplicity, then distrust it.

5. Kousser, "Ecological Regression," 247.
6. For other studies that document the importance of local environment, see Thomas B. Alexander *et al.,* "The Basis of Alabama's Ante-Bellum Two-Party System: A Case Study in Party Alignment and Voter Response in the Traditional Two-party System of the United States by Quantitative Analysis Methods," *Alabama Review,* XIX (1966), 243–76; and, for the modern period, David R. Segal and Marshall W. Meyer, "The Social Context of Political Partisanship," in Mattei Dogan and Stein Rokkan (eds.), *Quantitative Ecological Analysis in the Social Sciences* (Cambridge: M.I.T. Press, 1969), 217–32. If I had been able to locate a sufficient number of ward or beat returns for the January 2 election, it might have been possible to refine the analysis by looking at voting patterns within counties. Unfortunately, I could not locate such data.

The Data

For analysis, I used the election returns of January 2, 1861, which are the most generous estimate of the popular support for immediate secession.[7] To analyze the returns, I calculated the following measurements of important social, economic, and political variables in each county:

   1. *Slaves*—the proportion of slaves in the total county population; the data were taken from *Population of the United States in 1860; Compiled from the Original Returns of the Eighth Census . . . .* (Washington: Government Printing Office, 1864), 72–73, which was also the source for all the other population calculations;

   2. *Slaveholders*—the proportion of voters in the county in the 1860 presidential election who were slaveholders (Since I have assumed that all slaveholders in each county could vote in 1860 and did so, this figure is a maximum.); the data on slaveholders were obtained from *Agriculture of the United States in 1860; Compiled from the Original Returns of the Eighth Census . . . .* (Washington: Government Printing Office, 1864), 226–27, and the 1860 presidential returns were taken from Walter Dean Burnham, *Presidential Ballots, 1836–1892* (Baltimore: Johns Hopkins Press, 1955), 333–63, which was the source for all other calculations using the returns of presidential elections;

   3. *Planters*—the percent of county voters in the 1860 presidential election who were planters, *i.e.,* who held twenty or more slaves (Again, since I have assumed all planters voted, this is a maximum figure.); the data came from the same sources listed for item (2) above;

   4. *Wealth*—the aggregate estate value of the county in dollars per capita white; the aggregate estate value data came from *Statistics of the United States, (Including Mortality, Property, &c.), in 1860* (Washington: Government Printing Office, 1866), 298.

   5. *Staple crop production*—the total pounds of cotton, tobacco, and rice produced in the county per year per capita white; the crop production data were from *Agriculture . . . in 1860,* pp. 22–29.

   6. *Breckinridge voters*—the proportion of voters in the county who favored Breckinridge in the 1860 presidential election;

7. See Johnson, "A New Look at the Popular Vote for Delegates to the Georgia Secession Convention."

7. *Politics*—the mean percent of Democratic voters in the county in the presidential elections from 1836 through 1856; for the numerous counties which were created during that period, I calculated the returns for the years in which the county did not exist by taking the mean for those years from the means of the older counties from which a given new county was created; the information on the organization of counties was taken from Burnham, *Presidential Ballots,* pp. 904–905.

8. *Towns*—the proportion of county population which lived in a town or village; the town populations were taken from *Population of the United States in 1860,* p. 74.

9. *Manufacturing*—the dollar value of manufactured products produced in the county per year per capita white; the data on manufactures came from *Manufactures of the United States in 1860: Compiled from the Original Returns of the Eighth Census . . . .* (Washington Government Printing Office, 1865), 61–79.

Secession Election Data
Analysis

ALL COUNTIES

The correlation matrix in Table 1 shows that although there are a number of highly correlated variables, the correlation coefficients for the proportion of voters for secession are generally low, ranging from a high of .332 with the Breckinridge variable to a low of .079 with manufacturing.

To reduce the data and to ferret out the minimum number of factors, factor analysis was performed, using principal factoring with iteration and varimax orthogonal rotation. The resulting factor matrix is displayed in Table 2. It demonstrates that the variables are grouped into three factors: a slaveholding factor, a political factor, and a town factor. Again, the vote for secession has a low loading on all three factors. Thus, while factor analysis helps us see the factors that are measured by the independent variables, it does not indicate a strong relationship between any factor and the vote for secession. To illustrate the relationship that does exist, and to translate the correlation coefficients and factor loadings into more concrete terms, we can see how

Table 1
Correlation Matrix for All Counties
Pearson Product Moment Correlation Coefficients

	(1) Slaves	(2) Slave-holders	(3) Planters	(4) Wealth	(5) Staple Crop	(6) Breckin-ridge	(7) Politics	(8) Towns	(9) Mfg.	(10) Secession
1. Slaves	1.000									
2. Slave-holders	.902	1.000								
3. Planters	.908	.868	1.000							
4. Wealth	.883	.771	.847	1.000						
5. Staple Crop	.673	.568	.711	.674	1.000					
6. Breckin-ridge	-.379	-.358	-.287	-.350	.053	1.000				
7. Politics	-.434	-.417	-.328	-.332	-.104	.669	1.000			
8. Towns	.135	.047	.043	.322	.137	.010	.049	1.000		
9. Manufac-turing	.342	.270	.291	.435	.359	-.131	-.181	.523	1.000	
10. Secession	.239	.201	.182	.272	.242	.332	.127	.249	.079	1.000

Table 2
FACTOR MATRIX FOR ALL GEORGIA COUNTIES*

Factor Loadings

	Slaveholding Factor	Political Factor	Town Factor
Slaveholding Factor			
Slaves	.954	−.165	−.091
Slaveholders	.877	−.175	−.044
Planters	.956	−.072	.107
Wealth	.869	−.106	.010
Staple Crop	.744	.213	−.174
Political Factor			
Breckinridge	−.202	1.035	−.091
Politics	−.351	.660	−.044
Town Factor			
Towns	.056	.117	.909
Manufacturing	.313	−.033	.552
Secession	.254	.360	.176

*These factors are the result of principal factor analysis with iteration using varimax rotation. This method of rotation achieves maximum separation of factors. On the procedure used here, see Norman H. Nie, *et al.*, *SPSS, Statistical Package for the Social Sciences* (New York: McGraw-Hill, 1970), 208–44. On factor analysis in general, the best introduction is Rudolph Rummell, "Understanding Factor Analysis," *Journal of Conflict Resolution*, XI (1967), 444–80 or see *idem, Applied Factor Analysis* (Evanston, Ill.: Northwestern University Press, 1970).

the vote for secession varied with each of the variables within each factor.

Slaveholding Factor

The relationships between the popular vote for secession and the variables in the slaveholding factor are presented in Tables 3 to 7. One clear pattern that emerges is that the voters in the lowest categories in each table gave the least support to secession. While the converse pattern is less clear-cut, voters in the highest categories tended to give

Table 3

POPULAR VOTE FOR SECESSION IN COUNTIES
RANKED BY SLAVES*

Slaves	Percent of Voters for Secession	Number of Counties
0–14%	41	20
15–29%	48	30
30–44%	54	20
45–59%	61	37
60–80%	50	25

*Throughout the tables, I have rounded the percentages to the nearest integer. Not only does this make the tables easier to read, but it also provides a more realistic picture of the uncertainties contained in the estimated election returns.

Table 4

POPULAR VOTE FOR SECESSION IN COUNTIES
RANKED BY SLAVEHOLDERS

Slaveholders	Percent of Voters for Secession	Number of Counties
0–14%	34	13
15–29%	50	30
30–44%	57	34
45–59%	56	30
60–80%	53	25

Table 5

POPULAR VOTE FOR SECESSION IN COUNTIES
RANKED BY PLANTERS

Planters	Percent of Voters for Secession	Number of Counties
0– 3%	47	54
4– 7%	58	19
8–15%	52	29
16–25%	57	15

Table 6

POPULAR VOTE FOR SECESSION IN COUNTIES
RANKED BY WEALTH

Wealth	Percent of Voters for Secession	Number of Counties
$0– $600	43	44
$601–$1200	52	31
$1201–$1800	56	26
$1801–$2400	57	20
$2401–$4000	61	11

strong support to secession (see especially Tables 6 and 7). The tables also show that the popular vote for secession did not consistently increase with increases in the variables.

Political Factor

Tables 8 and 9 present the relation between the vote for secession and the variables in the political factor. In general, the areas that voted against Breckinridge gave the least support to secession, as did the areas that traditionally gave the least support to the Democratic party. On the other hand, traditionally Democratic areas and areas favoring

Table 7

POPULAR VOTE FOR SECESSION IN COUNTIES
RANKED BY STAPLE CROP PRODUCTION

Staple Crop Production (in lbs.)	Percent of Voters for Secession	Number of Counties
0– 24	41	16
25– 99	45	23
100– 200	55	15
201– 500	57	16
501– 900	52	27
901–1500	49	21
1501–9900	76	14

Table 8

POPULAR VOTE FOR SECESSION IN COUNTIES
RANKED BY BRECKINRIDGE VOTERS

Breckinridge	Percent of Voters for Secession	Number of Counties
0– 29%	40	17
30– 39%	42	16
40– 49%	49	18
50– 59%	55	35
60– 69%	64	22
70–100%	54	24

Breckinridge in 1860 supported secession. Again, however, support for secession does not consistently increase as the measured characteristics increased.

Town Factor

Tables 10 and 11 show the results for variables within the town factor. In general, voters in the countryside and in the lowest manufacturing areas opposed secession while town voters and voters in the higher manufacturing areas favored secession. Here, unlike in the other two factors, support for secession increased as the variables increased until, at the highest levels, the secessionist sentiment was very strong.

Table 9

POPULAR VOTE FOR SECESSION IN COUNTIES
RANKED BY POLITICS

Percent of Democratic Voters, 1836–56	Percent of Voters for Secession	Number of Counties
0– 39%	39	21
40– 49%	56	31
50– 59%	55	33
60–100%	51	47

Table 10
POPULAR VOTE FOR SECESSION IN COUNTIES
RANKED BY TOWN POPULATION

Town Population	Percent of Voters for Secession	Number of Counties	Towns in This Category
0	46	103	None
1– 10%	52	10	(A)
11– 30%	67	12	(B)
31– 60%	64	3	(C)
61–100%	77	4	(D)

(A) Alpharetta (200), Calhoun (187), Carrollton (319), Cassville (639), Darien (570), Gaines-ville (344), Oglethorpe (454), Sumnerville (350), Valdosta (166), Waynesboro (307)

(B) Albany (1,618), Bainbridge (1,869), Brunswick (825), Centre (356), Eatonton (2,009), Knoxville (1,811), Marietta (2,680), Milledgeville (2,480), Newnan (2,546), Palmetto (1,526), Rome (4,010), St. Mary's (650)

(C) Athens (4,721), Augusta (12,493), Macon (8,247)

(D) Atlanta (9,554), Columbus (9,621), Newton (3,225), Savannah (22,292)

Table 11
POPULAR VOTE FOR SECESSION IN COUNTIES
RANKED BY MANUFACTURING

Manufacturing	Percent of Voters for Secession	Number of Counties
$0–$14	48	71*
$15–$29	51	27
$30–$59	52	17
$60–$89	57	9
$90 and over	69	8

*This includes 23 counties for which the *Census* reported no returns.

Multiple Regression

Having surveyed measures of the strength of the relationship that exists between the vote for secession and other variables, we can use multiple regression analysis to investigate the form of the relationship. Specifically, we can learn how much of the variation in the vote for secession can be attributed to the measured variables as well as the relative contribution of each of the major variables to the regression equation.

Table 12 shows the variables that were entered into the stepwise multiple regression analysis. The slaveholder variable was chosen to represent the slaveholding factor even though it did not have the heaviest loading on the factor (see Table 2). The conceptual clarity of the proportion of slaveholders among the voters outweighed the relatively small difference between the slaveholding variable and the slave and planter variables. The political factor is represented by both the Breckinridge and politics variables. Both were used because they are separated widely in time. While all the variables in the slaveholding factor are contemporaneous, politics measures a twenty-year time span, 1836–1856, and Breckinridge refers only to 1860. Although there is a .669 correlation between these two variables, it is below a .700 cutoff for excluding variables on grounds of multicollinearity.[8] The town variable represents the town factor. Finally, the new variable *turnout* represents the proportion of the 1860 presidential voters who voted in the secession election.

As Table 12 shows, these variables accounted for just over 32 percent of the variation in the vote for secession. The beta coefficients demonstrate that the vote for Breckinridge was over twice as important as either the slaveholder or town variables and over seven times more important than past presidential preferences. Turnout had about the same impact as the town variable, but in the opposite direction.

The apparent unimportance of past political affiliation to the vote for secession is made more striking by its great importance to the vote for Breckinridge. As Table 13 shows, politics was the major variable in

8. See Charles M. Dollar and Richard J. Jensen, *Historian's Guide to Statistics, Quantitative Analysis and Historical Research* (New York: Holt, Rinehart and Winston, 1971), 88–90.

Table 12

STEPWISE MULTIPLE REGRESSION ANALYSIS OF SECESSION VOTE IN ALL COUNTIES

Dependent Variable: Vote for Secession

Variables	Multiple R	R Square	R-Square Change	Simple R	B	Standard Error of B	Beta
1. Breckinridge	.332	.111	.111	.332	.666	.130	.509
2. Slaveholder	.478	.228	.118	.201	.393	.119	.279
3. Turnout	.530	.281	.053	−.262	−.244	.090	−.211
4. Towns	.565	.320	.039	.249	.372	.136	.203
5. Politics	.568	.322	.002	.127	−.129	.190	−.070

accounting for the Breckinridge vote. By itself it accounted for almost 45 percent of the variation in the Breckinridge vote. In contrast, the town and slaveholding variables were much more important in the vote for secession than they were in the vote for Breckinridge, where their influence was almost negligible, at least compared to politics.

The general pattern revealed by the analysis so far is that (1) the vote for Breckinridge was the single most important influence on the vote for secession; (2) although the vote for Breckinridge was mostly influenced by past presidential preferences, the vote for secession was not—suggesting that in the vote for secession a new alignment of political forces was emerging; (3) in the new alignment, the town and slaveholding factors were much more important than they had been in the 1860 Presidential election.

Table 13

STEPWISE MULTIPLE REGRESSION OF BRECKINRIDGE VOTE IN ALL COUNTIES

Dependent Variable: Vote for Breckinridge

Variables	Multiple R	R Square	R-Square Change	Simple R	B	Standard Error of B	Beta
1. Politics	.669	.448	.448	.669	.892	.102	.631
2. Slaveholder	.675	.455	.008	−.358	−.101	.077	−.094
3. Town	.675	.455	.000	.010	−.023	.091	−.016

COUNTIES CATEGORIZED BY BRECKINRIDGE AND SECESSION VOTES

Since the vote for Breckinridge was the best single indicator of the vote for secession, we may study the impact of the 1860 presidential election in more detail by looking at those counties that voted in accordance with their 1860 vote and those that did not. Counties that voted more or less consistently can be divided into pro-Breckinridge-prosecession counties and anti-Breckinridge–antisecession counties. Pro-Breckinridge–antisecession counties and anti-Breckinridge-prosecession counties voted differently than we would have expected, given their 1860 presidential votes.

County Characteristics

Table 14 shows that pro-Breckinridge–prosecession counties differed from anti-Breckinridge–antisecession counties primarily by giving almost twice as many votes for Breckinridge, by having a history of preference for Democratic presidential candidates, by having a larger mean proportion of town population, and by giving well over twice as many votes for secession. Both sets of counties had about the same high proportions of slaves, slaveholders, and planters, and comparable wealth and staple crop figures, and about the same turnout.

Of the counties that voted against Breckinridge, those that voted for secession differed from those that opposed secession primarily in their higher wealth, their much higher proportion of town population, and in their resounding support for secession. Otherwise, anti-Breckinridge–prosecession counties shared the characteristics of anti-Breckinridge–antisecession counties: similar high proportions of slaves, slaveholders, and planters, similar staple crop production figures, the same low proportion of Breckinridge voters, the same history of opposition to Democratic presidential candidates, and very similar turnout rates. Thus, anti-Breckinridge–prosecession counties differed from pro-Breckinridge–prosecession counties in their opposition to Breckinridge and to other Democratic presidential candidates and in their higher proportion of town population.

The most strikingly different set of counties were those which voted

Table 14

CHARACTERISTICS OF COUNTIES CATEGORIZED BY
BRECKINRIDGE AND SECESSION VOTES

Means

	Pro-Breckinridge– Prosecession	Anti-Breckinridge– Antisecession	Anti-Breckinridge– Prosecession	Pro-Breckinridge– Antisecession
Slave	42%	47%	52%	19%
Slaveholder	43%	47%	48%	22%
Planter	7%	8%	10%	2%
Wealth	$1269	$1343	$2081	$520
Staple Crop	995 lbs	712 lbs	740 lbs	125 lbs
Breckinridge	61%**	32%*	32%*	59%*
Politics	56%	42%	42%	62%
Town	7%	1%	18%	2%
Turnout	76%	79%	76%	98%
Secession	70%*	31%*	63%*	36%*
N	57	32	14	29**

*These figures are not means. In each case they represent the actual percentage of the vote.

**In two counties, Banks and Forsyth, although 51% of the popular vote was for secession, one of the two convention delegates voted for cooperation (suggesting that the 51% secession majority may be an artifact created by a delegate elected as a cooperationist voting as a secessionist in the convention), and nearly three out of four voters in these counties favored Breckinridge in 1860. Therefore, the counties are included here.

for Breckinridge and against secession. These counties had less than half the number of slaves and slaveholders of the other sets of counties, less than a third as many planters, less than half the wealth, and less than a fifth the staple crop production. Yet these pro-Breckinridge–antisecession counties gave Breckinridge about the same proportion of their votes as did pro-Breckinridge–prosecession counties and they surpassed the latter's loyalty to Democratic presidential candidates of the past, although they gave about half the number of votes for secession, nearly matching the low figure for secession in anti-Breckinridge–antisecession counties. Finally, in these pro-Breckinridge–antisecession counties nearly every voter voted in the secession election who had voted in the 1860 presidential election. In these counties only two voters in one hundred failed to vote in the secession election while in the other sets of counties between twenty-four and twenty-one voters in a hundred stayed away from the polls.

Shifts of Voters Toward Secession

We would expect shifts of voters in anti-Breckinridge–prosecession counties and in pro-Breckinridge–antisecession counties and there may well have been voter shifts in the other, apparently consistent counties. Since we cannot know for certain exactly which 1860 voters voted in 1861, we must estimate the voter shift. If we want to measure the shift of voters toward secession (that is, from opposition to Breckinridge to support for secession) we can arrive at the *minimum* voter shift by subtracting the number of Breckinridge votes from the number of secession votes. If there were more secession voters than Breckinridge voters, then there had to be voters who voted for secession who had not voted for Breckinridge. Since turnout in the secession election almost never exceeded the 1860 turnout (*i.e.*, very few voters voted in the secession election who had not voted in 1860), it is reasonable to assume that these voters shifting toward secession had opposed Breckinridge in 1860. Table 15 shows that in anti-Breckinridge–prosecession counties a minimum of 2,710 voters shifted *toward* secession. The other sets of counties showed a minimum shift of voters away from secession, ranging from a high of 5,448 voters in pro-

Table 15

ESTIMATED VOTER SHIFT TOWARD SECESSION IN COUNTIES
CATEGORIZED BY BRECKINRIDGE AND SECESSION VOTE

	Voters		
	Minimum Estimate	Maximum Estimate	N
Pro-Breckinridge–Prosecession	−3255	+2738	57
Anti-Breckinridge–Antisecession	−1940	− 204	32
Anti-Breckinridge–Prosecession	+2710	+5283	14
Pro-Breckinridge–Antisecession	−5448	−5184	29

Breckinridge–antisecession counties to a low of 1,940 in anti-Breckinridge–antisecession counties.

While these minimum estimates measure the voter shift that certainly occurred, it is likely that the shift toward secession was in fact larger than the minimum because of the lower turnout in the secession election. That is, if a Breckinridge voter failed to vote in the secession election, but a Breckinridge opponent in the same county voted for secession, our minimum estimate would not count the voter who had in fact shifted toward secession. We can attempt to solve this problem by constructing a maximum estimate which takes turnout into account. If we assume that the turnout in a county was the same for both opponents and supporters of Breckinridge (that is, if a county had an 80 percent turnout, then the voters included 80 percent of the Breckinridge voters and 80 percent of the anti-Breckinridge voters), then we can calculate the Breckinridge voters we estimate to have voted in 1860, given the turnout (that is, we multiply the number of voters for Breckinridge by the turnout rate), and subtract that figure from the vote for secession to get an estimate of the *maximum* voter shift.

As Table 15 shows, the largest maximum voter shift toward secession (5283) was in anti-Breckinridge–prosecession counties, followed by a shift of 2,738 voters toward secession in pro-Breckinridge–procession counties. Anti-Breckinridge–antisecession counties displayed a very small shift of voters away from secession while in pro-Breckinridge–antisecession counties a maximum of 5,184 voters shifted away from secession. The reason there is relatively little difference between the maximum and minimum shifts in pro-Breckinridge–antisecession counties is the very high turnout in these counties—the maximum number of Breckinridge voters who failed to vote was very small.

Multiple Regression

As the R-square column of Table 16 shows, the variables account for a much greater proportion of the vote for secession in the anti-Breckinridge counties than in the pro-Breckinridge counties. The variables measured contribute only 3 percent to the vote for secession in the pro-Breckinridge–anti-secession counties. Although the variables are more important in the pro-Breckinridge–prosecession counties, accounting for about 14 percent of the variation, they fall far short of the 55 percent and 70 percent that they account for in the anti-Breckinridge counties. Turnout is the most important variable in all but the pro-Breckinridge–antisecession counties, its beta coefficient ranging from a −.843 in anti-Breckinridge–prosecession counties, through a −.299 in pro-Breckinridge–prosecession counties to a .461 in anti-Breckinridge–antisecession counties. In anti-Breckinridge–prosecession counties, which had an important town component, turnout alone accounted for almost 60 percent of the variation in the vote for secession. The negative sign of the beta coefficient in these counties indicates that as turnout increased, the vote for secession decreased. This suggests that in these counties, voters who opposed secession stayed away from the polls. In contrast, in the anti-Breckinridge–antisecession counties, which did not have a large town population, the beta coefficient is positive, which indicates that the vote for secession increased as the turnout increased, suggesting that the voters who stayed away from the polls were probably in favor of secession. Thus, even though we measured a maximum voter shift toward secession of −204 voters in these counties (Table 15), it is

Table 16

STEPWISE MULTIPLE REGRESSION ANALYSIS FOR COUNTIES
CATEGORIZED BY BRECKINRIDGE AND SECESSION VOTES

Dependent Variable: Vote for Secession

	Multiple R	R Square	R-Square Change	Simple R	B	Standard Error B	Beta
Pro-Breckinridge–Prosecession Counties (N=57)							
1. Turnout	.332	.110	.110	−.332	−.244	.111	−.299
2. Town	.366	.134	.024	.196	.182	.155	.153
3. Slaveholder	.372	.138	.004	.158	.064	.157	.057
4. Politics	.372	.138	.000	−.004	−.032	.211	−.020
Anti-Breckinridge–Antisecession Counties (N=32)							
1. Turnout	.646	.417	.417	.646	.378	.125	.461
2. Breckinridge	.721	.520	.103	.599	.421	.221	.365
3. Town	.730	.533	.013	.079	.374	.537	.094
4. Slaveholder	.737	.542	.009	−.150	.094	.137	.104
5. Politics	.741	.548	.006	.420	.107	.178	.096
Anti-Breckinridge–Prosecession Counties (N=14)							
1. Turnout	.771	.595	.595	−.771	−.692	.161	−.843
2. Breckinridge	.822	675	.080	−.008	−.283	.269	−.226
3. Slaveholder	.835	.698	.023	.277	.206	.227	.230
4. Town	.838	.703	.005	−.131	.057	.140	.096
Pro-Breckinridge–Antisecession Counties (N=29)							
1. Slaveholder	.070	.005	.005	−.070	−.145	−.232	−.140
2. Town	.104	.011	.006	.046	.287	.545	.120
3. Turnout	.142	.020	.009	.062	.098	.154	.148
4. Breckinridge	.172	.030	.009	−.048	−.128	.266	−.107

likely that there was a pronounced shift toward secession, but low turnout prevented that actual shift from being registered in the vote for secession. The difference in the impact of turnout on these two sets of anti-Breckinridge counties may well be related to the town factor, as we shall see.

COUNTIES CATEGORIZED BY SLAVEHOLDING

Having looked at the relationship between the Breckinridge vote and the vote for secession, we can turn next to slaveholding.

County Characteristics

Calling counties with less than 30 percent slaveholders *low slaveholding counties* and those with 30 percent or more *high slaveholding counties,* the characteristics of these two sets of counties are displayed in Table 17. As might be expected, low slaveholding counties were

Table 17
CHARACTERISTICS OF COUNTIES CATEGORIZED BY SLAVEHOLDING

	Means	
	Low Slaveholding	High Slaveholding
Slave	18%	50%
Slaveholder	18%	51%
Planter	1%	9%
Wealth	$489	$1556
Staple Crop	108 lbs	999 lbs
Breckinridge	58%*	44%*
Politics	62%	48%
Town	4%	6%
Turnout	89%	78%
Secession	46%*	55%*
N	43	89

*These figures are not means. In each case they represent the actual percentage of the vote.

relatively poor, averaging one-third the wealth of high slaveholding counties and only about one-tenth the staple crop production. They also differed from high slaveholding counties by having voted in favor of Breckinridge as they had voted for Democratic presidential candidates in the past while high slaveholding counties opposed Breckinridge as they had traditionally opposed Democratic presidential candidates. Yet low slaveholding counties opposed secession while high slaveholding counties favored it, with low slaveholding counties having a larger voter turnout.

Shifts of Voters Toward Secession

Table 18 demonstrates that in low slaveholding counties there was a decided shift of voters away from secession for both minimum and maximum estimates. Among high slaveholding counties, only those in the highest category showed a positive minimum shift toward secession although all high slaveholding categories showed pronounced maximum voter shifts toward secession.

Multiple Regression

Multiple regression analysis, summarized in Table 19, reconfirms the importance of the vote for Breckinridge, which is the most important variable in both low and high slaveholding counties. In low slavehold-

Table 18

ESTIMATED VOTER SHIFTS TOWARD SECESSION FOR
COUNTIES CATEGORIZED BY SLAVEHOLDING

	Voters		
Slaveholders	Minimum Estimate	Maximum Estimate	N
0–14%	−3063	−2947	13
15–29%	−3718	−1645	30
30–44%	− 544	+1737	34
45–59%	− 991	+2290	30
60–80%	+ 383	+2779	25

Table 19

STEPWISE MULTIPLE REGRESSION ANALYSIS FOR
COUNTIES CATEGORIZED BY SLAVEHOLDING

Dependent Variable: Vote for Secession

	Multiple R	R Square	R-Square Change	Simple R	B	Standard Error B	Beta
Low Slaveholding Counties (N=43)							
1. Breckinridge	.410	.168	.168	.410	.675	.153	.521
2. Slaveholder	.613	.376	.208	.404	1.075	.373	.358
3. Town	.689	.475	.099	.299	.531	.225	.288
4. Turnout	.704	.496	.020	−.325	−.191	.154	−.158
High Slaveholding Counties (N=89)							
1. Breckinridge	.429	.184	.184	.429	.615	.132	.441
2. Turnout	.494	.244	.060	−.209	−.249	.111	−.215
3. Town	.517	.267	.023	.221	.290	.170	.161
4. Slaveholder	.522	.273	.006	.041	.180	.219	.079

ing counties, the slaveholder variable was important, accounting for an additional 20 percent of the variation after the Breckinridge variable had entered the regression equation. In high slaveholding counties, however, slaveholding not only accounted for little variation when it was entered into the stepwise regression routine, but also its beta coefficient is less than one-fourth as large as in low slaveholding counties. Likewise, the town variable played almost twice as large a role in low slaveholding as in high slaveholding counties. Although turnout had a larger impact in high slaveholding counties, its importance there was relatively small.

COUNTIES CATEGORIZED BY POLITICS

If we define *Whig counties* as those which had a mean proportion of votes for Democratic presidential candidates between 1836 and 1856 of 50 percent or less and *Democratic counties* as those which a mean of over 50 percent, Table 20 displays the characteristics of the two sets of counties.

Table 20
CHARACTERISTICS OF COUNTIES
CATEGORIZED BY POLITICS

	Means	
	Whig Counties	Democratic Counties
Slave	50%	32%
Slaveholder	50%	32%
Planter	9%	5%
Wealth	$1556	$952
Staple Crop	844 lbs	609 lbs
Breckinridge	36%*	57%*
Politics	39%	62%
Town	5%	6%
Turnout	78%	84%
Secession	49%*	53%*
N	56	76

*These figures are not means. In each case they represent the actual percentage of the vote.

County Characteristics

Clearly, Democratic counties had fewer slaves, slaveholders, and planters, and less wealth and staple crop production than Whig counties. Yet Democratic counties as a group favored secession while voters in Whig counties opposed it. Since we already know that slaveholding had a considerable influence on the vote for secession, we might hold slaveholding constant and look at the vote for secession within Democratic and Whig counties. As Table 21 shows, the low slaveholding Whig counties opposed secession while the high slaveholding Whig counties gave secession a much larger proportion of their votes, although as a group their votes were evenly split. Likewise, only the lowest slaveholding Democratic counties opposed secession, while all other slaveholding categories favored it. In all slaveholding categories, the vote for secession in Democratic counties exceeded that in Whig counties.

Table 21

POPULAR VOTE FOR SECESSION IN COUNTIES
CATEGORIZED BY SLAVEHOLDING AND POLITICS

Percent of Voters for Secession

Slaveholder	Whig Counties	Democratic Counties
0–14%	– ⎫	34 ⎫
	⎬ 32	⎬ 46
15–29%	32 ⎭	51 ⎭
30–44%	55 ⎫	59 ⎫
45–59%	45 ⎬ 50	69 ⎬ 64
60–80%	50 ⎭	63 ⎭

Shifts of Voters Toward Secession

Having already seen the importance of voter shifts, Table 22 shows how voters moved within these sets of counties. At a minimum, 630 voters shifted toward secession in high slaveholding Whig counties, while the minimum estimates for all other categories were negative. The maximum estimates show large shifts toward secession in high slaveholding Whig counties and smaller but still sizable shifts in high slaveholding Democratic counties. In low slaveholding Democratic counties, the maximum estimate is −4515 compared to a minimum estimate of −6572.

Table 22

ESTIMATED VOTER SHIFTS TOWARD SECESSION FOR COUNTIES
CATEGORIZED BY SLAVEHOLDING AND POLITICS

Voters

	Minimum Estimate		Maximum Estimate	
Slaveholder	Whig Counties	Democratic Counties	Whig Counties	Democratic Counties
0–14%	–	−3063	–	−2947
15–29%	−239	−3509	− 121	−1568
30–44%	+270	− 814	+1268	+ 514
45–59%	−427	− 564	+1484	+ 700
60–80%	+787	− 404	+2417	+ 30

Multiple Regression

In Whig counties, as Table 23 shows, the vote for Breckinridge, which alone accounted for 28 percent of the variation in the vote for secession, was the most important variable, almost three times as important as the slaveholder variable and over three times as important as the town variable. In Democratic counties, on the other hand, turnout was the most important variable, although it only accounted for about 20 percent of the variation in the vote for secession. Table 24 further subdivides the counties by slaveholding. Since all but three Whig counties were high slaveholding, the Whig county entries in Table 23 are also appropriate for Table 24. Table 24 shows interesting differences between low and high slaveholding Democratic counties. The slaveholder, Breckinridge, and town variables all have a significant impact in low slaveholding Democratic counties, with the Breckinridge variable being the most important of the three. Yet in high slaveholding Democratic counties, the order of the variables entered into the regression equation is exactly reversed: turnout accounted for almost 19 percent

Table 23

STEPWISE MULTIPLE REGRESSION ANALYSIS FOR COUNTIES
CATEGORIZED BY POLITICS

Dependent Variable: Vote for Secession

	Multiple R	R Square	R-Square Change	Simple R	B	Standard Error B	Beta
Whig Counties (N=56)							
1. Breckinridge	.529	.280	.280	.529	.855	.169	.590
2. Slaveholder	.569	.324	.044	.076	.375	.220	.200
3. Town	.592	.350	.026	.175	.324	.224	.162
4. Turnout	.601	.361	.011	−.046	−.138	.147	−.109
Democratic Counties (N=76)							
1. Turnout	.441	.195	.195	−.441	−.337	.114	−.308
2. Slaveholder	.520	.270	.075	.400	.412	.146	.288
3. Breckinridge	.555	.308	.038	.169	.351	.164	.206
4. Town	.586	.343	.035	.297	.329	.170	.193

Table 24

STEPWISE MULTIPLE REGRESSION ANALYSIS FOR COUNTIES
CATEGORIZED BY SLAVEHOLDING AND POLITICS

Dependent Variable: Vote for Secession

	Multiple R	R Square	R-Square Change	Simple R	B	Standard Error B	Beta
High Slaveholding Whig Counties (N=56)							
All but three are high slaveholding; hence see the Whig Counties entry in Table 23							
Low Slaveholding Democratic Counties (N=40)							
1. Slaveholder	.459	.211	.211	.459	1.140	.379	.391
2. Breckinridge	.612	.374	.164	.364	.645	.167	.479
3. Town	.691	.477	.103	.304	.535	.230	.301
4. Turnout	.702	.493	.016	.339	−.166	.156	−.142
High Slaveholding Democratic Counties (N=36)							
1. Turnout	.432	.187	.187	−.432	−.391	.166	−.389
2. Town	.463	.214	.027	.244	.261	.253	.168
3. Breckinridge	.467	.218	.003	.096	.095	.309	.050
4. Slaveholder	.469	.220	.002	.121	.115	.396	.048

of the variation and had over twice the importance that it did in low slaveholding counties; the Breckinridge and slaveholder variables have beta coefficients of only.050 and .048 respectively, compared to.391 and .479 for low slaveholding counties.

Overall, the Breckinridge variable was most important in high slaveholding Whig counties, the slaveholding variable was most important in low slaveholding Democratic counties, and turnout was most important in high slaveholding Democratic counties.

COUNTIES CATEGORIZED BY TOWNS

Table 25 displays the characteristics of town and country counties. *Town counties* were defined as those with more than 10 percent of the county population living in towns. Those counties with 10 percent or less of their population in towns were defined as *country counties*. Although the 10 percent cutoff is somewhat arbitrary, I chose it because it included all counties with towns with a population of one thousand or more. Had I chosen a higher cutoff, I would have excluded

Table 25
CHARACTERISTICS OF COUNTIES CATEGORIZED BY TOWNS
Means

	Country Counties	Town Counties
Slave	38%	49%
Slaveholder	39%	45%
Planter	6%	8%
Wealth	$1078	$1984
Staple Crop	586 lbs	1434 lbs
Breckinridge	49%*	49%*
Politics	52%	54%
Town	0%	35%
Turnout	83%	75%
Secession	47%*	69%*
N	113	19

*These figures are not means. In each case they represent the actual percentage of the vote.

counties which clearly had towns. On the other hand, the 10 percent cutoff includes three villages with fewer than one thousand inhabitants (see Table 10).

County Characteristics

The most striking difference between town and country counties is in the vote for secession. A majority opposed secession in country counties while over two-thirds of the voters favored secession in town counties. Town counties also averaged more slaves, slaveholders, and planters, and almost twice the wealth and over twice the staple crop production of country counties. Yet the vote for Breckinridge was the same in the two sets of counties, closely matching the similar records of past presidential preferences.

If we hold politics constant, as in Table 26, we see that both Democratic and Whig town counties favored secession, although the level of support for secession was much higher in Democratic town counties. Country counties in both political categories opposed secession at about the same level.

Shifts of Voters Toward Secession

Looking at the shift of voters toward secession in Table 27, the minimum estimates show again an extremely large shift away from secession in country Democratic counties and a sizable shift toward secession in Whig town counties. The maximum estimates show a positive shift toward secession in both town and country counties.

Table 26
POPULAR VOTE FOR SECESSION IN COUNTIES
CATEGORIZED BY POLITICS AND TOWN

Percent of Voters for Secession

Town	Whig Counties	Democratic Counties
None	44 ⎫	48 ⎫
	⎬ 46	⎬ 48
1–10%	84 ⎭	45 ⎭
11–30%	49 ⎫	74 ⎫
31–60%	67 ⎬ 57	60 ⎬ 74
61–80%	50 ⎭	80 ⎭

Table 27

ESTIMATED VOTER SHIFTS TOWARD SECESSION FOR COUNTIES
CATEGORIZED BY POLITICS AND TOWN

	Town			
	Minimum Estimate		Maximum Estimate	
Town	Whig Counties	Democratic Counties	Whig Counties	Democratic Counties
0%	− 513	−6477	+2444	−4081
1–10%	− 24	−1200	+ 652	− 803
11–30%	− 314	− 589	+ 11	+ 811
31–60%	+1067	+ 164	+1548	+ 423
61–80%	+ 175	− 222	+ 368	+1511

Democratic town counties matched the Whig pattern, although Democratic country counties continued to show a sharp movement away from secession.

Multiple Regression

Table 28 shows that for town as well as for country counties, the Breckinridge variable is the best single variable for reducing the varia-

Table 28

STEPWISE MULTIPLE REGRESSION ANALYSIS FOR COUNTIES
CATEGORIZED BY TOWNS

Dependent Variable: Vote for Secession

	Multiple R	R Square	R-Square Change	Simple R	B	Standard Error B	Beta
Country Counties (N=113)							
1. Breckinridge	.295	.087	.087	.295	.653	.119	.510
2. Slaveholder	.453	.205	.118	.174	.454	.129	.335
3. Turnout	.493	.243	.038	−.222	−.273	.097	−.251
4. Town	.524	.274	.031	−.053	−3.104	1.44	−.184
Town Counties (N=19)							
1. Breckinridge	.563	.317	.317	.563	.716	.209	.618
2. Turnout	.723	.522	.205	−.487	−.626	.278	−.384
3. Town	.778	.606	.084	.160	.360	.195	.337
4. Slaveholder	.785	.617	.011	.248	.160	.257	.111

Table 29

STEPWISE MULTIPLE REGRESSION ANALYSIS FOR COUNTIES CATEGORIZED BY POLITICS AND TOWN

Dependent Variable: Vote for Secession

	Multiple R	R Square	R-Square Change	Simple R	B	Standard Error B	Beta
Whig-Country Counties (N=49)							
1. Breckinridge	.514	.264	.264	.514	.913	.201	.598
2. Slaveholder	.577	.333	.070	.064	.430	.244	.232
3. Town	.598	.358	.024	.274	3.621	3.054	.147
4. Turnout	.609	.371	.013	−.074	−.146	.151	−.120
Democratic-Country Counties (N=64)							
1. Turnout	.361	.130	.130	−.361	−.418	.115	−.408
2. Town	.517	.267	.137	−.236	−5.650	1.494	−.409
3. Slaveholder	.579	.336	.069	.343	.420	.149	.305
4. Breckinridge	.617	.381	.045	.152	.346	.167	.214

Whig–Town
Counties
(N=7)

1. Breckinridge	.612	.375	.375	.612	.636	.459	.658
2. Town	.792	.626	.252	.175	.553	.477	.496
3. Turnout	.863	.744	.118	.552	.971	.903	.415
4. Slaveholder	.874	.763	.019	.219	.376	.930	.204

Democratic-Town
Counties (N=12)

1. Turnout	.836	.700	.700	-.836	-1.040	.189	-.762
2. Breckinridge	.926	.857	.157	.412	.499	.223	.336
3. Slaveholder	.937	.878	.021	.489	.243	.197	.187
4. Town	.942	.887	.009	.182	.099	.136	.103

221

tion in the vote for secession. Yet in country counties the Breckinridge variable accounts for only about 9 percent of the variation while in town counties it accounts for nearly 30 percent. Also, in town counties the Breckinridge variable has a larger beta coefficient. Turnout is the next most important variable for town counties, while it ranks a poor third in country counties, being preceded by the slaveholder variable, which is about three times as important in country as in town counties. Finally, it is interesting that in country counties the higher the town variable, the lower the vote for secession, while in town counties, the higher the town variable, the higher the vote for secession.

If we further subdivide the counties by politics, as in Table 29, other interesting differences emerge. In country counties, for example, the Breckinridge variable is most important in Whig counties and least in Democratic counties. Conversely, turnout is most important in country Democratic counties and least in country Whig counties. Although the role of the slaveholder variable is about the same in the two sets of country counties, that of the town variable is very different. The villages in country Whig counties raised the vote for secession while they considerably lowered it in Democratic country counties.

The impact of the variables on Whig and Democratic town counties is also quite different. In Whig town counties the Breckinridge variable is the most important, followed by the town, turnout, and slaveholder variables. In sharp contrast, turnout is more than twice as important as the Breckinridge vote in Democratic town counties where it alone accounts for 70 percent of the variation. Strikingly, the negative beta coefficient indicates that in Democratic town counties opponents of secession stayed away from the polls while the positive beta coefficient in Whig town counties suggests that supporters of secession failed to vote in those counties.

Comparing Democratic counties, the role of turnout in town counties was nearly twice that in country counties, although in both sets of counties it was the most important variable. While the town variable slightly increased the vote for secession in Democratic town counties, it considerably depressed it in the villages in Democratic country counties. Among Whig counties, the most marked differences are in the roles of the town variable, which is more than three times as important in town counties, and the turnout variable, which depressed the vote for secession in country counties and elevated it in town counties.

COUNTIES CATEGORIZED BY SLAVEHOLDING, POLITICS, AND TOWN

Finally, we can categorize the counties by all three factors and create eight potential subdivisions, which are reduced to seven actual subdivisions, since there were no low slaveholding Whig town counties.

County Characterics

As Table 30 shows, the vote for secession was higher in the high slaveholding counties of both Whig and Democratic country counties and of Democratic town counties than in the respective low slaveholding counties. This illustrates the pervasive effect of the slaveholding factor. Likewise, Democratic counties consistently voted more strongly for secession than the corresponding Whig counties, illustrating the pervasive effect of the political factor. Finally, town counties consistently gave a substantially larger proportion of votes for seces-

Table 30

POPULAR VOTE FOR SECESSION IN COUNTIES
CATEGORIZED BY SLAVEHOLDING, POLITICS, AND TOWN

Percent of Voters for Secession

	Whig	Democratic
Country		
Low Slaveholding	32	42
High Slaveholding	47	58
Town		
Low Slaveholding	—	68 (A)
High Slaveholding	61 (B)	79 (C)

(A) The towns in this category are Atlanta, Marietta, Palmetto, Rome.

(B) The towns in this category are Athens, Augusta, Bainbridge, Brunswick, Eatonton, Milledgeville.

(C) The towns in this category are Albany, Centre, Columbus, Knoxville, Macon, Newnan, Newton, St. Mary's, Savannah.

sion than the corresponding country counties, illustrating the pervasive effect of the town factor.

Shifts of Voters Toward Secession

The minimum estimates in Table 31 demonstrate that Whig town counties exhibited a substantial voter shift toward secession, while the largest shift away from secession was in low slaveholding Democratic country counties. The maximum estimates illustrate the remarkable magnitude of the shift away from secession in these low slaveholding Democratic country counties as well as the shifts toward secession in Whig counties and town counties.

Multiple Regression

Table 32 highlights the difference between low slaveholding and high slaveholding Democratic country counties. The variables affected low slaveholding Democratic country counties in much the same way as they affected high slaveholding country Whig counties (see Table 29): note the primacy of the Breckinridge variable and the relative weight of each succeeding variable. Yet the voter shifts in Table 31 confirm that quite different processes occurred in each set of counties. In high

Table 31

ESTIMATED VOTER SHIFTS TOWARD SECESSION IN COUNTIES
CATEGORIZED BY SLAVEHOLDING, POLITICS, AND TOWN

Voters

	Minimum Estimate		Maximum Estimate	
	Whig Counties	Democratic Counties	Whig Counties	Democratic Counties
Country				
Low Slaveholding	−239	−6229	− 144	−4947
High Slaveholding	−298	−1448	+2683	+ 618
Town				
Low Slaveholding	—	− 313	—	+ 922
High Slaveholding	+928	− 334	+1530	+1153

slaveholding Democratic country counties, however, the town variable is most important, having a very large negative impact on the vote for secession, in marked contrast to the role of the town variable in Democratic town counties (see Table 29). Yet these high slaveholding Democratic country counties were almost identical to Democratic town counties in the large negative impact of turnout.

Turnout, then, seems to have been most important in Democratic town counties and high slaveholding Democratic country counties, where it depressed the vote for secession. In Whig town counties, in contrast, the higher the turnout, the higher the vote for secession. The Breckinridge variable had its greatest impact in Whig counties and in low slaveholding Democratic country counties. The influence of the town variable was greatest in high slaveholding Democratic country counties where it depressed the vote for secession while in all other categories it increased the vote for secession. Although the slaveholder variable was not primary in any set of categories, it was quite important in low slaveholding Democratic country counties.

TURNOUT

Table 33 shows the turnout in the secession election, computed as a percentage of the vote in the 1860 presidential election. Town counties contained the largest share of nonvoters, followed by high slaveholding country counties. Turnout was highest in low slaveholding Democratic country counties.

Analysis of Key Roll Call votes in the Secession Convention

Tables 34 to 37 demonstrate that the hard-core cooperationists in the secession convention–*i.e.,* those who voted against the secession ordinance—were consistently more strongly in favor of retaining or providing for traditional democratic political practices than were those cooperationists who voted for the secession ordinance.[9] Tables 35 and 37 show that on the votes to require state senators to reside at least one year in their districts and to allow superior court judges to be elected by

---

9. For the roll calls, see *Journal of the Convention,* 145–48, 251–53, 261–67.

Table 32

STEPWISE MULTIPLE REGRESSION ANALYSIS FOR COUNTIES
CATEGORIZED BY SLAVEHOLDING, POLITICS, AND TOWN

Dependent Variable: Vote for Secession

	Multiple R	R Square	R-Square Change	Simple R	B	Standard Error B	Beta
High Slaveholding-Whig-Country Counties							
All but three Whig-Country Counties were high slaveholding; hence see the Whig-Country Counties entry in Table 29							
Low Slaveholding-Democratic-Country Counties (N=36)							
1. Breckinridge	.475	.226	.226	.475	.615	.173	.495
2. Slaveholder	.634	.402	.176	.404	1.071	.393	.395
3. Turnout	.638	.408	.006	−.186	−.086	.164	−.078
4. Town	.640	.409	.002	−.002	.541	1.820	.041

High Slaveholding-
Democratic-Country-
Counties (N=28)

1. Town	.438	.191	.191	−.438	−10.128	1.969	−.773
2. Turnout	.769	.591	.399	−.376	−.660	.137	−.705
3. Breckinridge	.776	.602	.012	.003	.206	.257	.107
4. Slaveholder	.777	.603	.001	−.018	.079	.334	.032

High Slaveholding-
Whig-Town Counties

All Whig-Town Counties
were high slaveholding;
hence see the Whig-Town
Counties entry in
Table 29.

High Slaveholding-
Democratic-Town Counties

All but four Democratic-
Town Counties were high
slaveholding; hence see the
Democratic-Town Counties
entry in Table 29.

227

Table 33

TURNOUT IN SECESSION ELECTION IN COUNTIES
CATEGORIZED BY SLAVEHOLDING, POLITICS, AND TOWN

Percent

	Whig Counties	Democratic Counties
Country		
Low Slaveholding	89	93
High Slaveholding	75	79
Town		
Low Slaveholding	—	69
High Slaveholding	80	70

the voters, a heavy majority (66 and 65 percent, respectively) of the hard-core cooperationist delegates favored the motions which were opposed by a majority of both secessionists and cooperationists who had voted for the secession ordinance. On the residency requirement vote, the hard-core cooperationists were crucial to the narrow 116–112 victory of the motion. Tables 34 and 36 show that a majority of

Table 34

VOTE OF CONVENTION DELEGATES ON HANSELL'S MOTION
TO POSTPONE INDEFINITELY CONSIDERATION OF
LEGISLATIVE REDUCTION (In Percent of Those Voting)

	Secessionists	Cooperationists for Secession Ordinance	Hard-core Cooperationists	All Delegates
Delegates for Postponement	24 (N=33)	8 (N=3)	21 (N=17)	21 (N=54)*
Delegates Against Postponement	76 (N=107)	92 (N=33)	79 (N=64)	79 (N=206)†
Delegates Not Voting	(N=26)	(N=5)	(N=8)	

*Includes one delegate not voting on secession.

†Includes two delegates not voting on secession.

Table 35

VOTE OF CONVENTION DELEGATES ON AMENDMENT TO REQUIRE
STATE SENATORS TO RESIDE AT LEAST ONE YEAR IN THE
DISTRICT THEY REPRESENTED (In Percent of Those Voting)

	Secessionists	Cooperationists for Secession Ordinance	Hard-core Cooperationists	All Delegates
Delegates for Residency Requirement	46 (N=55)	42 (N=14)	66 (N=46)	51 (N=116)*
Delegates Against Residency Requirement	54 (N=65)	58 (N=19)	34 (N=24)	49 (N=112)†
Delegates Not Voting	(N=46)	(N=8)	(N=19)	

*Includes one delegate not voting on secession.

†Includes four delegates not voting on secession.

Table 36

VOTE OF CONVENTION DELEGATES ON AMENDMENT TO REQUIRE THE
ELECTION OF SUPREME COURT JUDGES BY THE STATE LEGISLATURE
(In Percent of Those Voting)

	Secessionists	Cooperationists for Secession Ordinance	Hard-core Cooperationists	All Delegates
Delegates for Election by Legislature	26 (N=28)	28 (N=8)	39 (N=26)	29 (N=63)*
Delegates Against Election by Legislature	74 (N=89)	72 (N=20)	61 (N=40)	71 (N=151)†
Delegates Not Voting	(N=49)	(N=13)	(N=23)	

*Includes one delegate not voting on secession.

†Includes two delegates not voting on secession.

Table 37

VOTE OF CONVENTION DELEGATES ON AMENDMENT
TO ALLOW SUPERIOR COURT JUDGES TO BE ELECTED
BY THE VOTERS (In Percent of Those Voting)

	Secessionists	Cooperationists for Secession Ordinance	Hard-core Cooperationists	All Delegates
Delegates for Election by Voters	42 (N=48)	39 (N=11)	65 (N=41)	49 (N=100)
Delegates Against Election by Voters	58 (N=67)	61 (N=17)	35 (N=22)	51 (N=106)
Delegates Not Voting	(N=51)	(N=13)	(N=26)	

hard-core cooperationists joined the majorities of the other two groups in defeating the motions to postpone legislative reduction and to allow supreme court judges to be elected by the voters. Yet on both these votes, the hard-core cooperationists had smaller majorities against these motions than did the cooperationists who voted for the secession ordinance.

Analysis of the Ratification Election

The county returns used for analysis were those published in the Augusta *Daily Constitutionalist,* August 17, 1861.

TURNOUT

The most striking feature of the returns is their magnitude, or lack of it. Only 26 percent of the voters who participated in the January election of delegates to the secession convention voted in the July ratification election. Table 38 shows that, although the turnout was generally low, again, the turnout in town counties was even lower than that in country counties. As in the secession election, the support for ratification decreased as turnout increased, as Table 39 makes clear. Table 40 demonstrates that in the counties which were most strongly opposed to ratification, the largest proportion of voters turned out, 45 percent of

Table 38

TURNOUT IN THE RATIFICATION ELECTION IN COUNTIES
CATEGORIZED BY SLAVEHOLDING, POLITICS, AND TOWN

	Percent	
	Whig Counties	Democratic Counties
Country		
Low Slaveholding	30	26
High Slaveholding	30	26
Town		
Low Slaveholding	—	16
High Slaveholding	20	23

Table 39

POPULAR VOTE IN FAVOR OF RATIFICATION IN COUNTIES
RANKED BY TURNOUT

Turnout	Percent Proratification	N
0	—	8
1–19%	66	37
20–29%	60	36
30–39%	51	24
40–49%	56	10
50% and over	33	17

Table 40

TURNOUT IN THE RATIFICATION ELECTION IN COUNTIES
RANKED BY THE PROPORTION OF PRORATIFICATION VOTERS

Percent of Pro-ratification Voters	Percent Turnout	N*
0– 29%	45	25
30– 49%	26	22
50– 69%	25	24
70– 89%	33	26
90–100%	25	27

*No votes were reported for eight counties.

those who voted in the secession election. But as the support for ratification increased, the turnout remained low, between a fourth and a third of the secession election voters.

Table 41 gives the distribution of the ratification vote by 1860 congressional districts. The strongest opposition to ratification and the highest turnout were in the Sixth District, which encompassed northeast Georgia. In contrast, the Fifth District, which included northwest Georgia, had the lowest turnout and a high proportion of proratification voters. In the Second, Third, Fourth, Seventh, and Eighth districts, which included most of the cotton-belt counties, the constitution did well, as it did in the First District, which included Savannah and the expanse of southeast and south central Georgia.

COUNTIES CATEGORIZED BY SLAVEHOLDING, POLITICS, AND TOWN

Although the turnout was quite low, the voting pattern established in the secession election held up remarkably well. Table 42 shows that, like in the secession election, low slaveholding country counties were the strongest opponents of ratification, town counties strongly favored the new constitution, and Democratic counties were more strongly proratification than the corresponding Whig counties.

Table 41
VOTERS FAVORING RATIFICATION AND TURNOUT,
IN CONGRESSIONAL DISTRICTS

Congressional District	Percent Proratification	Percent Turnout
1	59	30
2	64	24
3	78	25
4	70	18
5	61	17
6	16	45
7	65	32
8	50	21

Table 42

POPULAR VOTE IN FAVOR OF RATIFICATION

Percent of Proratification Voters

	Whig Counties	Democratic Counties
Country		
Low Slaveholding	17	39
High Slaveholding	46	77
Town		
Low Slaveholding	—	86
High Slaveholding	57	71

If the votes for Whig and Democratic counties are lumped together, we can look at the distribution of votes along the slaveholding and town-country axes. In country counties, low slaveholding counties gave 38 percent of their votes for the new constitution, high slaveholding counties, 56 percent; all together, 49 percent of country county voters favored ratification. In town counties taken as a group, 69 percent supported ratification. Likewise, if the counties are simply categorized by politics, Whig counties gave 45 percent of their votes for ratification, Democratic counties 57 percent.

Ideally, regression analysis would add to our understanding of the results of the ratification election. Unfortunately, the turnout was so small that a meaningful analysis is impossible. Of course it is possible to compute a regression equation. But, because of the low turnout, it would mean very little.

Bibliographic Note

Although the footnotes are a complete guide to the sources I found most valuable, an organized list of the primary sources I consulted may be of some interest. The footnotes are an adequate guide to the relevant secondary sources. The sources of the quantitative data are discussed in the Appendix.

Manuscript Collections

DUKE UNIVERSITY

Joseph Emerson Brown Papers
Robert Newman Gourdin Papers
Edward Harden Papers
Henry Washington Hilliard Papers
Nathan L. Hutchins Papers
Herschel Vespasian Johnson Papers
John McIntosh Kell Papers
S. H. Latimer Papers
Eugenius Artistedes Nisbet Papers
Joseph Belknap Smith Papers
Alexander Hamilton Stephens Papers

EMORY UNIVERSITY

John S. Dobbins Papers
Robert Newman Gourdin Papers
Iverson-Branham Papers
Alexander Hamilton Stephens Papers
Alexander Hamilton Stephens Papers (microfilm), Manhattanville College Collection

GEORGIA HISTORICAL SOCIETY

Mrs. M. P. Callaway Scrapbooks
George Galphin Nowlan MacDonell Diary
George Anderson Mercer Diary

UNIVERSITY OF GEORGIA

Colonel David C. Barrow Papers
Joseph E. Brown Papers, Felix Hargett Collection
Joseph Emerson and Elizabeth Grisham Brown Collection
Brown Family Papers
Nathan Atkinson Brown Papers
James Camak Collection
Carr Collection
Howell Cobb Papers
Thomas Reade Rootes Cobb Papers
Cobb-Erwin-Lamar Letters
Telamon Cuyler Collection
Rebecca A. Latimer Felton Letters
Charles Colcock Jones, Jr., Collection
Thomas Jones Family Papers
Gazaway Bugg Lamar Papers
Joseph Henry Lumpkin Papers
Margaret Branch Sexton Collection
Alexander H. Stephens Papers (microfilm), Library of Congress Collection
William Price Talmage Diary
Robert Toombs Papers

SOUTHERN HISTORICAL COLLECTION, UNIVERSITY OF
NORTH CAROLINA

John Macpherson Berrien Papers
William O. Fleming Papers
Duff Green Papers
Augustin Harris Hansell Papers (microfilm)
Mackay-Stiles Family Papers
William McKinley Book
Benjamin Cudworth Yancey Papers

Printed Primary Sources

Benning, Henry L. *Speech on Federal Relations, Delivered in the Hall of the House of Representatives, Nov. 6th, 1860. N. p., N. d.*

Brown, Joseph E. *Special Message to the Legislature of Georgia on Our Federal Relations, Retaliatory State Legislation, the Right of Secession, & c., November 7th, 1860.* Milledgeville, Ga.: Boughton, Nisbet, & Barnes, 1860.

Candler, Allen D. ed., *The Confederate Records of the State of Georgia.* Atlanta: Charles P. Byrd, 1909.

Cobb, Howell. *Letter to the People of Georgia on the Present Condition of the Country, December 6, 1860.* Washington: M'Gill & Witherow, 1860.

Cobb, Thomas Reade Rootes. "The Correspondence of Thomas Reade Rootes Cobb, 1860–1862," *Publications of the Southern History Association*, XI (1907), 147–85, 233–60, 312–28.

————. *An Inquiry into the Law of Negro Slavery in the United States of America*. Philadelphia: T. & J. W. Johnson, 1858; reprinted 1968.

————. *Substance of Remarks in the Hall of the House of Representatives, Monday Evening, Nov. 12, 1860*. Atlanta: John H. Seals, 1860.

Jackson, Henry R. *Letters to the Hon. Alexander H. Stephens*. Savannah: Steam Power Press, 1860.

Lipscomb, Andrew A. *Substance of a Discourse Delivered Before the Legislature of Georgia on the Occasion of the Fast Day Appointed by His Excellency Joseph E. Brown, November 28th, 1860*. Milledgeville, Ga.: Boughton, Nisbet, & Barnes, 1860.

Means, Alexander. *Diary for 1861*. Edited by Ross H. McLean. Emory University Publications, Sources, and Reprints; Atlanta: Emory University, 1949, Ser. VI, No. 1.

Meyers, Robert Manson, ed. *The Children of Pride: A True Story of Georgia and the Civil War*. New Haven: Yale University Press, 1972.

Phillips, Ulrich Bonnell, ed. *The Correspondence of Robert Toombs, Alexander H. Stephens, and Howell Cobb*. Washington: Government Printing Office, 1913.

Stephens, Alexander H. *Prophecy and Fulfillment: Speech of A. H. Stephens of Georgia, in Opposition to Secession in 1860*. New York: Holman, 1863.

————. *Extract from a Speech by Alexander H. Stephens, Vice-President of the Confederate States, Delivered in the Secession Convention of Georgia, January 1861*. N.p., n.d.

Toombs, Robert. *Speech on the Crisis, Delivered Before the Georgia Legislature, December 7, 1860*. Washington: Lemuel Towers, 1860.

Newspapers

Daily Chronicle and Sentinel, Augusta, Ga.

Daily Constitutionalist, Augusta, Ga.

Daily Enquirer, Columbus, Ga.

Daily Intelligencer, Atlanta, Ga.

Federal Union (Southern Federal Union after January 15, 1861), Milledgeville, Ga.

Morning News, Savannah, Ga.

Patriot, Albany, Ga.

Pilot, Upson County, Ga.

Republican, Savannah, Ga.

Southern Banner, Athens, Ga.

Telegraph, Macon, Ga.

Weekly Courier, Rome, Ga.

Index

Adams, John, 125

African slave trade, 128–30

Ailer, James W., 158

Alabama: secession of, xv, xxii, 111; commissioner of, 112, 113, 114

Albany, Ga., 5, 19

American Revolution: and secession, xxi, 85–87, 105–107; heritage of, in secessionist argument, 28–34; heritage of in Georgia, 87–94, 168

Anderson, Major Robert, 179

Andrews, Garnett, 118

Arkansas, 179

Athens, Ga., 22, 77, 124–26, 132, 139, 168, 183

Atlanta, Ga., 5, 19, 77, 108, 114, 117, 127, 137, 157, 184

Atlanta *Daily Intelligencer,* 157

Augusta, Ga., 5, 100, 138, 145

Augusta *Chronicle and Sentinel,* 159

Bartow, Francis S., 169

Bell, John: arguments of supporters in presidential campaign, 11–13, 16, 20; supporters of, 39, 71, 75, 81, 84, 94–95

Benning, Henry L.: advocates secession, 18, 30; on powers of convention, 163

Berrien, John M., 92

Breckinridge, John C.: arguments of supporters in presidential campaign, 11, 13–15, 20–21; supporters of, 39, 66–67, 71, 77, 83, 95

Brooks County, 162

Brown, John, 35

Brown, Joseph E.: announces secessionist majority, 7; supports secession, 17–18, 22, 27; social theory of, 42; appeal to nonslaveholders by, 48–51; reports secession election results, 64; a nonslaveholder responds to, 67–68; 1857 gubernatorial campaign of, 93; seated by secession convention, 113; social views of, 137–39; reports ratification election results, 183–84

Burson, Osborne, 133

Calhoun, John C., 69, 131

Charleston *Mercury,* 44

Chatham County, 39, 169

Chattahoochee River, 117

Civil War: and secession, xvii–xviii, 179, 187

Clinch County, 162

Cobb, Howell: 15–16; campaigns for secession in Georgia, 22–23, 27; on Republican patronage, 44; and Constitutional Union party, 92; and preconvention politics, 111; seated by secession convention, 113

Cobb, Mary Ann (Mrs. Howell), 19

Cobb, Thomas R. R.: 16; secessionist speech to legislature, 18; activities in campaign for secession, 20–23, 51; prosecession arguments of, 31, 33, 36–37; service of in Georgia and Confederate conventions, 124; as leader of Committee on Constitution, 125; assessment of secession, 126–27; opinion of Declaration of Independence, 136; utopian vision of, 126–27, 137–39; and equality of whites, 141; and piety of, 148; recommends voter ratification of new constitution, 163–64; requests revision of state constitution, 166; and legislative reduction, 168–69; on judicial reforms, 174–75; on new constitution, 176, 178, 180–81

Columbus, Ga., 25, 77, 137

Columbus *Daily Enquirer,* 181

239